T0261401

OBJECT-ORIENTED SIMULATION

OBJECT-ORIENTED SIMULATION
Reusability, Adaptability, Maintainability

Edited by

George W. Zobrist
University of Missouri—Rolla

James V. Leonard
Consultant

IEEE PRESS

The Institute of Electrical and Electronics Engineers, Inc., New York

This book may be purchased at a discount from the publisher
when ordered in bulk quantities. Contact:

IEEE PRESS Marketing
Attn: Special Sales
P.O. Box 1331
445 Hoes Lane
Piscataway, NJ 08855-1331
Fax: (908) 981-9334

For more information about IEEE PRESS products,
visit the IEEE Home Page:
http://www.ieee.org/

10   9   8   7   6   5   4   3   2   1

ISBN 0-7803-1061-6
IEEE Order Number: PC4150

Library of Congress Cataloging-in-Publication Data

Object-oriented simulation : reusability, adaptability,
maintainability / edited by George W. Zobrist, James V. Leonard.
   p.   cm.
Includes bibliographical references and index.
ISBN 0-7803-1061-6
1. Computer simulation. 2. Object-oriented programming (Computer
science) I. Zobrist, George W. (George Winston), (date).
II. Leonard, James V.
QA76.9.C65025   1996
003'.3511 — dc20
                    96-2228
                    CIP

Contents

Preface

Reusable simulation software! Now that's the edge needed by the simulation technologist in today's competitive environment. At present, large research organizations and industrial corporations are global in structure. As a result, units or modules of simulation code developed in the United States must be *reusable* in other parts of the world to realize this competitive cost edge. And, in the development of large systems, building a "breadboard" or engineering model is expensive, especially if it doesn't work as specified. When we simulate a large system (or any system, for that matter) on computers (or parallel processors), the system can be validated before we build it. Better yet, the simulated system can be "perturbed" to see how it reacts to real-world disturbances or out-of-tolerance conditions (lightning strikes, power outages, loss of signal, or lack of critical parts on the production line, for example). In order to perform large-scale simulations, our simulation techniques must be *adaptable* to real world situations. However, some philosophical analyses should be planned prior to application because, once a simulation program is in place, it must produce repeatable results. As we all know, "the only thing in this world that changes is change itself." So our simulation software must also be *maintainable*.

Reusability, adaptability, maintainability—that's the ticket in today's global economy. These standard software object-oriented design procedures can be applied to the development of simulation environments for separation of physical, control, and information elements of a system. *Object-Oriented Simulation: Reusability, Adaptability, Maintainability* is a valuable reference resource for the simulation developer who desires to work on the *leading edge* of simulation technology. The book was written for those professionally involved in computer simulation research as well as for designers, developers, producers, scholars, and managers. It will also benefit those preparing proposals for simulation techniques and those involved in research projects. It is particularly well-suited as an ancillary text for courses in object-oriented simulation and simulation methodology. The book contains specially-edited chapters on object-oriented simulation. Although such papers are presented in journals, special issues, and at conferences, it is difficult to find a single source that provides the foremost papers on the subject. In addition to presenting well-known software engineering techniques that are required in the design of a simulation environment, the information is presented in an object-oriented environment. Illustrated examples display the latest advances in object-oriented simulation techniques, which can help developers save countless research and development hours and increase productivity levels. The reader will gain a solid understanding of the concept of Object-Oriented Simulation (OOS), various applications utilizing the OOS environment, multilevel modeling and reusability in an OOS environment, object-oriented simulation testbeds, object-oriented concurrent programming for discrete event or behavioral simulation, and the use of object-oriented concepts throughout the lifecycle of software/model development. A particularly valuable feature is the variety of new simulation techniques described in the final three chapters.

An introductory survey is presented in Chapter 1 to offer the reader a good understanding of the basic concepts of OOS. Chapter 2 presents simulation languages based on C++. In Chapter 3, the Object Flow Model (OFM) and its contribution to simulation and conceptual modeling of database applications is examined. Discrete-event simulation is covered in Chapter 4, with a description of a methodology for developing reusable simulation models in an object-oriented framework. Chapter 5 discusses the issues involved in attempting to provide a multilevel simulation modeling capacity within object-oriented frameworks. In Chapter 6, a detailed account of a particular software integration environment, the Advanced AI Technology Testbed (AAITT) is reported. Chapter 7 reports further research on automating transformation schema execution. Then Chapter 8, building on the background gained from the previous seven chapters, presents a progression of steps for the application of object-oriented techniques to discrete-event or behavioral simulation problems, starting from simple objects (or actors) up to whole ecologies of reflective agents.

OBJECT-ORIENTED SIMULATION

Chapter 1

Object-Oriented Simulation and OPERAS

G. K. Yeh   *Space, Telecommunications,*
K. K. Bagchi   *and Radioscience Laboratory*
J. B. Burr   *Stanford University*
A. M. Peterson   *Stanford, California, USA*

Editor's Introduction ─────────────────────────────

*We start our monograph on Object-Oriented Simulation with a good intro-
ductory chapter that provides us with the basics for Object-Oriented Simulation (OOS). This chapter provides a brief survey of OOS concepts and
practices with a general review discussion. Simulation is regarded as a special kind of software design. Reusability, adaptability, and maintainability are
three standard software design features that should be supported by any simulation environment. OOS-based environments can provide inherent support
of these very important features, as well as other software design features.
After a brief review of the basic concepts of OOS, we examine various simulation languages, and then proceed to a specific application of OOS called
OPERAS (Objected-Oriented Power Estimating Restructurable Architecture
Simulation). OPERAS is an object-oriented system simulation that is reconfigurable and fast enough for a whole system simulation. Object-oriented
design and simulation allow for fast prototyping and simulation of very large
systems due to the ease of modeling. The benefit of the object-oriented view
of modules lies in the power of encapsulating the module as a flexible object,
capable of representing very complex objects such as a microprocessor to a
very simple object such as a logic gate.*

1.1. INTRODUCTION

Recently, Object-Oriented Simulation (OOS) has initiated a revolution
in simulation software design. With reusable and modular component
design as provided by concepts like encapsulation, inheritance, and

polymorphism, simulation software design has changed dramatically. Objects provide a better modeling of real-world entities than do traditional software modules, and an object-oriented simulator can closely model realistic systems. With a proper OOS framework, simulation can be made efficient to develop and maintain. As a result, OOS has become the state of the art in simulation design. OOS started with the development of Object-Oriented Programming (OOP) languages. SIMULA was the first language that contained the seed of OOS [9]. The growth of OOS started with the introduction of languages like Smalltalk, and modern, versatile programming languages like C++ are widely used to design OOS software. Object-oriented simulation software is likely to dominate the simulation software market in the near future.

In this chapter, we will describe the design of OPERAS (Object-Oriented Power Estimating Restructurable Architecture Simulator), which is motivated by the design of a low-power digital image signal processor. First, in Section 1.1, we make a brief survey of OOS concepts and practices. This is a general review discussion. This is followed by a detailed description of the OOS package OPERAS that has been in development at Stanford University's Space, Telecommunications, and Radioscience Laboratory, in Section 1.3.

1.1.1. What Is OOS?

The basic component of OOS is an object. Objects can be viewed as data structures that are allowed to have their own private variables and methods or procedures (using the familiar terms), invisible to other objects. The programmer detects the basic entities in any given domain to be modeled, develops corresponding classes to represent them in the simulation system, and plans how an object (instance) of a class will interact with other objects. This object-oriented simulation design is different from the traditional procedural approach of applying "separate procedures on separate data."

OOS and the State of the Art

Although simulation can be regarded as a special kind of software design, well-known software engineering techniques are not always applied for designing a simulation environment. In particular, reusability, adaptability, and maintainability are three standard software design features that should ideally be supported by any simulation environment for separation of physical, control, and information elements of a given system [54], [53], [62]. OOS-based environments can provide inherent support of these and other software design features. OOS falls well within the realm of OO software design, which, however, requires some special simulation techniques like the framework that essentially manages the simulation control mechanisms. Thus, for example, in implementing an event-driven simulation approach, a few major concepts need to be incorporated in OOS that outline the difference between OOP and OOS [41]. These are:

- Entities, which are active objects.

- An event, which represents a change in state of an object, and thus synchronizes the actions of two entities or passes messages between them. Consequently, event-list management is a major consideration in any such simulation design.

- The simulation time, which is a logical clock that is updated by events.

- Other data structures, such as ones for starting, conducting, and terminating simulation.

This may require simulation elements such as event, event queue, and event simulation time to be implemented in an OO environment, usually as objects. These objects are usually system objects, and so ideally should be transparent to end users.

As an example, let us consider a single-server, single-queue simulation. In this system, a customer arrives, receives service, and departs, and the server serves a queue where customers wait. In addition, a scheduler is needed to enforce a queue discipline policy and a clock is needed to measure simulation time. Events are denoted by arrival, service, and departure of customers. A root class can be defined that may contain methods and data common to a number of classes at higher levels. In the next stage, classes such as the following are needed:

- queue, which is used for waiting customers

- clock, which accumulates simulation time

- customer, for customers arriving for service

- server which serves

- simulation environment, an instance of which is created from input parameters like mean interarrival time, mean service time, and number of customers for the simulation run

- a class which handles arrival probability distribution.

For a detailed description of such a simulation in C++, refer to [22].

Some researchers also refer to simulation with OO Databases (OODB) as OOS [61]. The integrated environment of simulation and database systems using an OO approach is a powerful tool. In a traditional simulation environment, the objects disappear after the simulation run and need to be reconstructed each time, which means additional overhead in efficiency and effort. An OODB provides "persistence" of objects for simulation. Objects may vary in size and structure, and may hold text, numbers, and bit-mapped data created from prior modeling experiments. These can be combined in various ways, thereby saving design time and effort. The OODB should provide an easy method for storage and retrieval of such objects [49].

The developments of artificial knowledge representation schemes and OOS are very much interrelated. Much of the recent interest in OOS originated from knowledge-based simulation systems, which combine OO paradigms with production rules to model intelligent behavior. Knowledge can be modularized as objects, procedures, methods, or rules can be designed to perform the desired operations on them. Adapting this kind of OO-based implementation of rule-based knowledge systems is fairly standard. Expert system-based packages can act as a simulation aid in various stages of the simulation life cycle. Thus, for example, expert system packages can be used in the problem specification stage as well as for diagnosing possible problems in an integrated simulation environment. For a detailed discussion on the relationship between knowledge-based simulation and object-oriented structures, refer to [64]. In [70], an analysis of OOS model building is provided in the context of AI. "Logic graphics," a flowchart-like technique which represents systems logic graphically, is discussed there. One of the problems in modeling complex control structures with this kind of technique is the difficulty of mixing model control logic with model definition, and this is addressed using OOS in [54] and [17]. Reference [55] explores in detail the relationship between AI and simulation in general and OOS in particular.

Traditional objects are passive or reactive, since they only change state through received messages, i.e., act on messages sent. Accurate encapsulation and modularization of control mechanisms are not easy to achieve. This behavior of objects has been extended in recent years. An active object hides its capability to change state, can model actual systems more realistically, and provides high modularity [50]. Objects have also been made "proactive." Proactive objects continuously exhibit some behavior; messages may either modify that behavior or spawn a concurrent activity. Proactive objects have been used in an OOS, where free-form spreadsheet, animated graphics, and OOS have been combined to form a tactical simulation environment called AGcitePeMo88. These and other extended versions of objects continue to enrich OOS design.

Integrated system design based on simulation has become popular since it was suggested in [56]. Thus, consistent with the present focus on building an integrated environment for simulation, several tools supporting modeling and analyzing, simulation coding, animation, debugging, report generation, and verifying/validating of OOS are needed. Specific tools such as graphical interfaces, statistical analyzers, and database languages to manipulate objects are essential. Recent systems based on this are TESS, which is, however, not OO-based [72] and SAOS [50], which is OO-based. A discussion of what constitutes a set of requirements for a standard integrated simulation environment can be found in [75]. Integrating a heterogeneous set of models and modeling paradigms is not an easy task. In particular, all the models must be made explicit, and their explicit descriptions must be described in a way so that they can be plugged into a given environment with reasonable ease. These expert interfaces or "wrappings" are proving to be essential in any such integrated system design [37].

Another interesting related area in this connection is hardware and software codesign of systems, where OO-based schemes are used to help a designer to evaluate a codesign operation for final implementation in hardware or software. Codesign operations are those that can be implemented in either hardware or software. Detailed evaluation is usually needed before selecting the final implementation that optimally partitions a system into software and hardware components. OO specification and simulation schemes can be adapted for such hardware and software tradeoffs. Such a C++ based OOS scheme is described in [85].

1.1.2. Basic Concepts of OOS

Objects can be regarded as abstract data types. An object encapsulates both the data and the operations manipulating the data. Data encapsulated in an object can be changed only by their procedures/methods. Only parts for object interactions can be made visible. Objects communicate by sending messages to each other, much like procedure calls.

An important basic concept is that of a class. Object classes are templates that describe the general properties of objects. An instance of a class is an object that belongs to the class and resides in memory after being defined in the program. Each instance contains the same data structure of the class, but usually has different values for each element of the data structure.

Classes without any instances are called abstract classes. These are used for defining subclasses. A subclass or a child class is a class that is said to be inherited from a parent or superclass. A subclass has some additional or missing properties with respect to its superclass.

The two most important characteristics of OOP and OOS are inheritance and polymorphism. Each object inherits its parent object's properties, i.e., data structures and procedures. Multiple inheritance is the ability to inherit from more than one superclass. Polymorphism means "the ability to take more than one form." Polymorphism allows an instance to overrule the definition of an inherited procedure, and thus handles the same message differently in different objects.

Another important concept is that of dynamic binding or late binding. The selection of a particular method from a set of methods with the same name can be postponed to run time. Such a scheme helps in selecting and activating a proper method dynamically. Dynamic binding is associated with polymorphism and inheritance. Let us illustrate these features with an example from the domain of digital computer systems. Figure 1.1 shows the class digital computer system and the example objects or instances of it. Thus, typical data structures of the digital computer system could be

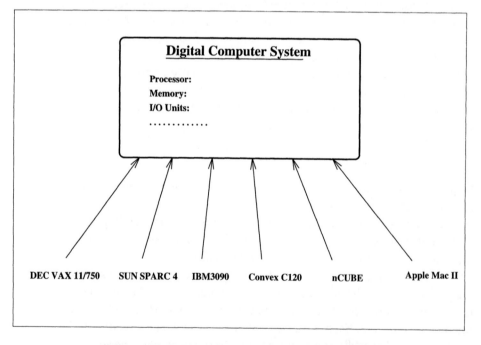

Figure 1.1 The digital computer system class and its instances.

processing unit, interface units, and memory unit, to name a few. Each instance of the class digital computer system such as IBM 3090, SUN SPARC 4, DEC VAX 11/750, Convex C120, nCUBE, or Apple Mac II gives different values of these data structures. A shared-memory multiprocessor system is a special type of multiprocessor system, and so inherits the properties of the multiprocessor system. It is called a subclass of the class multiprocessor, which is called the superclass. It may have some additional properties such as shared-memory interconnect, which may additionally refer to the specific interconnection pattern. Since a multiprocessor system is a digital computer system, a shared-memory multiprocessor system also inherits the features of a digital computer system.

OO theorists prefer OO analysis, design, and implementation as a total package for good OO system design as this makes the transition from one phase to another relatively easy. Thus, in the middle of an OO analysis, one can make parallel systems a superclass of multiprocessors and add on subclasses of multiprocessors such as distributed-memory multiprocessors. In this way, a detailed hierarchy chart like the one shown in Figure 1.2 can be built, which corresponds to the actual system chart and depicts the real relation between classes.

A **class** is sometimes derived from more than one **class**, and inherits the properties of all of its **superclasses**. Thus, the hybrid multiprocessor

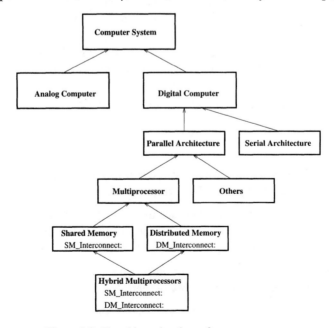

Figure 1.2 Class hierarchy chart of computer system.

class could be a subclass of a shared-memory multiprocessor and distributed memory multiprocessor, and inherits data structures like shared-memory interconnect and distributed-memory interconnect from each of its superclasses. This is an example of multiple inheritance (as shown in Figure 1.2). An abstract class in this example is Parallel Architecture which has no instances. It is used for defining subclasses.

Let us assume that a simulation program or method can be written to animate the execution of a computer program using these different digital computers. Thus, animate_execution can be a common name for the methods that belong to different objects and do similar things, but in different ways. This is an example of the polymorphic use of a method. Polymorphism can also be combined with dynamic binding. Let us assume that we want to run, on different windows on our computer screen, the animate_execution method of each parallel system class. To do it for all such systems, one can perhaps include within a "for loop" the invocation of the method animate_execution for all parallel system classes in a single statement. This means less code and clean design compared to the procedural version of the program. The OOS system will select the corresponding methods for each name during run time: an illustration of dynamic/late binding.

A framework is a set of objects and a set of rules of interactions. Frameworks are generic, and it helps in designing large systems rapidly. The ability of reusing and extending existing objects, object behavior, and object interactions is an important property of OOS [10] by allowing for rapid prototyping and construction of large simulation systems.

1.1.3. Advantages and Disadvantages of OOS

OOS has several attractive characteristics for extensive use. The most important ones are:

- Lego-like modeling/design using a building-block approach together with the use of abstract data types that allow easy integration.

- Information hiding, which hides internal object details from the external world with the class concept and provides encapsulation of structure and function within a single entity called an object.

- Modularity, with classes as modules and a proper design of objects (avoiding too many or too few objects).

- Hierarchical development and rapid prototyping with polymorphism.

- Software reusability by inheritance, which allows new object types to be defined in terms of already existing object definitions. Reuse can be made at both the class and framework levels.

- Identity, which permits distinction of each object from others, and allows a graph-structured representation of the system.

- Overloading, which is a technique to extend the behavior of an operator or a function, the use of the same name (function/operator) to do identical things to different objects.

Other advantages of OOS include clean design, flexibility, incremental modeling, less coding, portability, and maintainability [51].

The greatest disadvantage of OOS is the transition from a procedural design mode to an OO design mode, i.e., the process of "paradigm shift" as mentioned in [10]. Some claim that OOS is restricted in that it is difficult to answer questions beyond "what if" analysis, and thus needs to be extended with a deductive mechanism that can provide answers to more varied questions [66]. Another difficulty is the absence of an object library in many languages, but this has been increasingly addressed in recent times in languages like C++. Sometimes too many objects and too little structure can create an inefficient design.

Simulation using traditional non-OO schemes typically runs faster (20–25%) and generally requires less memory than an OOS system [51], [11], [47]. Still, the advantages outweigh the disadvantage of OOS.

1.1.4. Modeling Paradigms in OOS

Standard OO analysis and design schemes like Coad/Yourdon (CY), Booch, OOSD, etc., can also be applied to OOS design [20], [11], [47]. A brief discussion of these methods follows.

One fundamental aspect of any OO analysis and design is the graphical, model-independent representation that goes with any scheme. In any OO analysis phase, the key steps are:

- identify classes and objects

- define attributes

- define the functions done by the objects

- identify the relationship between various objects

- group objects.

The graphical representations (containing elements denoting classes, objects, inheritance, and the communication/relationship between objects/ classes) of an OO analysis/design vary quite a bit from one OO scheme to another. A brief discussion of two such schemes, CY and Booch, will illustrate this point. In Booch notation, a class is represented by a blob with dashed lines, whereas CY uses a rounded rectangle; data are represented within a class, and so are shown in the center of the rectangle. In Booch diagrams, data define relationships between classes, and are shown with two parallel lines terminating on a small circle. In the CY scheme, the functions or methods (in particular, public methods) of a class are considered encapsulated in a class much like data, and so are listed in the bottom portion of the class. Booch diagrams represent methods as sending messages to objects. Objects are represented in Booch by solid blobs, and in CY by rounded rectangles with two solid boundaries, thus denoting classes. Inheritance is shown in CY as a line with a semicircle on it, with the open end of the semicircle pointing toward the child class. Booch shows inheritance with solid pointed arrows between parent and child classes. Communication between objects is shown in both CY and Booch by arrows between object layers. Relationships between objects in CY are of two types: 1) whole–part, which is denoted by an arrow with a triangle from the part object to the whole, or 2) an instance relationship, which is represented by a single line connecting objects. Booch has a more rigorous representation that also shows relationships between classes. In brief, Booch diagrams are more complex but detailed, whereas CY diagrams offer simplicity at the expense of details. Both can be used in any object-oriented design (OOD). For further details, see [15].

The methods described above are usually applied to OOP design. However, they are equally applicable to OOS design. Several modeling methods specific to OOS also exist.

Ziegler's DEVS formalism specifies discrete-event systems in a hierarchical and modular form, and is based on system-theory concepts [89]. It is a model description language that allows event, activity, and process views and accommodates symbolic knowledge representations. The DEVS formalism permits two types of models: atomic and coupled. An atomic model is the elementary and basic one, with specific I/O. Its internal structure cannot be altered by the user. A coupled model can be formed by combining atomic and other coupled models with compatible I/Os. Its structure can be changed by the user. Coupled models can be used for designing larger coupled models, allowing systems to be designed in a hierarchical manner. A database of models and data is created for storage and reuse. This concept has been extended, for example, in [42], where the author proposes an extended environment with a model/database for holding an entire modeling environment for multiple analyses of a given problem.

OOS modeling with embedded production rules has been reported extensively in the literature. In this scheme, rules are used to define the behavior of objects, and simulation proceeds by execution of these rules. A rule is of the form: if *condition* then *action*.

The condition is usually a conjunction of predicates about system properties. The action is a specification of changes to the current state of the system [60]. This scheme is ideally suited for distributed simulation.

The client–server paradigm is also an OOS scheme. In this modeling scheme, there are two kinds of objects, clients and servers, that belong to a common class [8]. A client object gets activated by a start operation after its creation, and then acts independently (usually described by an iterating script). A client receives no messages. A server, on the other hand, only receives and serves requests from clients. A variant of this scheme is the actor–network model, where only one kind of object, an actor, acts and communicates with other actors, using explicit message-passing schemes. Both of these schemes are highly suitable for implementation on parallel architectures, using a parallel/distributed simulation scheme, as discussed in the Beehive system simulation [7].

1.1.5. OOS Languages versus Simulation Languages

Although in earlier stages, traditional high-level languages like PASCAL, Modula-II, Ada, and C were used for OOS, they needed to be extended with OOS facilities. Earlier examples can be found in [26], [25], and [63]. A recent example is a C-based OO system named Calico that supports all OO facilities including multiple inheritance [23]. However, at present, with the emergence of many OOP and OOS languages, these above-mentioned languages are not that popular among designers, and either a special-purpose simulation language or a general-purpose OO language is used. The selection of an OOS implementation language depends on, among other things, flexibility, expressive power, portability, library support, and run-time performance [61].

Simulation Languages

Languages like SIMULA, GPSS, SIMSCRIPT, and SLAM are available for simulation system development [39]. Most of these are inefficient or inadequate for OOS, except SIMULA. SIMULA-67 is the first language that contained the seed of OOP with concepts like data abstraction, encapsulation, polymorphism, and inheritance. However, SIMULA has not found wide usage due to its Algol-like structure, which is not popular among a large number of designers/programmers who are FORTRAN/COBOL/C structure-oriented, and due to the fact that it cannot be easily integrated with other systems.

General-Purpose OO Languages

Languages like C++, Objective-C, and CLOS can be adapted suitably for performing OOS. Of these, the most frequently used languages are C++ and its variants. C++ is the most versatile and popular of these for OOS. A good review of OO modeling using C++ can be found in [22], [14], and [68]. In SimPOL, SIMULA-like simulation primitives have been added on top of C++ for ease of simulation [44].

Many designers prefer icon-based OO languages like Object Vision for ease of design [29]. Finally, instance-based OO languages like SELF [79] are emerging, where new objects can be created easily by composition and specialization of existing objects. These can be readily used for simulation purposes.

AI-Oriented OO Languages

Languages such as Flavor, Scheme, and SCOOPS, which are LISP-based, entity-oriented, modular, and interactive, have also been used [38], [69]. These have facilities for defining classes, generic functions, and methods. Some of these have been updated with the DEVS formalism. The resulting systems, such as DEVS-SCHEME/DEVS-CLOS [88], are more appropriately geared toward modeling and simulation. The main problems of LISP-based systems are that they are often slow, and may not integrate well with other components in an overall integrated simulation system. Finally, MODL is a Prolog-based OOS environment that combines simulation, reasoning, and graphics to make the simulation more powerful [66].

Other Special OOS Languages/Packages

Several languages, including ROSS, Smalltalk-80, ModSim/ModSim II, SIMPLE++, and SIM++, have been developed for OOS. The ROSS language, developed at the RAND Corporation, was one of the earlier simulation languages that supported multiple inheritance [35]. Smalltalk-80 has a number of advantages, including rapid prototyping and the associated integrated environment. It provides different classes for discrete-event simulation and probability distributions. Smalltalk-based simulation can be either process-interaction-based or event-driven. The disadvantages of

Smalltalk are the absence of multiple inheritance and no general mechanism for access-based activation. ModSim is a language sponsored by the U.S. Army for OOS applications. ModSim II is a compiled, modular OO language that supports multiple inheritance [6]. Simple ++ is an OOS package that supports simultaneous modeling, simulation, and animation, with an easy-to-use graphical user interface [1]. DEVSIM++ is a C++ implementation of the DEVS formalism [34]. SIM++ is a package based on C++ that supports event-oriented OO sequential or parallel simulation, and provides a set of simulation primitives [41].

1.1.6. Applications Using OOS

Although OOS is used in almost every type of application, a large percentage of OOS simulation work is built around the modeling of production/manufacturing systems, battlefield and other defense-related simulation, and spacecraft simulation. Other widely differing application areas where OOS has been applied include superconducting collider modeling, flowshop, real-time and process-control, ecology, and management education and training [4], [28].

Digital systems span a wide range, including simulators for microarchitectures [78], multiprocessor systems like MUDS [58], Mentat [30], and a LISP-based system in [76]. Network modeling using OOS is described in [5], [21]. PRISM [80] and DOSE [43] have been reported for a simulator of queue networks. SESAME [77] has been reported for modeling neural nets.

We are interested in OOS of VLSI-realizable digital systems. In order to create a framework for this type of design, the first step is to identify various objects at different levels, and then create a database and a uniform framework for conducting simulation with the object database. Design objects can be of various types, corresponding to various levels of VLSI design: synthesis, RTL, logic, and circuits. Various objects result from using different technologies and design approaches (for example, sequential versus parallel/systolic). Furthermore, multiple versions of a typical design may result from a design scheme that may optimize, for example, area, power, or speed or a suitable combination [3]. A classification of objects by building some kind of hierarchy is desirable. Object models at various levels of VLSI design have been developed recently. At the synthesis level, for example, Ptolemy is a C++ based tool that supports modeling and simulation of typically single-processor and shared-memory multiprocessor DSP systems [16]. At the hardware logic level, VHDL is a frequently used language/tool that allows structured and hierarchical object composition. However, inheritance is not supported in VHDL, and sequential processes are used to model the behavior of active components [50]. OPERAS, the tool we describe in this chapter, is targeted toward low-power VLSI DSP system design at a coarser grain level [87].

1.1.7. Parallel and Distributed OOS

Providing each simulated object a real processor, although attractive in theory, may not work well in many applications due to practical constraints, especially when a complex system with many objects is modeled. OO Parallel Simulation (OOPS) allows one to have more hardware resources like memory and processing power at the designer's disposal, which can be used to reduce simulation run time or conduct large-scale simulation [41]. OOS is usually sequential in nature. Efforts to make it parallel/distributed have been made using traditional distributed simulation techniques [32] or distributed decision-making schemes by associating production rules [45], [71]. Therefore, any such OOPS requires a few desirable properties. First, one must ensure that the program is designed so that it can run on any architecture, using any number of processors (one to many). Second, one must ensure that the program produces the same results in various runs, with identical input. This means that the run-time executive needs to be designed carefully. Some argue that concurrency-hiding abstractions are useful for such designs, while others prefer high-level techniques to handle such issues.

Concurrent versions of some standard OO languages and new concurrent OO languages like Concurrent Smalltalk, Emerald, Gnu C++, and COOL have emerged in recent years that may be used for OOPS. Such various languages can be classified based on process-management-related properties, such as granularity, or activation/termination conditions. See [86] for a description of 14 such languages.

OOPS packages/environments worth mentioning are Synapse [82] and a concurrent logic language KL1-based simulator [45].

In the next section, the features of C++ will be described in some detail, as this is the language of implementation of the package described in this chapter, OPERAS.

1.2.   FEATURES OF C++

As already mentioned, C++ is one of the main OO languages in use today. In this section, the main features of C++ will be reviewed in some detail, since this is the implementation language of the package described in this chapter.

In addition to data abstraction and encapsulation, inheritance, and poly-morphism facilities, C++ allows function/operator overloading, in-line functions, strong typing, and modularity, among other things. Also, C++ is compatible with C. The fundamental elements of C++ are *classes* and *objects*.

1.2.1. Class and Object

The class construct supports data abstraction by data hiding. A *class* is a user-defined data type in C++. It can consist of members that are either methods (similar to functions) or data. The scope of the class is dependent on the keyword *public*. All declarations not declared as *public* are local and private to the class, and only methods (functions) belonging to that class are capable of accessing the *private* variables and methods. A *class* is somewhat similar to *struct*, with the great difference that *struct* allows full access to its members whereas *class* can restrict access.

For example, one may define the class of digital computers as

```
class Digital_Computer {
        char name[20];
        int  year;
        float price;
};
```

A function or a method can instantiate a class in two ways: it can simply declare an object on the stack like a normal local variable, or it can use the *new* operator to dynamically allocate the object from heap memory.

The visibility of a data member of a class is implemented by an ac-cess mechanism which can be one of three types: *private*, *protected*, or *public*. Private data members of a class are protected by the *private* dec-laration in a class. The *private* members belonging to a class can only be accessed by the methods of that same class. This is known as "data hiding." The *public* keyword is used in front of those data members that can be accessed from anywhere in the program. The default access type is *private*. A *protected* member can be accessed by member functions of its own class, as well as by member functions of classes derived from this class.

For example, one may write

```
class Digital_Computer {
private:
        char name[20];
        int  year;
        float price;
```

```
public:
    //member function declarations
    init(char*, int, float);
           . . . .
}
```

An object is an instance of a class, and performs the behavior of the class with specific data values. Thus, the instantiations of the Digital_Computer class could be written as

```
Digital_Computer digitalcomputer1, digitalcomputer2,
                 digitalcomputer3;
```

The operators are symbols such as +, *, &, and %. Member functions define the behavior of a class and operate on global and object data, and are the interface between the data and outside world. A member function can have an argument list which allows the rest of the program to pass values to its objects. For example, the member function *init()* declared in the code segment above could be defined as

```
void Digital_Computer::init(char N[], int x, float y) {
    strcpy(name, N); //copy from N to name
    year = x;
    price = y;
}
```

A class declaration with a member function prototype can be made, and the member function's code can be included in the same file or linked by the linker. If the body of the member function is defined outside the class declaration, then the scope resolution operator "::" needs to be used in front of the body of the function, as shown above. This binds the member function with the class. Objects instantiated from that class such as *digitalcomputer1* may execute the *init()* method by preceding the call with the corresponding object name and a dot operator as follows:

```
main() {
    Digital_Computer digitalcomputer1, digitalcomputer2,
                     digitalcomputer3;

    digitalcomputer1.init("sun_sparc_4.", 1988, 100000);
    digitalcomputer2.init("IBM_3090.", 1987, 50000);
    digitalcomputer3.init("Apple_MacII.", 1989, 3000);
}
```

In object-oriented terminology, the method invocation shown is referred to as message passing to an object. Message passing is the basic method of communication between objects in C++. Specific messages are passed between objects by invoking the corresponding methods in the object. A class declaration, which shows the public methods' interfaces and the public data members, is sufficient to use an object of that class. A class library containing various class definitions can therefore supply the building blocks for program development.

Encapsulation allows one to model a program as a collection of smart objects (with behaviors and attributes) by combining (binding together) the data members and member functions within a class. Therefore, a program can be created that does not directly access any data member of a class, but simply directs the objects to perform user tasks by sending messages to objects. These member functions of the class take care of all tasks such as initialization, updating, data error checking, or printing, as needed. A user only needs to concentrate on the method defining the object interface. This separation of object data definition from object interface allows the programmer to concentrate on the overall software design of object interactions via methods. OO languages also make programming easier because they facilitate reusing of code, modularity, and data hiding. A program can be broken up into independent parts and developed separately. Only the interfaces need to be common for communication between various objects. The separate code modules can be redesigned and changed if needed, keeping the interface portions unchanged. Sharing or reusing code can be done by extending a base class suitably with data and methods. Classes can also be derived to make new classes.

1.2.2. Variable and Function Bindings

C++ provides a new reference variable type not found in the C language. This type acts like a pointer because it refers to a variable location as opposed to a variable value. The reference variable can be used like a regular variable in the program syntax, and does not require explicit dereferencing as C++ will automatically dereference a reference-type variable.

Sometimes the efficiency of a program is increased by in-line substitution of code. The *in-line* keyword can be used to define in-line methods:

```
inline void Digital_Computer::init(char N[], int x, float y) {
    strcpy(name, N);
    year = x;
    price = y;
}
```

When this method is referred to, message/function call overhead is eliminated by substituting the code itself in place of the call.

Function overloading in C++ refers to the redefinition of a function with another function of the same name, but with a different number and different types of arguments. In the example below, two function prototypes *printChar()* have the same name but different argument types and number of arguments, and they perform entirely different functions. This is often referred to as the "Polymorphism with Overloaded Functions." Polymorphism means having more than one form. C++ will bind the correct form of *printChar()* automatically.

```
//example of function overloading
#include <iostream.h>

void printChar(char);              //declaration
void printChar(char, int);         //declaration

void main() {
    printChar('<');                // call
    printChar('=',25);             // call
}

void printChar(char ch) {          //function definition
    for(int k=0; k<35; k++)
    cout << ch;
    cout << endl;
}

void printChar(char ch, int i) { //function definition
    for(int k=0; k<i; k++)
    cout << ch;
    cout << endl;
}
```

The output from this sample program is

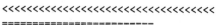

```
<<<<<<<<<<<<<<<<<<<<<<<<<<<<<<<<<<<<<
=========================
```

Operator overloading redefines the meaning of traditional C++ operators by extending their definitions to user-defined data types. For example, the arithmetic operator + can be overloaded to add two or more strings or extended to other completely unrelated operations between two classes.

1.2.3. Class Inheritance

Inheritance is the behavior and data that a class gets from another class, and is explicitly supported in C++. In Coad and Yourdon's terms, it is the "Gen-Spec" relationship. The derived class retains all the features of the parent class, and may contain some additional features of its own. In the following code, the effects of inheritance are emulated, although the inheritance mechanism is not actually used. Parallel_Architecture is a child/derived class of the base class Digital_Computer, and so inherits all of its data and method members, including any other base class of Digital_Computer if Digital_Computer is itself derived from other base classes. In addition, additional members can be defined that are particular to the Parallel_Architecture derived class.

```
///////////First example////////////////////
// Showing effects of class inheritance //
class Digital_Computer {
private:
     char name[20];
     int  year;
     float price;
public:
     //member declarations
};

class Parallel_Architecture {
private:
     char name[20];
     int  year;
     float price;
     float performance;
     int number_of_processors;
     char interconnect_type[20];
public:
     //member declarations
};
```

To use the C++ inheritance mechanism, Parallel_Architecture should be declared as

```
class Parallel_Architecture : Digital_Computer {
private:
     float performance;
     int number_of_processors;
     char interconnect_type[20];
public:
     //member declarations
};
```

In the second C++ example, the classes Header1 and Header2 are derived from the Base class. Note the *public* declaration, the ":" symbol, and the name of the base class "Base" in the declaration of the

derived classes, Header1 and Header2, which establishes the relationships
between the classes. Note the two method calls to *prnt_head()* from the
main routine. The method *prnt_head()* has the same name, argument, and
return types in parent and child classes. However, the overloading feature in C++ enables the execution of the functions in the derived classes
first.

```
/////////Second Example////////////////
// used as base class for inheritance
class Base {
    public:
        void prnt_head()
            { cout << "This is not printed\n";}
};

//derived class header1
class Header1: public Base {
    public:
        void prnt_head()
            { cout << "List of Computers\n";}
};

//derived class header2
class Header2: public Base {
    public:
        void prnt_head()
            { cout << "End of Report\n";}
};

void main() {
    Header1 hdr1;       // object of derived header1 class
    Header2 hdr2;       // object of derived header2 class
    Header1* ptr1;      //pointer to the class header1

    ptr1 = &hdr1;       //address of hdr1 in pointer
    ptr1->prnt_head(); //Calls hdr1.prnt_head();

    Header2* ptr2;

    ptr2 = &hdr2;       //address of hdr2 in pointer
    ptr2->prnt_head(); //Calls hdr2.prnt_head();
}
```

Thus, the printout will be

```
                    List of Computers
                    End of Report
```

In addition to single inheritance, multiple inheritance is possible in C++. A class can be derived from more than one base class. The derived class inherits properties from multiple base classes. This process is known as "multiple inheritance." In the example below, the class Hybrid_Multiprocessors is derived from the classes Shared_Memory and Distributed_Memory. The parent classes are listed after the ":" symbol in the declaration of the inherited class Hybrid_Multiprocessors.

```
class Hybrid_Multiprocessors :
    private Shared_Memory, private Distributed_Memory {
    . . . .
    Body the Derived Class Declarations
    . . . .
};
```

Also note below how calls to functions in the classes Shared_Memory and Distributed_Memory are made from the interconnect() function in the class Hybrid_Multiprocessors. The language will automatically bind the correct message method in each case. In the case of an identical method name in the two parent classes, the programmer must explicitly invoke the correct message.

```
class Shared_Memory {
private:
    char name[20];
    int  year;
    float price;
    float performance;
    int number_of_processors;
public:
    //member declarations
    void SM_interconnect();
};

class Distributed_Memory {
private:
    char name[20];
    int  year;
    float price;
    float performance;
    int number_of_processors;
public:
    //member declarations
    void DM_interconnect();
};
```

```
class Hybrid_Multiprocessors :
    private Shared_Memory, private Distributed_Memory {
private:
    char interconnect_type[20];
public:
    //member declarations
    void interconnect();
};

void Hybrid_Multiprocessors::interconnect() {
    if(number_of_processors<1000)
        Shared_Memory::SM_interconnect();
    else
        Distributed_Memory::DM_interconnect();
}
```

It should be mentioned that there is some controversy regarding the use of multiple inheritance in C++. Some programmers argue that a single inheritance can deal with all inheritance situations in C++, and that although the concept of multiple inheritance is powerful and simple, the implementation can give rise to unusual complications. For a detailed discussion, see the references.

Friend Functions

Friend functions are used when a nonmember function or method needs to access the private data or methods of a class. In such cases, the function/method that is permitted to access the private members is declared by placing the *friend* keyword in front of the functional prototype in the class declaration. For example, suppose the object details of the *Digital_Computer* class are needed by the *print_detail()* global function. Then the code that allows access to the private data members of *Digital_Computer* is as follows:

```
//Digital_Computer class declaration
class Digital_Computer {
public:
    void init(char N[], int x, float y);
    friend void print_detail(const Digital_Computer comp);
    . . . .
}

//Main routine
main() {
    Digital_Computer digitalcomputer1, digitalcomputer2,
                     digitalcomputer3;
```

```
digitalcomputer1.init("sun_sparc_4.", 1988, 100000);
digitalcomputer2.init("IBM 3090.", 1987, 50000);
digitalcomputer3.init("Apple MacII.", 1989, 3000);

print_detail(digitalcomputer1); //call by a friend
print_detail(digitalcomputer2); //call by a friend
print_detail(digitalcomputer3); //call by a friend
return 0;
}


//global function print_detail()
void print_detail(const Digital_Computer comp) {

//Accessing the private data members of Digital_Computer objects
cout << "Computer name:    " << comp.name << "\n";
cout << "Computer year:    " << comp.year  << "\n";
cout << "Computer price:   " << comp.price << "\n\n";
}
```

In this code segment, the *print_detail()* global function can access the private data members of the Digital_Computer class such as name and price. This access is allowed because the *Digital_Computer* class has declared *print_detail()* to be a friend function.

1.2.4. Constructor and Destructor

C++ has two special types of members called constructor and destructor. When an object is created, a constructor is invoked automatically, and when an object is destroyed, the corresponding destructor is invoked. For example, the allocation of memory space from the heap memory for an object's use may be done through constructors when the object is created. A constructor can also initialize the members of a class, and performs other necessary processing before the object instantiation is completed. A constructor has the same name as its class. Moreover, the memory space the object allocated is released when the object goes out of scope. A destructor performs the necessary "garbage collection" before the object is destroyed, and it has the same name as its class with an additional tilde in front:

```
class Digital_Computer{
private:
    char name[20];
    int  year;
    float price;
```

```
public:
    //member etc., function declarations
    void init(char N[], int x, float y);
    Digital_Computer();    //Constructor
    ~Digital_Computer();   //Destructor
};
```

Note that the constructor and destructor cannot be invoked directly by the programmer, but they are automatically invoked when the object is created or destroyed.

1.2.5. Virtual Functions and Late Binding

As mentioned previously, polymorphism allows one to refer to methods, functions, and operators that have the same name but perform different functions, depending on the associated object or parameters. This feature is implemented with overloading in C++. Overloading of operators/functions makes it possible for the same operator/function to perform different operations/functions, with different or additional meanings. Another form of polymorphism is the automatic resolution and binding of the correct methods between the derived and base class when methods of identical name and parameters are defined both in the base class and in the derived class. This mechanism is implemented through the virtual function feature of C++. Virtual functions are member functions defined in a base class with the *virtual* attribute. This method, with identical name and parameter list, can be redefined by a derived class, and C++ will automatically bind the correct method to a method call. In the example below, the function prnt_head() is a virtual function.

```
//Base Class Declaration
class Base {
    public:
        //virtual function
        virtual void prnt_head()
            { cout << "This is never printed\n";}
};

//Derived Class Declaration
class Header1: public Base {
    public:
        void prnt_head()
            { cout << "List of Computers\n";}
};
```

```
//Derived Class Declaration
class Header2: public Base {
    public:
        void prnt_head()
          { cout << "End of Report\n";}
    };

//Main Program
main () {
    //Virtual function for header
    Header1 hdr1;      // object of derived header1 class
    Header2 hdr2;      // object of  derived header 2 class
    Base* ptr;         // pointer to the class Base

    ptr = &hdr1;       // address of hdr1 in pointer
    ptr->prnt_head(); // execute printing of header

    ptr = &hdr2;       // address of hdr2 in pointer
    ptr->prnt_head(); // execute printing of end-message
}
```

First, assume that the keyword *virtual* is NOT used in front of the function prnt_head() in the Base class declaration; then the program output from the function call ptr->prnt_head() would be

```
This is never printed
This is never printed
```

Even though the ptr points to an object of class Header1, it is itself of class Base, so the access resolution will access the Base class' prnt_head() method. The function ptr->prnt_head() in the base class is executed twice.

With the *virtual* declaration, the function becomes a virtual function, and the call to each member function is automatically resolved and bound to the correct method in the derived class. In this case, the member functions of the derived classes are executed using the same function calls, and the output is

```
List of Computers
End of Report
```

1.2.6. Summary

In this section, we have developed a simple C++ program modeling the different classes of computer systems. The summary of the program is outlined as follows.

```
//An example illustrating various OO-features of C++
//The program prints a simple report on digital computers
//First the declaration of header files follows

#include <iostream.h>
#include <iomainp.h>
#include <string.h>

//////// class declarations ////////
class Digital_Computer {
private:
    char name[20];
    int  year;
    float price;
public:
    //member and friend function declarations
    void init(char N[], int x, float y);
    friend void print_detail(const Digital_Computer comp);
    Digital_Computer(void);   //this is a constructor
    ~Digital_Computer();      //this is a destructor
};

class Base {        // used for virtual function
public:
    virtual void prnt_head() //virtual function
       { cout << "This is never printed\n";}
};

class Header1: public Base {
public:
    void prnt_head()
       { cout << "List of Computers\n";}
};

class Header2: public Base {
public:
    void prnt_head()
       { cout << "End of Report\n";}
};

//////// init() method definition ////////
void Digital_Computer::init(char N[], int x, float y) {
    strcpy(name, N);
    year = x;
    price = y;
}
```

```
//////// class declarations ////////
class Shared_Memory {
private:
    char name[20];
    int  year;
    float price;
    float performance;
    int number_of_processors;
public:
    //member declarations
    void SM_interconnect();
};

class Distributed_Memory {
private:
    char name[20];
    int  year;
    float price;
    float performance;
    int number_of_processors;
public:
    //member declarations
    void DM_interconnect();
};

class Hybrid_Multiprocessors :
    private Shared_Memory, private Distributed_Memory {
private:
    char interconnect_type[20];
public:
    //member declarations
    void interconnect();
};

void Hybrid_Multiprocessors::interconnect() {
    if(number_of_processors<1000)
        Shared_Memory::SM_interconnect();
    else
        Distributed_Memory::DM_interconnect();
}

//////// Overloaded Global Functions ////////
void headoutline(char);
// declaration of head outline--overloaded
void headoutline(char, int);
// declaration of head outline--overloaded
```

```
///////////////////// Main Program/////////////////////////
main() {
    //objects of class Digital_Computer
    Digital_Computer digitalcomputer1, digitalcomputer2,
                      digitalcomputer3;

    headoutline('<'); //call of headoutline--overloaded
    headoutline('=', 25); //call of headoutline--overloaded

    //Virtual function for header
    Header1 hdr1; // object of derived header1 class
    Header2 hdr2; // object of derived header2 class
    Base* ptr; //pointer to the class Base
    ptr = &hdr1; //address of hdr1 in pointer
    ptr->prnt_head(); //execute printing of header
    //End of virtual function

    //Execution of ....
    digitalcomputer1.init("sun_sparc_4.", 1988, 100000);
    digitalcomputer2.init("IBM 3090.", 1987, 50000);
    digitalcomputer3.init("Apple MacII.", 1989, 3000);

    print_detail(digitalcomputer1); //call by friend function
    print_detail(digitalcomputer2); //call by friend function
    print_detail(digitalcomputer3); //call by friend function

    // Virtual function for end-message
    ptr = &hdr2; //address of hdr2 in pointer
    ptr->prnt_head(); //execute printing of end-message
}

// text of header outline function--overloaded
void headoutline(char ch) {
    for(int k=0; k<35; k++)
    cout << ch;
    cout << endl;
}

void headoutline(char ch, int i) {
    for(int k=0; k<i; k++)
    cout << ch;
    cout << endl;
}

// text of friend function
void print_detail(const Digital_Computer comp) {
    cout << "Computer name:     " << comp.name << "\n";
```

```
        cout << "Computer year:    " << comp.year  << "\n";
        cout << "Computer price:   " << comp.price << "\n\n";
}
```

The output of the program is

```
              List of Computers
              Computer name:    sun_sparc_4.
              Computer year:    1988
              Computer price:   100000

              Computer name:    IBM 3090.
              Computer year:    1987
              Computer price:   50000

              Computer name:    Apple MacII.
              Computer year:    1989
              Computer price:   3000

              End of Report
```

1.3.   DESIGN OF OPERAS

In the first section, a brief survey on the general OOS concepts was presented, and a simple overview of the C++ language features followed in Section 1.2. These two sections are by no means exhaustive, but rather a bird's-eye view of the field.

In this section, the design of a specific OOS named OPERAS is described in the context of design choices and tradeoffs of an object-oriented simulation system. In particular, the selections of basic implementation and simulation languages for simulation are critical. The pioneering SIMULA language will be used as a starting point for the discussion of simulation languages. After discussing the selection process of simulation language, the OPERAS is used to illustrate the design of an object-oriented simulation system in the domain of the signal processing electronic system design.

1.3.1. Simulation Language

Two main usages of simulation language can be identified. First, the simulation language is a vehicle through which the user models the system under simulation. The systems range from digital circuits or manufacturing processes to large battlefield simulations and socioeconomic systems. Consequently, the generality, simplicity, and expandability of the simulation language are important to allow for simple yet accurate modeling of the system. SIMULA is an example of such a general-purpose modeling and simulation language. In more specialized simulation applications, special modeling syntax may be implemented to facilitate the modeling activity. In other simulation tools, the user supplies the parameters to the model as inputs, which are simply interpreted by the simulation system to complete the simulation models. Typically, such input specifies only the parameters of an existing model, and it is not a simulation language since it lacks many programming language constructs. The computer program that interprets the parameters contains the actual language-based models of the system under study. In many modern simulation systems, the use of user-friendly graphic user interface also aids in the modeling activities. Examples of a special simulation system include many electronic schematic capture and simulation programs. SPICE is a popular circuit simulation program in which the input description is a list of circuit elements and associated parameters. The input description can be typed in by a user or automatically generated from a graphical schematic entry tool. SPICE simply reads the description and constructs the circuit network. Then the simulation is conducted according to a set of stimuli supplied by the user.

Second, the simulation languages are often used to program the computer to conduct the simulation using one of the simulation principles. For example, time-sequencing simulation updates the time in fixed increments, and the model descriptive data are updated at each time step. Differential equation-based models are often simulated in this manner. The simulation program describes data management and numerical calculation based on the model. Event-sequencing simulation models the continuous process as a list of events separated by varying intervals. At each event time, the model data are updated, and new events may be generated and scheduled in the future. In this usage, the simulation language is often used to describe the required list processing algorithm or events and simulation methods.

The early development of the simulation language essentially parallels the development of a general-purpose programming language. SIMULA is extended from ALGOL, and SIMSCRIPT II is Fortran-like. The reason for this closeness is that many of the desirable traits of a good programming language are also desirable in a simulation language. In fact, a simulation language may be considered as a superset of most general-purpose programming languages. The desirable traits of simulation/programming languages are paraphrased from [57]:

- *Generality* means that the same language can be used for many different applications.

- *Simplicity* means that the language has a well-thought-out, simple but general, and basic structure.

- *Expandability* allows one to achieve both generality and simplicity by allowing for special-purpose language extension to meet the special requirements.

- *Model closeness* means that an accurate and intuitive model of the problem can be expressed in a readable form.

- *Program structuring* means that programs can be broken down into manageable size for easy integration, debugging, and readability.

- *Security* means that the compiler and run-time systems can detect as many programming errors as early as possible.

- *Efficiency* means that the language allows the compiler to generate code with fast execution speed and resource efficiency.

- *Compatibility* means that the language allows for easy portability of programs across hardware platforms.

- *Special requirements* include facilities for numerical calculations, string handling, list structures, debugging, etc. Also, simulation capabilities are desirable.

Simulation systems have been implemented using the simulation languages, as well as the general-purpose programming language. Although simulation languages are considered as a separate type of computer language, the ideas and requirements of simulation applications have a great impact on the development of the general-purpose language. In fact, SIMULA contains many ideas that are central to the modern object-oriented programming paradigm.

Object-Oriented Language Features

SIMULA is a pioneering language in that some of the modern object-oriented language's basic features are found in SIMULA [57]. Specifically, SIMULA has data structures that allow for object class inheritance and protection. These ideas are extended in an object-oriented language as object polymorphism and object encapsulation. The protection and inheritance features of SIMULA make large simulation possible by minimizing the possibility of errors. The useful features making SIMULA popular are also driving the current interests in object-oriented simulation. In addition, SIMULA defines processes as a means of specifying the system under study. Each process runs autonomously, but interacts with others to make the simulation possible. SIMULA was defined with many of the basic desired properties of a modern simulation language.

Since the introduction of SIMULA, the state of software engineering has progressed to include many popular general-purpose languages such as C, PASCAL, Ada, Smalltalk, and C++. Among these, object-oriented languages are ideally suited for simulation because, in addition to the reasons mentioned above such as protection and inheritance, full object encapsulation and polymorphism make reliable and efficient programming easier. Also important, the widespread use of the standard programming environment means easy portability, integration, and management of the simulation system that uses the modern general-purpose languages.

Unlike SIMULA, the concept of concurrency is not commonly built into the current generation of the object-oriented language because parallel hardware is not commonly available and process concurrency is already implemented within the operating systems. Consequently, simulation system programmers implementing concurrency must write their own code or use the operating system's facilities. Other researchers have defined or extended the existing programming languages to allow for simulation such as parallel discrete-event simulation [2]. Parallel object-oriented language is an emerging area of research which may also address the lack of built-in concurrency of current object-oriented languages.

1.3.2. Object-Oriented Simulation System Design

OPERAS is an OOS package for designing low-power digital signal processing (DSP) systems. The low-power DSP design optimizes the energy consumption and performance of the signal processing system over a set of image processing benchmarks. By accurately estimating the power behavior of a whole system, one can optimize the system design choices using energy consumption criteria, as well as area and performance. The system design choices include partitioning of algorithms, architecture, as well as hardware and software partitioning of each system component.

In addition to algorithm and architecture, new circuit technologies also influence the power and performance behavior of a system. For example, low-voltage circuit techniques dramatically reduce system power because power is proportional to the square of the supply voltage [18], [81]. However, reduced supply voltage increases signal latency in CMOS circuits, and the system slows down. The modeling of interactions between performance and power with the parameter *supply voltage* is a goal of OPERAS. Furthermore, the simulator can also accommodate systems with mixed supply voltages and systems with scalable supply voltage.

Object-oriented modeling provides a powerful and flexible tool for expressing system design. Simulation for different domains such as mixed analog and digital systems as well as hardware/software cosimulation is possible by restructuring the simulator [48]. The simulator demonstrates how object-oriented modeling of complex systems allows for accurate simulation through an event-driven mechanism. OPERAS uses the efficient C++ compiler to generate a fast and efficient simulator which allows for the simulation of a large number of virtual machine cycles [74], [12].

For the remainder of this chapter, the "designer" will refer to the designer, and the "user" is the user of the OOS package for modeling and simulation.

The Structure and Simulation Flow

Figure 1.3 shows the overall simulation environment of OPERAS. The user describes the system design by defining a group of modules using the OPERAS input language (OSDL). As shown, each module has an interface specification, functional description, performance information, and energy estimation function. Furthermore, each module may also contain instantiations of other modules.

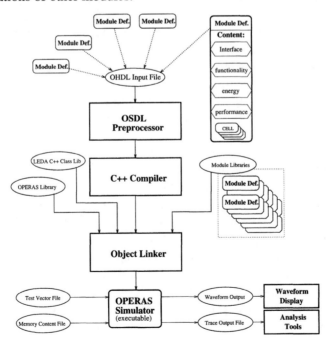

Figure 1.3 The structure of OPERAS.

The whole system is represented as a module at the root level of the hierarchical tree. The module definition contains other components called *cells* or *stdcells*. A cell is an instantiation of a user-specified module definition, and an stdcell is an instantiation of a module definition from the module libraries. In OPERAS, the user-defined module specifications are implemented as class definitions in C++, and instantiations of *cells* correspond to object instantiation within the class definition of a parents module. The module that defines the cell can consist of still other cells. The whole design is described in this hierarchical manner as each instantiated cell is a descendant, and complex systems can be formulated and modeled. Although nested structures are not new in programming languages, the use of constructors in C++ allows the designer to control the initialization simply and exactly.

All modules are derived classes of a basic *Module* class. The common methods and data members of all module objects are encapsulated within the base module class. The derived module's methods override the original module's methods through the use of a C++ virtual function mechanism. Consequently, each module can be treated in the same way through a common method interface, while the behavior of a particular module may be customized by overriding a subset of the methods. The user specifies only those portions of the model that are relevant by first deriving from the base module, and then specializes or extends the relevant class members. For example, the behavioral model of the module is encapsulated in the *execute()* virtual function. As the user creates or extends modules with different behavior, the *execute()* method is modified in the derived module class, and the new method definition overrides the old one. This is an example of polymorphism in the object-oriented paradigm because all module objects respond to the *execute()* message, but the actual behaviors are specified by the user. Furthermore, the OO inheritance and polymorphism mechanisms are used to handle the simulation as well as design specification and evolution, which will be elaborated on later.

The design of a new user-defined module can be inherited from an existing module, and only the aspects of the modules that are different are changed. While the performance and energy methods may be changed, the functional specification may remain unchanged. For example, a new adder design can be inherited from an old adder design by taking an existing adder module and modifying the power estimation algorithm without affecting the rest of the original adder implementation. Only the relevant changes need to be made, and this allows for fast design by reusing existing modules. A user may also add additional methods and data members through the

OSDL description, and the power of the C++ inheritance mechanism is provided for these new members.

Since OPERAS is a simulation package designed for a particular domain of application, a special language extension to facilitate the modeling of systems is defined. The additional syntax shields the user from the unnecessary details of the underlying simulation language, allowing the user to focus on the modeling. Yet, through the use of a preprocessor, the underlying C++ language is still available for the user to use. By extending the syntax, the user has to learn something new, but the total simulation system achieves the goals of model closeness, better program structuring, and being less error-prone.

After the input description is preprocessed by the OSDL preprocessor which automatically generates the C++ code, then the C++ code is compiled to generate the module object codes. The object linker is invoked to link the object codes with the module libraries, the OPERAS library, and the LEDA library. Module libraries contain the previously defined library modules. Additional simulator functionalities such as the event-driven simulation are contained within the OPERAS library. The LEDA C++ class library contains the standard implementations of common data structures which are used within OPERAS [52].

The user can direct the simulation by providing the test vectors and initial contents to the memory modules. The information is stored on the host machine file system, and the test vector and initialization information are handled by the pattern generator and memory objects, respectively. For example, the constant coefficients (called twiddle factors) for an FFT can be stored in a file. When the simulator starts to run, the twiddle factor can be read by the internal memory module. Currently, to implement persistent objects across simulation sessions, OPERAS saves the state of simulation objects onto the host file system. However, a complete object-oriented database system would be able to interface with OPERAS to store complete objects with state and interfaces. An object-oriented database system would also allow for dynamic construction of the system using parts from the database.

OPERAS generates output that describes the output waveform, and the waveform can be displayed by a standard waveform display program [46]. Output traces of selected nodes within a design can be generated to monitor for correctness and other analysis. Also, the trace output can be used to drive other simulation tools.

A major advantage of the C++ based simulation is that the existing development environment allows for integrated simulation with many other tools. For example, OPERAS has been applied to the simulation of a mesh-connected array of processors. The interconnection network has been modeled using a C-based simulator, and the combined simulation under OPERAS' control is achieved by linking the two simulators' object codes.

The object-oriented simulation structure of the OPERAS with suitable extension allows for distributed simulation. Extending the current generation of object-oriented programming language for efficient concurrent execution is an active area of research [83], [33]. By distributing objects to different machines, parallel simulation of a very large system is possible. However, the synchronization requirements make distributed simulation of tightly coupled systems difficult. In the case of large parallel systems, course grain synchronization between processors makes object-oriented distributed simulation feasible.

OSDL Input Description

As mentioned above, the OSDL module description consists of several parts: module interface, instantiation of new nets, cells, initialization information, and additional functions (methods). From the description, the preprocessor can generate the C++ code that implements the OPERAS internal representation of interconnected nets and modules. The bus width of the net object is specified in the net instantiation.

The module defined within the module libraries can be used as a database of existing module designs. First, the library modules can be instantiated as stdcell and used within the user-defined module. Second, the user can extend or modify the existing module using the C++ inheritance mechanism as described in the previous section. To use these module libraries, the user specifies the name of the libraries so that proper files will be included during the compilation and linkage. Furthermore, mature designs of user-defined modules can be collected to form new module libraries.

In addition to module functionality, the performance information is modeled by a delay method associated with each output of a module. This delay information can be implemented as a function or a lookup table of dependent variables such as temperature, supply voltage, process parameter, and circuit technology. This capability allows for modeling of a system consisting of mixed operating environment and circuit technology.

An example of OSDL description of an 8 b ALU is presented and the corresponding schematic of an 8 b ALU is shown in Figure 1.4. The power estimation method, *update_energy()*, produces an estimate of energy consumed each time the module's function is executed, and the user provides

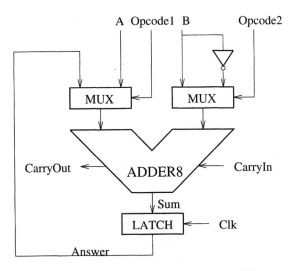

Figure 1.4 Schematic of the 8 b ALU (ALU8).

the C or C++ code which describes the energy estimation method. The estimation method can be derived from detailed circuit analysis and simulation, or from high-level energy models. Like the delay specification, the power estimation method can also have complex dependent variables from supply voltage to technology.

The interface section declares input and output nets, and the net section defines new net objects. The cell section instantiates other modules as new cell or stdcell and defines the interconnections. Then the necessary definitions of stdcells from the module libraries are included in the *hinclude* statement. Finally, the logic, performance, and energy estimation methods are defined by *execute()*, *delay()*, and *update_energy()*, respectively. Note that a private data member called *overflowCount* is introduced to keep track of how often the ALU units overflow. Also, a public method member called *getOverflowCount()* is available to access the encapsulated *getOverflow-Count*. All of the object-oriented mechanisms available through C++ can be applied to these user_defined members.

```
module ALU8 {
    desc {
    An 8-bits ALU unit
    }

    //* Interface Section *****
    output {Answer}
    output {CarryOut}
    output {Overflow}
```

```
       input {A}
       input {B}
       input {CarryIn}
       input {Opcode1}        //select input mux
       input {Opcode2}        //select input mux
       input {Clk}            //clock output latch

       //* Net Section ***********
       net {Addin1[8]}        //Specified with bus width
       net {Addin2[8]}
       net {Bbar[8]}
       net {Sum[8]}

       //* Cell Section **********
       cell MUX_8 {muxA (Addin1,Answer,A,Opcode1)}
       cell MUX_8 {muxB (Addin2,B,Bbar,Opcode2)}
       cell ADDER_8 {adder8 (Sum,CarryOut,
                       Addin1,Addin2,CarryIn)}
       stdcell LATCH{latch(Answer,Sum,Clk)}
       stdcell NOT {inv  (Bbar,B)}

       hinclude {<STDC/gate.h>,<STDC/latch.h>}

       private {
           int  overflowCount;
       }

method getOverflowCount{
    access { public }
    code {
        //* Legal C or C++ Code */
        //. . . Return overflowCount
    }
}

//* Performance as Delay Method *********
delay Overflow {
    //* Legal C or C++ Code */
        . . . . .
}

//* Functionality as Execute Method *********
execute (output Overflow,input Sum,
           input Addin1,input Addin2) {
    //* Overflow Detection Logic */
    Overflow = (
```

```
        !((Addin1>>7)&0x1 ^ (Addin2>>7)&0x1) &
        ((Addin1>>7)&0x1 ^ (Sum>>7)&0x1)) ? 1 : 0;
}

//* Energy Estimation Method *****
update_energy {
    /* energy estimation function */
    //* Legal C or C++ Code */
        . . . . .
}
}
```

OPERAS Class Hierarchy

Figure 1.5 shows the class hierarchy of the simulator. All classes are derived from the *GenCl* class which serves as a superclass of all simulation objects. The hierarchical class structure allows for the inheritance of common interfaces and data structures from the parent class. By deriving all the objects from a common base class, OO programming is made easier as all objects share common attributes and have the same basic interfaces. This common interface makes the whole simulation framework very extensible to other closely related domains such as modeling of software components of a system. For example, the *Hardware* class or classes

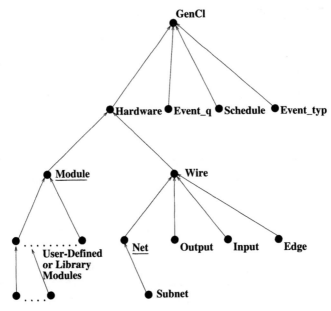

Figure 1.5 OPERAS class inheritance relationships.

derived from *Hardware* contain a name and a common method for obtaining the object name (e.g., *whoami()*). The name and the *whoami()* method are both inherited by all descendants of the *Hardware* class. Similarly, the *Wire* class encapsulates methods and data that are common to all wire objects. The *Event_q*, *Schedule*, and *Event_typ* classes implement the event-driven simulation mechanism.

In OPERAS-based design, the whole system is described in a concise, hierarchical, and modular manner through two fundamental object classes: *Module* and *Net*. The detailed behavior of a module is specified by the user using the C or C++ code, and the C or C++ code is encapsulated within the methods of *Module* class. Net objects are used to interconnect the modules, and each net object can be defined as a single wire or a bus of wires. The *Subnet* class is used to connect one or multiple wires within a bus to a module. For example, in a processor design, the wires representing the source register number can be extracted from a net that contains the whole processor instruction. OPERAS models the hardware concurrency and conducts the event-driven simulation through this simple system of modules and nets. The objects of *Input*, *Output*, and *Edge* classes are used within the internal implementation of the module class to interface with the net objects, and they will be described in the next section.

1.3.3. System Modeling and Simulation

In the design of the OOS system, arriving at the correct object-oriented model is important for concise and precise modeling and simulation. References [20] and [11] provide guidance in this. The system modeling activities were found to be naturally and smoothly described in a hierarchical fashion. However, the directed graph, with the module being nodes and the arcs representing input–output relationships, was found to be a natural representation of systems. The graph representation can model the complex interactions between modules in a clean and efficient way. Consequently, the event-driven simulation is conducted over a graphlike internal representation. Using the C++ constructor, the internal directed graph representation is generated from the hierarchical description. After the design transformation, the hierarchical user view is preserved through the naming of modules and nets.

Figure 1.6 illustrates the internal representation of the 8 b ALU example. The OSDL code of the ALU unit is shown in a subsection of Section 1.3.2, and the schematic of the ALU unit is shown in Figure 1.4. For Figure 1.6, the 8 b adder is assumed to be constructed out of two 4 b adders.

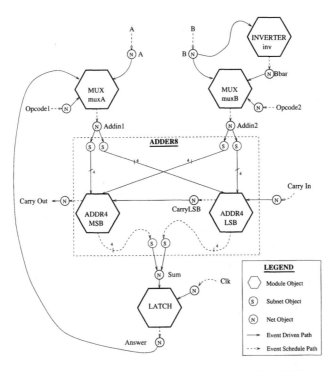

Figure 1.6 OPERAS' internal representation of the ALU8 datapath circuit.

In a hierarchical representation, the 4 b adders would be represented as cells (instantiated modules) within the 8 b adder. Consequently, the design details of the 8 b adder are hidden in the hierarchical representation. The figure shows the actual directed graph representation that is generated and stored within the design database.

Each module can logically represent a wide range of objects with a varying degree of complexity. For example, the system model can be an array of signal processors, with each module representing one processor. On the other hand, a module may represent a gate-level model of an adder circuit. A module just needs to have standard interface methods to the simulator structure for the simulation to work [89]. Consequently, the module structure allows for the study of a gate-level module, with the rest of the system represented by other high-level behavioral modules. This flexibility allows for detailed and efficient exploration of different system structures.

The ALU8 input signals such as *A*, *B*, and *CarryIn* can be driven from other modules or from the test vectors defined by the user. In addition to *Module* and *Net* objects, the diagram also shows one additional class of objects: *Subnet*. The figure shows that the 4 b adder inputs need to be taken from two separate nets by first splitting each net into the most significant portion (MSB) and the least significant portion (LSB). The sums by the MSB adder and by the LSB are then combined at the output. In both the splitting and merging cases, the subnet object is used to handle those abstractions.

Module Modeling

Once the system model is derived, then the details of how the module interfaces with the rest of the systems need to be defined. In the OPERAS-based design, the module interfaces with nets through three classes of objects: *input*, *output*, and *edge*. The input object serves as an interface to propagate signal transitions from a net to an instantiated modules. For example, the net object updates all the associated input objects when the net transitions to a new value. A module's input may be sensitive to the input transition rather than the input level. For example, an edge-triggered latch would need special handling at the clock input. Such input is modeled through the *edge* object. Figure 1.7 shows the object-oriented view of two

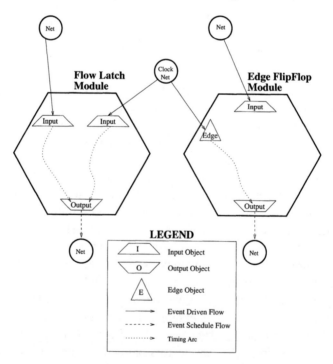

Figure 1.7 Interface relationships between modules and nets.

modules. The first module is a level-sensitive flow latch circuit, and the second module is an edge-triggered flip-flop. The two modules share the same clock signal.

Shown in Figure 1.7, the nets propagate the events to the *input* or *edge* objects within the module. When a module is ready for execution, the module's *go()* method obtains the current input values from the *input* or *edge* to start execution.

Each *output* object detects whether the corresponding output node has transitioned due to the module execution. If the transition has occurred, the new event is scheduled for the net corresponding to the output object. Each *output* object can have an associated delay method, and the delay method implements timing arcs between related input and output within a module. For example, in the figure of the edge-triggered flip-flop, the timing arc only exists between the edge object and the output object because the output delay is only affected by the edge of the clock signal. The delay methods within the flow latch and flip-flop modules would implement the different types of timing arcs. The delay method can be a complex function of circuit technology, supply voltage, or other system parameters to allow for complex delay modeling.

Event-Driven Simulation

The simulation is conducted in an event-driven manner, advancing time in nonuniform increments, skipping over time when system has no activity [24]. The event-driven simulation allows for the accurate modeling of delays and strict orders of events. Each module models the functionality, delay, and energy based on input events, and these methods are evaluated when an event arrives.

Although the event-driven simulation algorithm can be written in a non-OO fashion, the simulation entity such as events and event queue can naturally be represented as objects because, in addition to containing vital state information such as time, associated net, and scheduled transition, they also possess behaviors that interact with the rest of the system. For example, the global event queue advances the global clock sequentially from one time slot to another, and it will accept newly scheduled events as well as deactivate cancelled events. The global event queue is implemented as a linked list object of schedule objects sorted according to time. Each schedule object represents a point in time where at least one event is pending, and since additional events may be pending at that time, each schedule has a linked list of pending events.

Not all scheduled events are activated because a previous scheduled event can be cancelled by a subsequent event. When a net having a scheduled event is reevaluated to have a new event, and the new event is to take effect before some of the already scheduled events, the simulator will schedule the new event and deactivate the originally scheduled events after the new event. This well-known effect is due to the different delay paths through a module [13], [67].

The event-driven simulation engine of the simulator interacts with the system model by accepting events from the module and stimulating the nets that have an activated event. Each event is associated with a net, and an activated event will cause the net object to propagate the new value to the modules. The intervening *Subnet* objects also forward the new value. After all the events have been activated and propagated to the proper modules, the affected modules are executed to produce the new outputs. If an output has transitioned to a new value, the module schedules a new event at the net corresponding to the output. For example, when the 4 b LSB adder produces a new output, the change to the *Sum* net is scheduled as an event to the least significant *subnet of Sum*. When the event is activated, the new value is sent to the *subnet of Sum*, which forwards the new value to *Sum* net and *Latch* module. The event-scheduling flow between module output and net object is shown as dashed lines, and the event-driven flow is shown as solid lines in Figure 1.6. The stimulus inputs to nets such as *A* and *B* can be driven from other modules or a test vector generator.

The event-driven simulation is an integral part of modeling systems. The delays through a module provide detailed insight into the actual operational performance and energy behavior. For example, in the process of performance tuning for a pipelined system, known as retiming, detailed knowledge of delay is necessary. In low-power design, the designer wants to avoid unnecessary signal transitions because these cause unnecessary dynamic power in switching the node capacitance. The detailed modeling of delay is important to balance signal delay into a module and to avoid false transitions.

Simulation Interface

The OPERAS simulation results can be displayed on waveform display programs. Currently, OPERAS adapts the analyzer program of IRSIM [67] for waveform display. Figure 1.8 shows the waveform output from a simulation of the 8 b ALU, and each signal corresponds to a net object of Figure 1.6.

The *Answer* waveform has been annotated to show the ALU operations and results, and the *CarryOut* and *Overflow* show the status resulting from

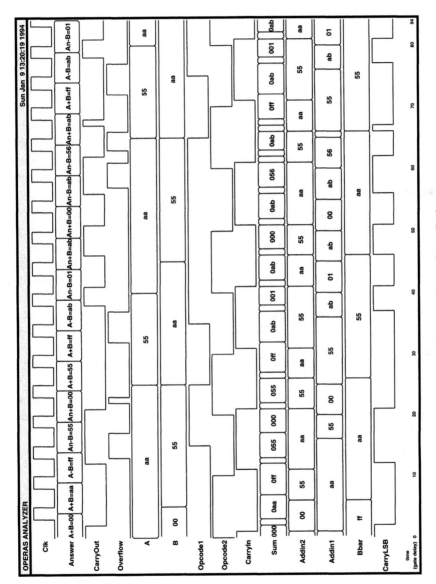

Figure 1.8 OPERAS waveform display.

45

the operations. For example, the third cycle of the simulation shows the answer from *A–B*, and the fourth cycle shows the result of subtracting *B* from the previous answer *(An–B)*. *A, B, Opcode1, Opcode2*, and *CarryIn* are the waveforms of the input test vectors. The rest of the waveforms are from the internal signals of the 8 b ALU design.

1.3.4. OPERAS Summary

OPERAS is an object-oriented system simulator that is reconfigurable and fast enough for a whole system simulation. With the increasing integration of systems and needs for low-power design, OPERAS offers a unique holistic approach to overall system simulation, design, and optimization through the use of object-oriented technology. Object-oriented design and simulation allow for fast prototyping and simulation of very large systems due to the ease of modeling through the mechanism such as object encapsulation, class hierarchy, class inheritance, and polymorphism. The benefit of the object-oriented view of modules lies in the power of encapsulating the module as a flexible object capable of representing very complex objects like a microprocessor to very simple objects like a logic gate. At the same time, hardware concurrency can be efficiently modeled by the network of *nets* and *modules*. With the wide availability of fast object-oriented languages such as C++, object-oriented simulation tools such as OPERAS is within easy reach of many DSP system designers.

OSDL is a design language interface to OPERAS which allows the designer to describe the whole system without having to deal with the details of the C++ language syntax. The OSDL language is designed to allow users to concentrate on the design of the system. At the same time, OSDL offers an interface to the underlying C++ object-oriented mechanisms. OPERAS/OSDL is being extended to model software components of systems. Future work also includes extension to the OSDL that allows for interfaces to an object-oriented database, object-oriented graphic interface, and concurrent object-oriented simulation.

1.4.   CONCLUSION

In this chapter, a brief survey of the OOS arena was presented, followed by a review of C++ features. An object-oriented DSP system modeling and simulation tool called OPERAS was described in Section 1.3.

As pointed out by several researchers, future research in OOS can be performed in many directions. First, with the present focus on building an

integrated environment for simulation, specific tools like graphical interfaces, statistical analyzers, and database languages to manipulate objects
are essential with the simulation system, as mentioned in [56]. The communication models of OOP are changing, and the changes are likely to
have an effect on OOS languages. Parallel/distributed OOS techniques are
important as many simulation programs are large in size and need parallel
distribution. Icon-based OOS has already emerged as a reality, and this
trend is likely to continue. AI-based simulation and OOS have many things
in common, and further integration of these two systems can be made. Improved performance (higher speed, less memory) OOS system design is
yet another possible area of investigation. New OOS design methods are
also important as some traditional ways of performing OOS may not find
favor among present and future designers. Validation techniques of OOS
systems are rarely discussed in the literature and are a good area of future
research. Finally, one needs to agree to some common terminology in the
context of OOS, and hence the need for research in this area is felt. There
are some disagreements even on basic terms like encapsulation in OOP
[14] that also may arise in the OOS domain. Some standard works have already started in the OOP area. These can be used in a standardization work
for OOS to avoid unnecessary nontrivial human communication problems
in OOS [84].

Many textbooks on OO design and principles include a chapter or discussion on OOS. In particular, books on OO design written by Booch [11],
Cox [20], and Meyer [47] can be consulted for getting started. For recent
surveys/tutorials, one can read [31], [84], and [19]. For a tutorial paper
on OOP, refer to [73]. A book on the premier simulation language, SIM-
ULA, like the one written by Birtwisle, is also worth reading [9]. Ziegler's
book on OOS could be a good starting point for those who want to design
hierarchical systems using a formalism like DEVS [89]. Review papers
that contain good material on OOS are [29], [10], [65], and [60]. Journals and books like *Journal of OOP, International Journal in Computer
Simulation (IJCS), Simulation, IEEE Software, IEEE Computer, CACM,
Progress in Simulation Series* [90], and others [36], [15], [59] contain arti-
cles related to OO design and simulation. The Object-Oriented Simulation
Conference (OOS'90–93) [25]–[28], sponsored annually by SCS, is entirely dedicated to the topical theme. Other conferences like OOPSLA,
Annual Simulation Symposium, Winter Simulation Conference, and Mascots Workshop all contain papers on various aspects of OOS from time
to time.

Acknowledgments

The first author is supported by a NASA Global Change Graduate Fellow-ship (NASA Grant NGT30115). The authors would like to acknowledge Drew Wingard and Masataka Matsui for their help in obtaining and adapting the IRSIM analyzer display. The OPERAS preprocessor program is derived from the Ptolemy [40] preprocessor program from the University of California, Berkeley.

References

[1] AESOP, Simple ++ is a product of AESOP, Stuttgart, Germany.

[2] R. L. Bagrodia, V. Jha, and J. Waldorf, "The Maisie environment for parallel simulation," in *Proc. 27th Annu. Simulation Symp.*, 1994, pp. 4–12.

[3] D. Batory et al., "Modeling concepts for VLSI CAD objects," *ACM Trans. Database Syst.*, vol. 10, Sept. 1985, pp. 322–346.

[4] J. Baveco and A. Smeulders, "Objects for simulation: Smalltalk and ecology," *Simulation*, Jan. 1994, pp. 42–57.

[5] M. Beckers, J. Peeters, and F. Verboven, "OO modeling, simulation and implementation of an NMS," in *Proc. Mascots'94*, 1994, pp. 222–228.

[6] R. Belanger, "MODSIM II—A modular OO language," in *Proc. 1991 Winter Simulation Conf.*, Sept. 1984, pp. 87–92.

[7] J. Bezivin, "Some experiments in OO simulation," in *Proc. OOPSLA'87*, 1987, pp. 394–405.

[8] J. Bezivin, "Design and implementation issues in OO simulation," *SIMULET-TER*, vol. 19, June 1988, pp. 47–53.

[9] G. Birtwisle, *Discrete-Event Modeling in SIMULA*. New York: Macmillan, 1979.

[10] D. Bischak and S. D. Roberts, "OO simulation," in *Proc. 1991 Winter Simulation Conf.*, 1991, pp. 195–203.

[11] G. Booch, *Object-Oriented Design with Applications*. New York: Benjamin Cummings, 1991.

[12] G. Booch, *Object-Oriented Analysis and Design with Applications*. New York: Benjamin Cummings, 1994.

[13] M. A. Breuer and A. D. Friedman, *Diagnosis & Reliable Design of Digital Systems*, 2nd ed. Rockville, MD: Computer Science Press, 1976.

[14] D. Breugnot et al., "GAME: An OO approach to computer animation in flexible manufacturing system modeling," in *Proc. 1991 Annu. Simulation Symp.*, 1991, pp. 217–223.

[15] D. Brumbaugh, *OO Development: Building CASE Tools with C++*. New York: Wiley International, 1994.

[16] J. Buck et al., "Ptolemy: A platform for heterogeneous simulation and prototyping," in *Proc. European Simulation Conf.*, June 1991.

[17] J. Burns and J. D. Morgensen, "An OO world-view for intelligent discrete, next-event simulation," *Management Sci.*, vol. 34, Dec. 1988, pp. 1425–1440.

[18] J. B. Burr and A. M. Peterson, "Ultra low power CMOS technology," in *NASA VLSI Design Symp.*, Oct. 1991, pp. 4.2.1–4.2.13.

[19] T. Corson and J. McGregor, "Understanding OO: A unifying paradigm," *Commun. ACM*, vol. 33, no. 9, 1990, pp. 40–60.

[20] B. J. Cox, *Object-Oriented Programming: An Evolutionary Approach*. Reading, MA: Addison-Wesley, 1986.

[21] W. Dobosiewicz and P. Gburzynski, "SMURPH: An OOS for communication networks and protocols," in *Proc. Mascots'93*, 1993, pp. 351–352.

[22] D. L. Eldredge et al., "Applying the OO paradigm to discrete event simulations using the C++ language," *Simulation*, 1990, pp. 83–91.

[23] S. Engelstad et al., "A dynamic C-based OO system for UNIX," *IEEE Software*, May 1991, pp. 73–85.

[24] D. Ferrari, *Computer Systems Performance Evaluation*. Englewood Cliffs, NJ: Prentice-Hall, 1978.

[25] Society for Computer Simulation, Ed., *Collection of Papers, Proc. OOS'90*, San Diego, CA: SCS Press, Jan. 1990.

[26] Society for Computer Simulation, Ed., *Collection of Papers, Proc. OOS'91*, Anaheim, CA: SCS Press, Jan. 1991.

[27] Society for Computer Simulation, Ed., *Collection of Papers, Proc. OOS'92*, SCS Press, Jan. 1992.

[28] Society for Computer Simulation, Ed., *Collection of Papers, Proc. OOS'93*, La Jolla, CA: SCS Press, Jan. 1993.

[29] J. Giron-Sierra and J. Gomez-Pulido, "Doing OO-simulation: Advantages, new department tools," in *Proc. 1991 Annual Simulation Symp.*, 1991, pp. 177–183.

[30] A. Grimshaw, "Easy-to-use OO parallel processing with Mentat," *IEEE Computer*, May 1993, pp. 39–50.

[31] B. Henderson-Sellers and J. Edwards, "The OO system life cycle," *Commun. ACM*, vol. 33, no. 9, 1990, pp. 143–169.

[32] D. Jefferson et al., "Supercritical speedup (discrete event simulation)," in *Proc. 24th Annu. Simulation Symp.*, 1991, pp. 159–168.

[33] D. Kafura, M. Mukherji, and G. Lavender, "ACT++: A class library for concurrent programming in C++ using actors," *J. Object-Oriented Programming*, Oct. 1993, pp. 47–55.

[34] T. G. Kim and S. Park, "The DEVS formalism: Hierarchical modular systems specification in C++," in *Proc. 1992 European Simulation Conf.*, 1992, pp. 152–156.

[35] P. Klahr, "AI applied to simulation," in *Proc. 1984 UKSC Conf. Comput. Simulation*, Sept. 1984, pp. 87–92.

[36] R. Lafore, *OOP in Turbo C++*. Waite Group Press, 1991.

[37] C. Landauer, "Incorporating simulation in a design environment," in *Proc. 1991 Winter Simulation Conf.*, 1991, pp. 1180–1185.

[38] T. S. Larkin et al., "Simulation and Object-Oriented programming: The development of SERB," in *Simulation Symp.*, vol. 51, no. 3, 1988, pp. 93–100.

[39] A. M. Law and W. Kelton, *Simulation Modelling and Analysis*. New York: McGraw-Hill, 1991.

[40] E. A. Lee, "A design lab for statistical signal processing," in *Int. Conf. Acoust., Speech, Signal Processing*, Mar. 1992, pp. 81–84.

[41] G. Lomow and D. Baezner, "A tutorial introduction to OO and Sim++," in *Proc. 1991 Winter Simulation Conf.*, 1991, pp. 157–162.

[42] J. Luna, "Application of hierarchical modeling concepts to a multi-analysis environment," in *Proc. 1991 Winter Simulation Conf.*, 1991, pp. 1165–1172.

[43] V. Mak, "DOSE: A modular and reusable OOS environment," in *Proc. OOS'91*, 1991, pp. 3–11.

[44] B. Malloy et al., "The implementation of a simulation language using dynamic binding," in *Proc. OOS'93*, 1993, pp. 3–8.

[45] Y. Matsumoto and K. Taki, "Adaptive time-celling for efficient parallel discrete event simulation," in *Proc. OOS'93*, 1993, pp. 101–106.

[46] *Sigview User Manual*, MCNC, Research Triangle Park, NC, 1991.

[47] B. Meyer, *OO Software Construction*. Englewood Cliffs, NJ: Prentice-Hall, 1988.

[48] G. De Micheli, "Extending CAD tools and techniques," *IEEE Computer*, Jan. 1993, pp. 85–87.

[49] J. Miller *et al.*, "Query driven simulation using active KDL," *IJCS*, vol. 1, no. 1, 1991, pp. 1–30.

[50] T. Minoura et al., "Structured active object systems for simulation," in *Proc. OOPSLA'93*, 1993, pp. 338–355.

[51] L. Mollamustafaoglu, "OO design of output analysis tools for simulation languages," *Simulation*, Jan. 1993, pp. 6–15.

[52] S. Naher, *LEDA User Manual*, Max Planck Inst., 1992.

[53] R. Nance and J. Arthur, "The methodology roles in the realization of a model development environment," in *Proc. 1988 Winter Simulation Conf.*, 1988.

[54] M. Ogle, T. Beaumariage, and C. Roberts, "The separation and explicit declaration of model control structures in support of OO simulation," in *Proc. 1991 Winter Simulation Conf.*, 1991, pp. 1173–1179.

[55] R. O'Keffe, "Simulation and expert systems—A taxonomy and some examples," *Simulation*, Jan. 1986, pp. 10–16.

[56] T. I. Oren and B. P. Zeigler, "Concepts for advanced simulation methodologies," *Simulation*, Mar. 1979, pp. 69–82.

[57] J. Palme, "SIMULA 67—An advanced programming and simulation language," Tech. Rep., Swedish Res. Inst. of National Defence, 1970.

[58] M. Papazoglou, "Experiences from using simulation tools for the design of multiprocessor and distributed systems," *IJCS*, vol. 3, no. 2, 1993, pp. 181–209.

[59] G. Perry, *Teach Yourself OOP with Visual C++ 1.5*. SAMS Publishing, 1994.

[60] L. Pollacia, "A survey of DES and state-of-the-art discrete event languages," *SIMULETTER*, vol. 19, no. 2, June 1988, pp. 8–25.

[61] D. Popken, "An OO simulation environment for airbase logistics," *Simulation*, 1992, pp. 328–338.

[62] D. Pratt et al., "A framework for highly reusable simulation modeling: Separating physical, information, and control elements," in *Proc. 1991 Winter Simulation Conf.*, 1991, pp. 254–261.

[63] S. Raczynski, "Process hierarchy and inheritance in PASION," *Simulation*, vol. 50, no. 6, June 1988, pp. 249–251.

[64] R. Reddy, "Epistemology of knowledge based simulation," *Simulation*, 1987, pp. 162–166.

[65] S. Roberts and J. Heim, "A perspective on OO simulation," in *Proc. 1988 Winter Simulation Conf.*, 1988, pp. 277–281.

[66] J. Rothenberg, "Knowledge-based simulation at RAND," *SIMULETTER*, vol. 19, no. 2, June 1988, pp. 54–59.

[67] A. Salz and M. A. Horowitz, "IRSIM: An incremental MOS switch-level simulator," in *ACM/IEEE Design Automation Conf.*, 1989, pp. 173–178.

[68] D. P. Sanderson, "OO modeling using C++," in *Proc. Annu. Simulation Symp.*, 1988, pp. 143–156.

[69] S. Sevine, "Extending common LISP object system for DE modeling and simulation," in *Proc. 1991 Winter Simulation Conf.*, 1991, pp. 204–206.

[70] R. Shannon, "Models and AI," in *Proc. 1987 Winter Simulation Conf.*, 1987, pp. 16–23.

[71] P. Sheu and L. Peterson, "An OO parallel simulation environment," in *Proc. OOS'93*, 1993, pp. 113–118.

[72] C. R. Stanridge, "Performing simulation projects with the extended simulation system (TESS)," *Simulation*, vol. 45, Dec. 1985, pp. 283–291.

[73] B. Stroustrup, "What is OOP," *IEEE Software*, vol. 5, pp. 10–20, May 1988.

[74] B. Stroustrup, *The C++ Programming Language*, 2nd ed. Reading, MA: Addison-Wesley, 1991.

[75] O. Tanir and S. Sevinc, "Defining requirements for a standard simulation environment," *IEEE Computer*, Feb. 1994, pp. 28–34.

[76] M. Thapar and B. Delagi, "Simulation of cache coherence protocols on an instrumented simulator," *IJCS*, vol. 3, no. 2, 1993, pp. 165–180.

[77] C. Tietz, A. Linden, and T. Sudbrak, "SESAME—An OOS tool for design, simulation, analysis of neural nets," in *Proc. Mascots'93*, 1993, pp. 339–340.

[78] J. Turner and R. Yavatkar, "Constructing microarchitecture simulators using OO building blocks," in *Proc. Mascots'93*, 1993, pp. 359–360.

[79] D. Unger and R. Smith, "SELF: The power of simplicity," in *Proc. OOPSLA'87*, 1987.

[80] P. Vaughan et al., "PRISM: An OO system modeling environment in C++," in *Proc. OOS'91*, 1991, pp. 32–42.

[81] E. A. Vittoz, "Micropower techniques," in Y. Tsividis and P. Antognetti, Eds., *Design of MOS VLSI Circuits for Telecommunications*. Englewood Cliffs, NJ: Prentice-Hall, 1985.

[82] D. Wagner, "The design of an OO parallel simulation environment," in *Proc. OOS'91*, 1991, pp. 201–205.

[83] P. Wegner, "Dimensions of object-oriented modeling," *IEEE Computer*, Oct. 1992, pp. 12–20.

[84] R. J. Wirfs-Brock and R. Johnson, "Surveying current research in OO design," *Commun. ACM*, vol. 33, no. 9, 1990, pp. 105–124.

[85] N. Woo, A. Dunlop, and W. Wolf, "Codesign from cospecification," *IEEE Computer*, Jan. 1994, pp. 42–47.

[86] B. Wyatt, K. Kavi, and S. Hufnagel, "Parallelism in OO-languages: A survey," *IEEE Software*, Nov. 1992, pp. 56–66.

[87] G. Yeh et al., "OPERAS—An OO signal processing system architecture simulator," in *Proc. 1994 Annu. Simulation Symp.*, Apr. 1994.

[88] B. Zeigler, "OO paradigms for model development environments," in *Proc. Mascots'93*, 1993, pp. 384–389.

[89] B. P. Zeigler, *Object-Oriented Simulation with Hierarchical, Modular Models*. Orlando, FL: Academic, 1990.

[90] G. Zobrist et al., *Progress in Simulation Series*. Ablex Publishers, 1992.

Chapter 2

Object-Oriented Simulation Languages and Environments
A Four-Level Architecture

John A. Miller
Walter D. Potter
Krys J. Kochut
Deepa Ramesh*

*Department of Computer Science
and Artificial Intelligence Center
University of Georgia
Athens, Georgia, USA*

Editor's Introduction

In the previous chapter, we were introduced to simulation languages such as C++. In this chapter, we will focus on simulation languages based on C++. Since C++ is extensible (via classed, template, and operator overloading), it is often the case that a complete language is not defined, but rather a library, and possibly a preprocessor are provided to extend the language. This has the advantage of simplicity, ease of learning, and ease of portability. These are the types of simulation languages (or more properly, language extensions) that we will focus on in this chapter. Concepts and features will be discussed within the context of explaining the object-oriented paradigm and its advantage for simulation.

An important theme of the chapter is the use of object-oriented concepts throughout the life cycle of software/model development. In software engineering, Object-Oriented approaches to requirements Analysis (OOA), Design (OOD), and Programming (OOP) are meeting with success.

Key Words

Integrated information systems, Object-oriented databases, Object-oriented simulation, Repositories, Simulation modeling environments.

---

*Not associated with Artificial Intelligence Center at the time of this writing.

2.1.   INTRODUCTION

Simulation modeling and analysis are very complex undertakings. Their primary purpose is to provide useful and accurate information to designers and decision makers. As such, they can be viewed, combined, as a special type of information system. Since the centerpiece of modern information systems is advanced Database Management Systems (DBMSs), such as Extended Relational DBMSs or Object-Oriented DBMSs, they should also play this role in simulation environments. A variety of other tools and systems are also vitally important in today's information systems (those for development as well as those for end use). To provide an Integrated Information System (IIS), these tools and systems need to be kept track of, managed, and glued together in a loosely coupled fashion. As an emerging technology, metadatabases or repositories are beginning to be used for this purpose. In this chapter, we present a four-level architecture for loosely coupled, database-centered simulation environments.

Recently, object-oriented programming techniques have been increasingly applied to simulation, using languages such as C++ [44] and Mod-Sim II [4]. The benefits of utilizing this programming paradigm are being realized in the simulation area as they have been in the software industry in general. It is, however, somewhat misleading to imply that simulation is following this general trend in software development. In the mid-1960s, a pioneering simulation language called SIMULA-67 [2], [3] was developed. Motivated by the need to more faithfully model entities or objects in the real world, the designers of SIMULA-67 introduced the core concepts that now form the object-oriented paradigm. SIMULA-67 also strongly influenced the designs of Smalltalk and C++, the two languages that are primarily responsible for the enormous popularity of object-oriented programming today. Therefore, it is only natural for object-oriented programming to be important in simulation, as that is where it originated.

In this chapter, we will present a four-level architecture suitable for object-oriented simulation languages/environments. The goal of this architecture is to provide a framework in which a Query-Driven Simulation (QDS) system can be built. Users see a QDS system as an integrated information system that is able to present the results of simulations in an understandable manner, and if adequate results are not available, it can execute simulation models to produce an adequate set of results [23], [24], [35], [25], [18], [26], [27], [36], [28], [38]. Much of our previous work has focused on developing a tightly coupled system based on using an object-oriented database system (ActiveKDL [25]) which includes a database programming language that is sufficiently powerful to express simulation models. (Note that ActiveKDL is an extension to KDL, which was designed by Potter and Kerschberg [32]–[34], [37].)

We now feel that although the tightly coupled approach is viable, it may be unwieldy. The trend today is to provide interoperable components that fit within a superstructure. Components should be able to work independently as well as in an integrated fashion. It should also be possible to replace components with superior ones (i.e., unplug an old component and plug in a new replacement). Consequently, the focus of this chapter will be on providing a framework suitable for a loosely coupled QDS system. Object-oriented approaches provide the necessary foundation for this degree of modularity and reusability. Note that this is important in both developing a QDS system, as well as in developing simulation models using a QDS system.

Foundational capabilities will be provided via C++, the most widely used object-oriented programming language. The loosely coupled system that we are developing extends the base capabilities of the language by including some widely available class libraries (a general-purpose one, the Gnu C++ Library [20], and two simulation-oriented ones, SimPack [9] and AWESIME [12], [13]. An overview of the simulation libraries is provided in the Appendix.

In this chapter, we use a few simple mathematical tools to build an architecture for a loosely coupled simulation support environment based on QDS. The architecture is built up by using these tools to construct a *four-level framework*. This framework is based on emerging international standards which are intended to be used to build standardized environments for both software engineering and integrated information systems. In both cases, *repositories* are used to maintain the information in the upper levels of the framework. A repository can be thought of as a metadatabase. Just as a data dictionary keeps track of the types of information available in a database system, a repository provides this capability on a much larger scale, for an entire information system. In addition to keeping track of the types of available information, a repository must also keep track of the tools, systems, and applications that access and manipulate this information, as well as keep track of design information and activities (see [15], [29], [30], [45]).

2.2.   BACKGROUND

2.2.1. Integration of Data, Knowledge, and Model Management

A logically centralized repository can serve as the foundation for comprehensive information management and tool integration. Recently, several commercial repository products [30] have been developed to facilitate integration for enterprise-wide information systems. Because of the necessity for breadth in such systems, it is difficult to explore certain deeper issues. Therefore, our approach would be to limit the breadth, while increasing the depth. The area of simulation is ideal for this since there are many stereotypical kinds of objects and interactions involved in simulation modeling. A QDS system requires sufficient metadata to facilitate on-the-fly selection of simulation models, as well as composition of simulation models from model components stored in the repository. It should also provide a simulation analysis interface that is as easy to use as querying an ordinary database.

Our loosely coupled approach provides the flexibility to purchase and include a full-blown repository manager. (Because of their currently high cost, we are not doing this in our prototype.) Ideally, like the state-of-the-art repository vendors, one should provide repository capabilities using an Object-Oriented Database Management System (OODBMS) (e.g., ObjectStore, ONTOS, UniSQL, or ActiveKDL). Our initial prototype will, however, use a slightly extended Relational Database Management System (RDBMS) (Oracle, Version 7). (Oracle, Version 7, includes some capabilities found in OODBMSs.) The DBMS will be used to represent information in a variety of different forms, including Stored Data, Rules, Constraints, and Models (e.g., simulations). These forms allow information to be retrieved, derived, checked, and generated.

2.2.2. Query-Driven Simulation

Query-Driven Simulation (QDS) is based on the following simple notion: simulation analysis involves the retrieval and manipulation of simulation data. Because of the complexity of simulation programs, these data should not be thrown away, but should be stored in a database. This is being done to a limited extent today using Relational DBMSs. It can be done more fully using OODBMSs. This is the first step of QDS; all simulation data, no matter how complex their structure, should be stored in a database. Therefore, more simulation data would become available. If the necessary information is not available, a QDS system will analyze the user's query to try to find a model to instantiate, and execute it in order to fill in the missing data. This is step two, which requires models, as well as formal descriptions of models, to be stored in a highly organized fashion in the repository. Finally, step three of QDS facilitates the rapid development of simulation models/programs via model composition and even model synthesis.

Layered on top of the DBMS and the repository manager will be a collection of tools and interfaces that support the notion of Query-Driven Simulation (QDS). Simulation data will be stored in the DBMS, while information about these data (i.e., metadata) will be stored in the repository. In addition, information about development tools, simulation analysis tools, and simulation models (abstraction of a simulation program), as well as the definitional aspects of the simulation programs themselves, will be stored in the repository. The repository will be the vehicle for the integration of fundamentally different types of data/knowledge. Users' queries may be answered by simple data retrieval, complex query processing, querying requiring heuristic knowledge and inference, or even model instantiation and execution. This will provide a testbed for experimentation with accuracy–time tradeoffs involved with retrieval versus information derivation/generation.

The technological foundation for QDS consists of the following technologies:

1. Object-Oriented Programming Languages and Translators

2. Object-Oriented Database Management Systems

3. Object-Oriented Repository Managers.

In particular, the DBMS and the Repository Manager support QDS by providing access to integrated knowledge, data, and model bases.

Using these technological foundations, a QDS system can be built to provide a variety of different types of users (e.g., simulation model builders, simulation analysts, and even business end users) with a powerful, yet easy-to-use environment for simulation modeling and analysis. In a QDS system, users will predominantly interact with the system by formulating queries to retrieve stored data, data inferred from knowledge, or data generated from models. The system allows access not only to data, but also to knowledge and models. Information of vastly different character can be integrated using both algorithmic and AI-based techniques. Queries formulated using the query language (or GUI-based query tool) will allow users to retrieve information about the behavior of systems under study. Data from simulation runs will be stored by the system. If the information requested by a query is already stored in the database, more or less conventional query processing techniques will be applied. If rules are available to derive the requested information, then they will be fired and the results will be presented. However, if the amount of information retrievable (either stored or derived) is below a user-settable threshold, model instantiation and execution may be automatically carried out to generate the desired information.

Model instantiation occurs when the DBMS does not have sufficient data or knowledge to provide a satisfactory answer. In such a case, the QDS system will automatically create model instances that are executed to generate enough data to give a satisfactory answer to the user. The process centers around the creation of sets of input parameter values which are obtained by schema and query analysis. Model instantiation has the potential to require an enormous amount of computation in response to a query. Therefore, user-settable thresholds, as well as more sophisticated information generation rules incorporating user preferences, are provided to control the amount of computation. If the threshold is at 100%, then all parameter sets implied by the query whose results are not already stored in the database are used to instantiate models. At the opposite extreme, if the threshold is at 0%, then only data generated from previous simulation runs will be retrieved.

2.2.3. Comparison with Other Ongoing Research

Some of the most closely related work to our QDS approach was presented in two sessions on Database-Centered Simulation Environments held at the 1993 Winter Simulation Conference (organized and chaired by Professor Miller).

1. *The Object Flow Model for Data-Based Simulation*, by Lois M. L. Delcambre (Oregon Graduate Institute) and Lissa F. Pollacia (Northwestern State). "The Object Flow Model uses an object-oriented database to describe entities and methods for manipulating entities and provides a visual formalism called the Object Flow Diagram (based on network-based process-oriented discrete event simulation languages) to describe the dynamic processing of an application" [8].

2. *Databases: Designing and Developing Integrated Simulation Modeling Environments*, by Martha A. Centeno and Charles R. Standridge (Florida State). "Database management systems (DBMS) provide robust information storage, retrieval, and indexing functions needed by a simulation modeling environment (SME)" [5]. Their work has been to develop

ever-increasingly more sophisticated prototypes of SMEs. Notably, Dr. Standridge, while working for Pritsker and Associates (Slam), developed the first commercial SME (called Tess [43]) back in the mid-1980s. Tess used a custom-built DBMS. Dr. Centeno (1990) was one of the first to build a prototype SME based on a commercial relational DBMS, namely, Oracle. (Another major effort along these lines was by Balci and Nance [1]; they used Ingres.)

3. *Applying Active Database Models for Simulation*, by Aloysius Cornelio (Bellcore) and Shamkant B. Navathe (Georgia Tech). "In this paper we propose a data model for simulation which builds on object oriented and active database principles to represent physical systems in terms of its structure and function" [7]. Dr. Navathe is one of the leading researchers on database systems, and is the only one we know of applying his expertise to simulation.

4. *Employing Databases for Large Scale Reuse of Simulation Models*, by Martin Hitz, Hannes Werthner, and Tuncer Oren (University of Vienna). "To enhance reusability in the field of simulation, model bases must be equipped with powerful tools for retrieval, modification, and aggregation of simulation models. In this paper, the role of database management systems supporting a modeling environment is discussed and reuse oriented query interfaces are presented" [14]. Their future work includes replacing their Relational DBMS with an Object-Oriented DBMS.

5. *The Concept of Views in Simulation*, by Margarita Rovira, David Spooner, and Jorge Haddock (Rensselaer). "The concept of views is widely used in the database community as a tool to reorganize and extend a database. It allows different users to look at the same data in different ways without changing the original data or violating its integrity. The same concept can be applied to a simulation model to find new high level interaction patterns among the components of a model without having to define new models and in a way that maintains consistency among the results" [40].

6. *A Prototype Implementation of a Model Management System for Discrete-Event Models*, by Melanie Lenard (Boston University). "The conceptual foundation for this MMS is Structured Modeling (SM) and Extended Structured Modeling (ESM). Using the SM and ESM frameworks makes it possible to take an integrated approach to representing and managing both models and data" [21].

Most of the important related work is reported in earlier papers by these authors. We also mentioned above the work of Balci and Nance. More distantly related to our QDS research is the work done on knowledge-based simulation. This work is highlighted by the following important projects: KBS [39], [10], Ross [22], and SES/MBase [50], [49], [51]. Finally, a life-cycle perspective is given in a special issue on object-oriented simulation and simulation support [31].

2.3.   THE OBJECT-ORIENTED PARADIGM AND THE CORE MODEL

In the last several years, the Object-Oriented Paradigm has emerged as one of the most successful approaches to software development. The collection of technologies and methodologies that embody it have matured sufficiently to make the object-oriented approach appropriate for numerous situations: systems programming/development, applications programming/development, and, of course, simulation. Reports from industry have indicated that the benefits provided by the object-oriented approach (better modularity and code reusability) have yielded substantial productivity gains [48].

Both Object-Oriented Programming Languages (OOPLs) and (OODBMSs) share a common conceptual framework. This framework is often referred to as the core model, and it consists of the following conceptual elements.

1. *Objects.* The principal construct for the creation of programs, applications, or systems is that of an object. An object has a state and a set of well-defined operations (or methods). The state is made up of attribute or data values. The collective action of the methods over time defines the behavior of the object.

2. *Object Identity.* The object itself is uniquely identifiable, irrespective of the values (or state) it contains. (This is in sharp contrast to the notion of keys which are used for these purposes in relational databases.)

3. *Classes.* Objects are classified or grouped into classes. The particular class that they are an *instance-of* constrains their state and defines (or at least governs) their behavior.

4. *Encapsulation.* Objects can function correctly only if their state is not corrupted. An object is said to be fully encapsulated if its state is accessible only via the object's methods. An object is partially encapsulated if exceptions to this are allowed (e.g., public attributes or read-only attributes).

5. *Information Hiding.* This takes encapsulation one step further. Not only can the state of an object never be accessed directly, but its form is to

be known only by the class implementor. This has very practical benefits for large systems; if a change to the form or structure of the state is made, the impact is minimal (e.g., primarily relinking instead of recompiling all modules).

6. *Message Passing.* A single uniform syntax is used for invoking all methods, whether the actual implementation corresponds to a regular function call (early binding), an indirect function call (late binding), or a remote procedure call (rpc) involving the transport of a packet over a Local-Area Network. The syntax should also be suggestive of the fact that one object is requesting another object to do something. The syntax is generally of the form `object method parameters` with suitable intervening punctuation.

7. *Inheritance.* Since the form and function of objects are specified by the classes, much of system development centers on specifying (e.g., in `.h` files) and implementing (e.g., in `.cc` files) classes. Inheritance is a mechanism by which new classes can be readily built (or derived) from existing classes. In particular, if a derived class `inherits-from` a base (or parent) class, it inherits all the attributes and methods of the base class. The derived class has the option of redefining (or overriding) any of these, as well as adding new ones.

8. *Polymorphism.* C++ allows base class pointers to point at an object of this or any derived class. Pure polymorphism comes into play when a method is to be invoked. If the statement `ptr->Display();` (where `ptr` is of type `Person*`) is to be executed, then which `Display()` method should be invoked, the one defined for the `Person` class, or the one defined for a class derived from `Person`? Since `ptr` can point at objects of type `Person` or any type derived from it, typically, it is most useful for the particular method invocation to be determined on the basis of the type of object pointed to, rather than the type of the pointer. This will be the case in C++ if `Display()` is defined to be a virtual member function. This requires a method to be invoked by an indirect function call (late binding) since the specific type of an object must be determined at run time.

2.4.   MULTILEVEL FRAMEWORK

Tools and facilities in a loosely coupled QDS system need to be carefully organized into a multilevel framework. The bottom levels of the framework will contain facilities such as programming language compilers and database management systems. In both cases, from an object-oriented point of view, we are dealing with objects and their types (or classes). Higher levels in the framework will contain facilities such as Data Dictionaries (DDs), Repository Managers (RMs), Model Management Systems (MMSs), and Computer-Aided Software Engineering (CASE) tools.

At this point, we go into a more detailed analysis of what constitutes a repository. The organization of a repository is best understood as a multilevel framework. We motivate this by considering the general concept first. A database is a large integrated collection of information which is organized according to type. Consequently, it is a two-level concept, with instances (actual data) forming the lower level, and type information (schema specification) forming the upper level. Modern databases view this type information as important enough to store data about these types in a separate small database, known as a data dictionary. Since a data dictionary is itself a database, it is again a two-level concept. Therefore, modern databases actually consist of two databases: a database storing the application data, and a database storing data about this application data (in other words, metadata). These notions can be clarified with a diagram consisting of three levels (see Figure 2.1).

Dictionary Schema	Metamodel	
Dictionary Data	Metadata	Application Schema
	Data	Application Data

Figure 2.1 Three-level framework.

The top level, the metamodel level, simply defines a type structure, but contains no data. Therefore, the metamodel specifies the type structure for the metadata. Relevant types include `Table` (or `Class`), `Column`, and `Constraint`. (`Class` in an OODBMS is analogous to `Table` in an RDBMS.) The instances that fill up these types would be stored at the level below. Examples of instances of `Class` type that one might find in, say, a QDS system consisting of transportation system simulators are the following:

`Person, Employee, Department, Car, Engine, Body.`

Again, these instances at the metalevel represent types for the level below. Instances for the `Employee` type might include `employee A`, `employee B`, and `employee C`.

Multilevel frameworks, such as the one above, exhibit an interesting regularity. Each of the middle levels viewed from below represents type information, while viewed from above represents instances. The exceptions are the topmost and bottommost levels. At the data level, there is no view from below, so that the type viewpoint does not exist. Similarly, at the metamodel level, there is no view from above, so no instance (or data) viewpoint exists.

The above discussion may lead one to ask how the metamodel is itself structured. The answer is that it is fixed and hard-coded. The vendor decides what kind of metadata is needed for its product and supplies this. However, to meet the special demands of some of its customers, some vendors allow their data dictionary to be extended. A natural way to do this is to let the structuring information for the metadata (i.e., the metamodel) be defined in yet another database, which is conceptually one level higher. Consequently, one ends up with a four-level framework, as shown in Figure 2.2.

	Metametamodel	Definition Schema
Dictionary Schema	Metamodel	Definition Data
Dictionary Data	Metadata	Application Schema
	Data	Application Data

Figure 2.2 Four-level framework.

This new fourth level provides for extensibility and interoperability. Since this upper level database is relatively small, its structure can be fully specified in standards, and even if there are multiple standards, translations between these standards will be facilitated. An example of data at this fourth level might be the data that fill in a type called Metaclass which could consist of instances such as Table, Column, and Constraint. If an enterprise wishes to include information on application programs, it can extend the dictionary by adding an instance called Application to the Metaclass.

In summary, we now have three databases: an Application Database, a Dictionary Database, and a Dictionary Definition Database, with each database consisting of a lower level (instances) and an upper level (types). We can think of these two levels as forming level-pairs, called Definition, Dictionary, and Application. Hence, we have four levels and three level-pairs. This highly useful framework is the basis for several International Standards [46]:

1. IRDS (Information Resource Dictionary System). This standardization effort was sponsored by ANSI (American National Standards Institute). A standard was completed in 1988 [19], but there are several proposals

under review which would extend the standard. A draft of ANSI IRDS V2 [16], [11] which includes the ATIS (A Tool Integration Standard) specifications developed by DEC and Atherton Technologies has recently been produced [15]. Requirement #4 (of 259) for IDRS2 states that: "the IRDS shall be object-oriented, with multiple inheritance and complex objects" [11].

   2. PCTE (Portable Common Tool Environment). This standardization effort was sponsored by ECMA (European Computer Manufacturer's Association). Standards documents [42] were produced in 1986 (PCTE V1.4), 1988 (PCTE V1.5 and PCTE+), and 1991 [a joint report by both ECMA and NIST (National Institute of Standards and Technology)]. Extensions are ongoing today; for example, a language-specific binding to C++ is currently under development. Recently, IBM has announced support for PCTE within their proposed AIX repository [47].

   3. CDIF (Case Data Interchange Format). This standardization effort was initiated by a group of CASE vendors and was sponsored by EIA (Electronics Industry Association). The standard specifies a common format for import/export files.

   Within these standards, the names for the levels vary, but the concepts remain the same. The various names are shown in Table 2.1.

Table 2.1   Standard Terminology for Levels

GENERAL	IRDS	PCTE	CDIF	QDS
Metametamodel	Fundamental	Metaschema	Metameta	Metametaclass
Metamodel	IRD Definition	SDS	Meta	Metaclass
Metadata	IRD	Object	Model	Class
Data	Application	(Undefined)	Application	Object

Note: IRD stands for Information Resource Dictionary, while SDS stands for Schema Definition Set. In the section below, we develop our QDS framework, level by level, starting with the object or bottom level.

2.5.   LEVELS IN A QDS SYSTEM

As shown in Table 2.1, the four QDS levels are, from bottom to top: the object-level, the class-level, the metaclass-level (or just metalevel), and finally, at the top, the metametaclass-level (or simply just metameta-level). At each level, we are interested in three particular notions: the notion of an instance, the notion of a class extent, and the notion of a full extent. At the object-level, an instance simply corresponds to an object. All of the objects in the system constitute the full extent (i.e., the set of all objects). At the class-level, an instance corresponds to a class, while the full extent is the set of all classes. The same idea applies at the next two levels. Table 2.2 summarizes the situation.

Table 2.2   Level-by-Level Notation

LEVEL	INSTANCE	CLASS EXTENT	FULL EXTENT
Metametaclass	μ_i^2	—	—
Metaclass	μ_i	M_j	M
Class	κ_i	K_j	K
Object	θ_i	Θ_j	Θ

As yet, a connection between the levels has not been formally established. The mechanisms of instantiation and classification provide one clean way to establish the connection. These ideas are easiest to understand when dealing with the class–object level-pair.

For the class–object level-pair case, given a class κ_j, an application of the *instantiation* mechanism will produce some unique object θ_i. Minimally, this will require that space (volatile and/or persistent) be allocated for the object and its object identifier maintained. Typically, much of its state will be initialized at this time. Abstractly, this process adds another ordered pair to the *instance-of* function.

$$instance\text{-}of : \Theta \rightarrow K.$$

The *instance-of* function maps every $\theta_i \in \Theta$ to a unique $\kappa_j \in K$. This instantiation process then establishes the link between the object-level and the class-level. The information stored about a class is used to give form and function to an instantiated object. It may also put constraints on the values that make up the state of the object.

Since the *instance-of* function is not injective, the inverse of this function produces what we call a *classification* relation. Corresponding to each class κ_j will be a set of objects (i.e., all instances of κ_j). We may therefore define the *class extent* for, say, κ_j to be the following set:

$$\Theta_j = \{\theta_i | instance\text{-}of\,(\theta_i) = \kappa_j\}.$$

Clearly, the union of all the class extents Θ_j is equal to the full extent Θ.

The instantiation mechanism can be applied for higher level-pairs as well. For the metaclass–class level-pair, a metaclass μ_j can be used to instantiate an ordinary class κ_i. Various techniques for producing new classes are encoded as methods of the metaclass called Class (see Section 2.5.3).

Finally, at any level, there are a variety of ways to establish collections of instances. For example, at the object-level, a collection of objects can be established by drawing objects from some Θ_j. Typically, collections are either sets, bags, or lists. Bags and lists allow an object to be drawn more than once, while a set does not. In addition, the objects in a list are totally ordered.

2.5.1. The Object-Level and Its Relationships

Beyond the core model, there are conceptual elements that elaborate and differentiate the way in which objects can be related to each other. Although more relevant to database systems, these concepts are becoming more common in programming languages, and in particular in OOD. For example, the Object Modeling Technique [41] is a design methodology that incorporates many of these elements, and is used to design object-oriented implementations in languages such as C++. A great deal of work on semantic data models has contributed to the understanding of how objects relate to each other [17]. (Note that while objects are named using noun phrases, relationships are named using verb phrases.)

Several types of relationships are generally recognized as being useful. Directed graphs will be used to formally model these relationships. A *Directed Graph* (or Digraph) $G(N, E)$ consists of a set of nodes N and a set of edges (ordered pairs of nodes) E. ($G.N$ and $G.E$ denote the graph's node and edge set, respectively.)

Aggregation

One of the strengths of the object-oriented approach is that it allows complex objects to be built up from other objects. In the real world, objects contain subobjects which themselves are made up of subobjects. This process can continue indefinitely or until one reaches the level of fundamental particles (i.e., the limit of our knowledge). In practice, the process stops when one reaches the point where the next level of subobjects is not important for the purpose at hand. The objects that are not further decomposed are referred to as atomic objects. Those that are composed of subobjects are referred to as composite or complex objects.

Given an object θ_i, its aggregation subgraph is a directed graph consisting of it and all of its subobjects. These form the nodes of the graph. The edges in the graph represent has_a relationships, that is, the edge (θ_i, θ_j) means that object θ_i contains subobject θ_j, which is read "θ_i has_a θ_j." Objects for which there are no incoming aggregation (or has_a) edges are said to be independent objects. Otherwise, objects are dependent on the objects that contain them. If all of the objects on which θ_j is dependent are deleted, then θ_j should be deleted. (Note that the commonly used is_part_of relationships are simply the inverse of has_a relationships.)

A complete *aggregation graph* is simply the union of the subgraphs for each independent object in the system. The directed graph is *Acyclic* since it makes no sense for an object to be a subobject of itself. Thus, in general, aggregation graphs are Directed Acyclic Graphs (DAGs). Let us consider some other potential properties for the graph:

1. Connected. Although there are likely to be connected components, in a large system, it is unlikely for the entire graph to be connected.

2. Planar. In a theoretical sense, this is irrelevant, but in a practical sense, it is desirable as it enables CASE tools to display the graph without crossing lines.

3. Hierarchical. If the structure must be hierarchical, then an object may not be a part of more than one object. That is, there would be no *sharing* of subobjects. This implies that the in-degree of each node is at most one. Combined with the fact that the graph is acyclic, this means that the graph is a forest (or collection of trees). Some systems enforce this restriction, but more commonly, it is a constraint that can be added (or left out) at the discretion of the designer.

Let us consider a simple example of a C++ class that could be used in a simulation of transportation systems (see Figure 2.3). One type of transportation vehicle to be used is a Car. From this class specification, actual cars or car objects may be created. The attributes are shown as protected members, while the methods are shown as public members. Public members are generally accessible, while protected members are only available to objects of type Car (or types derived from Car).

The attributes car_Engine and car_Body are examples of subobjects. Therefore, aggregation relationships will exist between car objects and engine objects (and between car objects and body objects). Consequently, if the destructor (~Car()) for a car object is executed, car_Engine and car_Body will also be deleted.

```
class Car {
protected:
    String        model;           // Attributes
    String        year;
    String        VIN;             // Vehicle ID No.
    Engine        car_Engine;      // Aggregation
    Body          car_Body;
    Manufacturer* make;            // Association
    Person*       owner;
    Person*       driver;
    Person*       passenger [3];
public:
    Car  ();                       // Methods
    ~Car  ();
    Boolean Enter  (Person* p, Boolean is_Driver = FALSE);
    Person* Exit  ();
    Drive (double delay);
}; // Car

class Engine {
protected:
    int horsepower;
    ...
public:
    ...
}; // Engine

class Body {
protected:
    Color paint;
    ...
public:
    ...
}; // Body

class Person {
protected:
    int ssn;
    ...
public:
    ...
}; // Person

class Manufacturer {
protected:
    String name;
    ...
public:
    ...
}; // Manufacturer
```

Figure 2.3 Example classes.

Association

Sometimes the notion of association is not differentiated from the notion of aggregation. In complex systems, it may be important to do so. The idea is that an object can participate in associations when deemed appropriate, that is, it can be formed and disbanded at any time without impacting the existence of any of the participating members. The most common forms of associations can also be modeled as digraphs.

An *association graph* consists of all the objects in the system forming the nodes, and all of the associations forming the edges. In particular, a directed multigraph is needed since a given pair of objects (θ_i, θ_j) can participate in multiple associations.

In the association graph, it is also very useful to include identifying edge labels. An edge label indicates which type of association an edge represents. For example, department objects may be involved in a few kinds of associations with employee objects (e.g., employs associations and is_managed_by associations). Although specifying the endpoints (θ_i, θ_j) will not select a unique edge, adding the edge label $(\theta_i, \theta_j; k)$ will.

In addition, the graph should be directed since the objects play different roles in the association. The designer should choose the object playing the more significant role to be the source, and the other object to be the destination. For example, since money flows from a department θ_i to an employee θ_j, a reasonable choice for a designer would be to specify associations as follows: $(\theta_i, \theta_j;$ employs$)$ which reads "department θ_i employs employee θ_j." (Similarly, $(\theta_i, \theta_j;$ is_managed-by$)$ reads "department θ_i is_managed-by employee θ_j.") Note that, unlike edges in aggregation graphs, the direction of edges in association graphs may at times be somewhat arbitrary. Because of this arbitrariness, it is possible for an association graph to be cyclic. (Some systems may wish to eliminate this possibility since it complicates the management of objects. This control can be exercised during schema design.)

The example in Figure 2.3 has attributes that represent association relationships. These are the driver and passenger attributes. Clearly, the existence of a passenger should not depend on whether one has entered or exited a car.

2.5.2. The Class-Level and Its Relationships

Class-level graphs can be derived from corresponding object-level graphs in relatively straightforward ways. Their utility is twofold: they provide a broader picture of the system, and more importantly, they can be used to constrain and/or give form to the lower level. The form of each association is defined in a class-level schema specification.

Association

Class-level associations provide the principal tool for designing database systems. Indeed, the Entity-Relationship Model [6] is built primarily on this concept. A class-level graph may be constructed as follows. If a labeled edge in the object-level graph touches any object in some class κ_i, then there will exist a corresponding edge in the class-level graph.

The form of the association determines what classes the participating objects must come from. For example, an association (with label k) defined on classes κ_i and κ_j is a subset of

$$\{(\theta_l, \theta_m; k) | \theta_l \in \Theta_i, \theta_m \in \Theta_j\}$$

where Θ_i is the class extent of κ_i and Θ_j is the class extent of κ_j. Note that it is not necessary for κ_i and κ_j to be different.

In addition to edges having labels, edges in the class-level graph also have an important property called cardinality. Given an edge in the class-level graph, (κ_i, κ_j), there are four possible values this property (the cardinality property) can take on.

1. One-to-One. For all edges $(\theta_i, \theta_j; k)$ with the same label k, there is at most one θ_j for a given θ_i, and vice versa.

2. One-to-Many. For all edges $(\theta_i, \theta_j; k)$ with the same label k, there may be many θ_js for a given θ_i, but only one θ_i for a given θ_j.

3. Many-to-One. This is just the flip side of the previous case.

4. Many-to-Many. For all edges $(\theta_i, \theta_j; k)$ with the same label k, there may be many θ_js for a given θ_i, and vice versa.

Since associations among objects within the same class are not uncommon, such graphs may be cyclic. Also, since we are restricting ourselves to graphs, we are not able to model higher arity relationships such as ternary relationships found in Entity-Relationship (ER) Models. It is straightforward to extend our approach by using hypergraphs to represent higher arity relationships. We chose not to do so, feeling that the marginal value of introducing higher arity relationships is outweighed by their negative impact on complexity.

Aggregation

The class-level aggregation graph is constructed in much the same manner. If there is a has_a edge (θ_i, θ_j) in the object-level graph, there must be an edge (κ_i, κ_j) in the class-level aggregation graph. Although it makes no sense for an object to be part of itself, having cycles at the class-level is not unusual. For example, if one were modeling Pascal procedures, one component of a procedure could be another procedure since Pascal supports nested procedures.

Inheritance

An *inheritance graph* is a Directed Acyclic Graph (DAG) where each node corresponds to a class and each edge (κ_i, κ_j) indicates that class κ_j directly inherits-from κ_i. If a system does not support multiple inheritance (i.e., it supports only single inheritance), then the additional constraint that each node has an in-degree ≤ 1 makes the DAG into a forest (collection of trees). Unlike association or aggregation graphs, inheritance graphs cannot be derived from the object-level. (Note that in the case above, it is commonly said that κ_j is a specialization of (or is-a) κ_i, or conversely, that κ_i is a generalization of κ_j.)

Since inheritance is a transitive property, the transitive closure of the inheritance graph will show the totality of inheritance. Given a class-level inheritance graph, G_{CI}, the transitive closure of this graph is denoted by G^*_{CI}.

If κ_j inherits-from κ_i, we often refer to κ_i as the superclass and κ_j as the subclass. Since the subclass can add features (attributes, methods, and constraints), the subclass will typically have more features than its superclass. If we move down a level, though, and look at the corresponding class extents, Θ_i and Θ_j, the more specific class extent Θ_j is a subset of the more general class extent Θ_i ($\Theta_j \subseteq \Theta_i$).

If κ_i has another subclass, say κ_k, then both Θ_j and Θ_k are subsets of Θ_i. It is often useful to allow the designer to selectively apply additional constraints on this subclassing, such as requiring the subclasses to be disjoint. As an example, let us consider two subclasses of Person, namely, Employee and Customer, as shown in Figure 2.4.

Because of the typing rules used by C++, it is not possible to create an object that is common to both Employee and Customer. However, if the designer specifies a third class called *Emp_Cust* that is derived (using multiple inheritance) from both Employee and Customer, then it is possible to have objects common to both (Figure 2.5).

Some additional terminology is in order here. If object θ_i is an *instance-of* Emp_Cust, then it is also a member of all the superclasses, Person, Employee, and Customer. It is an *instance-of* the unique class from which

```
class Employee : public virtual Person {
protected:
        int         salary;
        Department* home_Department;
        . . .
public:
        . . .
}; // Employee

class Customer : public virtual Person {
protected:
        string credit_Rating;
        . . .
public:
        . . .
}; // Customer
```

Figure 2.4 Examples of single inheritance.

```
class Emp_Cust : public Employee, public Customer {
protected:
        int discount;
        . . .
public:
        . . .
}; // Emp_Cust
```

Figure 2.5 Example of multiple inheritance.

it was constructed. More formally, we may define the closure of a class extent Θ_j as follows:

$$\Theta_j^* = \cup\{\Theta_k | k = j \text{ or } (\kappa_j, \kappa_k) \in G_{CI}^*.E\}.$$

Communication

An additional type of relationship between classes is depicted by the *communication graph*. The nodes in the graph represent classes. The existence of a directed edge between κ_i and κ_j, (κ_i, κ_j), means that there exists a flow of control (thread path) that will result in an object θ_i, an *instance-of* κ_i, sending a message to θ_j, an *instance-of* κ_j. This graph can be produced, for example, by performing a static source code analysis of C++ implementation files. Unfortunately, finding a minimally sufficient graph is an undecidable problem. However, a close-enough approximation (which is still sufficient) can be built by assuming that: 1) every condition in the program can be evaluated to both TRUE and FALSE values, and 2) where polymorphism is possible, all relevant virtual functions can be invoked. Note that, as with the inheritance graph, the communication graph has no object-level equivalent. (Some systems may indeed have an object-level equivalent if authorizations are necessary for accessing objects.)

Binding Energy

Each type of relationship has a different degree of binding energy or cohesive force. From strongest to weakest, we have inheritance, aggregation, association, and then communication.

2.5.3. The Metalevel and Its Relationships

The metalevel is conceptually produced via the classification/instantiation mechanism which groups abstractly related classes together. As shown in Table 2.2, for every class-level class extent K_i, there is a corresponding metaclass μ_i. An *instance-of* a metaclass is an ordinary class, and the fact that it is implies that it must conform to the abstract specifications given by the metaclass. In other words, metaclasses can impose constraints on the form and function of ordinary classes. This is analogous to the influence that classes have over objects, just at a higher level of abstraction.

From an object-oriented point of view, programs written in languages like C++ consist primarily of classes as well as functions. Clearly, we would then need metaclasses for these. Each of these metaclasses would contain descriptive information about actual classes. In particular, for example, the metaclass called *Class* would contain attributes and methods. An instance of this metaclass would be a *fully elaborated* class specification. From this, a standard class specification (e.g., in the form of an .h file) can be generated. In addition to standard information found in .h files, the fully elaborated specification could include the following: documentation on the purpose and use of a class, diagrammatic information suitable for CASE tools, and information about relationships with other classes.

Because of the complex nature of ordinary class specifications, the Class metaclass will have many attributes and methods. These will involve other metaclasses such as Attribute, Method, Type, and Function. Furthermore, the Class metaclass will have several submetaclasses derived from it. This allows additional information and control to be maintained over a set of classes that share a common abstract behavior. This more detailed information is also the basis for computer-aided simulation model development. Useful submetaclasses include

Event_Class	Thread_Class
Entity_Class	Monitored_Class
Persistent_Class	Class_Template
Abstract_Class	

Let us examine the details of what would appear in some of the metalevel classes. Probably the most important metalevel class is the one called Class. A specification of this metaclass would look something like the following (Figure 2.6). Note that for the sake of brevity and simplicity, the methods for these metaclasses are left out.

```
class Class : public Type {
protected:
    Set<Attribute> new_Attribute;    // New attributes
    Set<Attribute> red_Attribute;    // Redefined attributes
    Set<Method>    new_Method;       // New methods
    Set<Method>    red_Method;       // Redefined methods
    Set<Assertion> new_Invariant;    // New invariants
    Set<Assertion> red_Invariant;    // Redefined invariants
    ...
public:
    ...
}; // Class

Set<Class> Class_Collection;    // Full Extent for Class-Level
```

Figure 2.6 The principal metaclass.

Some of the important methods for metaclass Class are methods to retrieve information from the graphs (inheritance, aggregation, association, and communication; see Figure 2.8 below). There would be a method to return a string that contains a definition of the class suitable for a compiler to process. In addition, methods to support schema evolution are very important. Schema evolution embodies technologies and methodologies that extend, adapt, and change schema. There needs to be methods to do the following:

1. Create a class.

2. Remove a class.

3. Derive a subclass using the inheritance mechanism.

4. Generate a class by instantiating a class template.

5. Add a feature (`Attribute`, `Method`, or `Assertion`) to a class.

6. Remove a feature from a class.

7. Turn assertion checking on or off.

Of these, deriving (sub) classes from superclasses and generating (template) classes from class templates provide the greatest opportunity of code reuse. Class derivation using the inheritance mechanism has been explained before. However, a short explanation of templates is in order. In C++, templates can be used to generate functions and classes. An example of a class template is shown in Figure 2.7. The unique aspect of the template is that the Set data structure is parameterized by type. Actual classes can be generated from this template as follows.

```
template<class T> class Set { ... };

Set<int>     Integer_Set;
Set<Person>  Person_Set;
```

Figure 2.7 Example of a template.

The class-level graphs (inheritance graph, aggregation graph, association graph, and communication graph) are maintained by the metalevel classes as shown in Figure 2.8.

A complete specification of the metalevel would be quite involved. We will thus limit ourselves to some metaclasses related to the metaclasses given in Figure 2.9.

Recall that definitions such as the ones above really relate to a level-pair, in this case, the metaclass–class level-pair. The type specifications are properly at the metalevel, while the instances (or sets of instances) are the level below, the class-level. For example, the instances of the Class metaclass (call it μ_1) constitute the set called Class_Collection $= K_1 =$ K. Subclasses of Class, for example, μ_i, will produce subsets (K_i) of Class_Collection. The situation is the same for the class-level graphs which record the relationships between ordinary classes. Their form is specified at the metalevel, while the actual data are stored as class-level information.

Note that what is important here are the concepts, and not the particular syntax. Since we have a loosely coupled system, we could have just as well defined Class as an Oracle, Version 7, table, or as a class using the syntax

```
class Digraph {
protected:
    Set<Adjacency_List> out_Node_List;
public:
    . . .
}; // Association

class DAG : public Digraph {
public:
    . . .        // Methods will be redefined to prevent cycles
}; // DAG

class Multigraph {
protected:
    Set<Labeled_Adj_List> out_Node_List;
public:
    . . .
}; // Multigraph

class Adjacency_List {
protected:
    Class       source;
    Set<Class> dest;
public:
    . . .
}; // Adjacency_List

class Labeled_Adj_List {
protected:
    Class           source;
    Set<Label_Class> dest;
public:
    . . .
}; // Labeled_Adj_List

class Label_Class {
protected:
    String edge_Label;
    Class  node;
public:
    . . .
}; // Label_Class

Dag        Inheritance_Graph;      // Instances
Digraph    Aggregation_Graph;
Multigraph Association_Graph;
Digraph    Communication_Graph;
```

Figure 2.8 Metaclasses for graphs.

```
class Class_Template : public Class {
protected:
    Set<Parameter> argument;
public:
    . . .
}; // Class_Template

class Type {
protected:
    String name;
    String description;
public:
    . . .
}; // Type

enum Protection_Level { public, protected, private };

class Attribute {
protected:
    String           name;
    String           description;
    Type             domain;
    Protection_Level visibility;
public:
    . . .
}; // Attribute

class Method {
protected:
    String           name;
    String           description;
    Set<Assertion>   pre_Conditions;
    Set<Assertion>   post_Conditions;
    Set<Parameter>   parameter;
    Type             return_Type;
    Protection_Level visibility;
public:
    . . .
}; // Method
```

Figure 2.9 Other related metaclasses.

of ONTOS or ObjectStore. In the latter two cases, no major changes to the code given above would be needed since their schema definition languages are based on C++.

As one might expect, a rich set of relationships is possible at this level, the metalevel. For one, since we are using C++ syntax at this level to define metaclasses, it should be apparent that graphs analogous to those provided at the class-level (namely, inheritance, aggregation, association, and communication graphs) are useful at this level also. These higher-level graphs keep track of relationships between metalevel classes. Some examples of such relationships are the following:

1. An edge in the metalevel inheritance graph is (Type, Class). This edge indicates that the metaclass Class is derived from the meta-class Type.

2. An edge in the metalevel aggregation graph is (Class, Method). This edge indicates that the metaclass Method is a part of the meta-class Class. Furthermore, a property of this aggregation is that methods cannot be shared.

It is also possible to conceive of metalevel graphs whose chief purpose is not to structure the metalevel, but rather to provide abstract constraints on the graphs at the level below. For example, there might be a type of aggregation graph at the metalevel that indicates what family of ordinary classes can come together to produce composite classes. These families of classes could be specified by choosing appropriate submetaclasses of Class. That is, for some μ_j, the class extent K_j would define a family of classes.

In summary, all four types of metalevel graphs (inheritance, aggregation, association, and communication) are useful at this level. The data for these graphs are stored as metalevel information, while their form (or type) is specified at the metameta-level.

2.5.4. The Metameta-Level

The principal reasons for having this even more abstract level are interoperability and extensibility. Conceptually, it is much like the metalevel. The goals at these two levels are, however, different. The metalevel should be comprehensive in that one should be able to store all varieties of metadata, and should be able to tailor and extend the capabilities to match current demands. In contrast, the metameta-level should be minimalistic and standardized.

The metameta-level is conceptually produced via the classification/instantiation mechanism that groups abstractly related metaclasses together. As shown in Table 2.2, for every metaclass-level class extent M_i, there is a corresponding metaclass μ_i^2. An *instance-of* a metameta-class is a metaclass, and the fact that it is implies that it must conform to the abstract specifications given by the metameta-class.

Essentially, the main purpose of the metameta-level is to provide a fixed set of modeling facilities to allow metalevel modeling facilities to be defined, extended, and processed. The fact that two systems share the same top-level modeling facilities and have the ability to process (e.g., translate) instances from the level below makes it easier for them to interoperate. In particular, the fact that the level below (i.e., the metalevel) is fully defined in terms of this standardized topmost level means that general-purpose translators can be constructed. Consequently, new special-purpose translators do not need to be developed every time there is a new (or upgraded) tool or package to integrate into a system, as is the current state of affairs.

Previously, standards organizations have based the modeling facilities for the metameta-level on Extended Entity-Relationship (EER) Models. However, their new draft proposals are based on Object-Oriented (OO) Models. The most important metameta-class is the class called `Metaclass`. This records information about the actual metaclasses available (e.g., `Class`, `Digraph`, `Attribute`, `Method`). The metalevel can be extended simply by adding a new instance to `Metaclass` (e.g., `Function`).

In any event, the fixed set of modeling primitives provided by the metameta-level should be powerful enough to allow the metalevel to be created using the four fundamental types of relationships (inheritance, aggregation, association, and communication).

2.6.   SUMMARY AND CONCLUSIONS

Before we become *level-lost*, let us review the situation. The easiest way to see the connections is to consider the three level-pairs and the instantiations that provide the interlocking.

1. Metameta-Class–Metaclass Level-Pair. A metaclass $\mu_j \in M$ is an *instance-of* some metameta-class μ_i^2.

2. Metaclass–Class Level-Pair. An (ordinary) class $\kappa_k \in K$ is an *instance-of* some metaclass μ_j.

3. Class–Object Level-Pair. An object $\theta_l \in \Theta$ is an *instance-of* some class κ_k.

Perhaps the easiest way to understand all of the graphs is also in terms of level-pairs. Recall that each of the levels except the topmost (the metameta-level) had a variety of types of graphs. For each of these levels, the graphs record and depict the relationships between instances (be they objects, classes, or metaclasses). It is also important to realize that the form (or type) of the graph is determined by the level above (e.g., for a class-level graph, the instances are classes while the form of such a graph is specified as, or at least deducible from, metalevel information). We summarize this situation in Table 2.3, which for each level-pair shows the types of graphs to be found.

Table 2.3 Graphs for Each Level-Pair

LEVEL-PAIR	ASSOCIATION	AGGREGATION	INHERITANCE	COMMUNICATION
MMclass–Metaclass	D M	D G	D A G	D G
Metaclass–Class	D M	D G	D A G	D G
Class–Object	D M	D A G	—	—

Key: D: Directed, A: Acyclic, G: Graph, M: Multigraph

In this chapter, we have outlined a four-level architecture for simulation environments. Some of the advantages of this approach are the following:

1. Object-Oriented. The object-oriented approach has been shown to be successful in software development [Analysis (OOA), Design (OOD), and Programming (OOP)], in Database Management (OODBMS), and in Simulation (OOS). It thus should be the basis for most integrated information systems.

2. Database-Centered. Databases and metadatabases should be critical elements (if not the centerpieces) of any complex integrated information system, such as a QDS system.

3. Loosely Coupled. The wide variety of useful tools, systems, and applications available today argues for a loosely coupled approach to integration, where components can be mixed and matched.

4. Relationship-Rich. The considerable body of research on semantic data models indicates that important benefits accrue by providing a full palette of relationships (inheritance, aggregation, and association). Because OODBMSs have methods, it is also beneficial to keep track of their pattern of message passing via the communication relationship.

5. Flexible and Comprehensive Metalevel. As is the case in emerging repository technology, we have split the metainformation into two parts: a

small standardized top level called the metameta-level, and an extensible and comprehensive lower level called the metalevel.

2.7. APPENDIX: EXAMPLE C++ PACKAGES

Two of the widely available (and free) packages suitable for providing the foundation of the simulation language component of the QDS environment are SimPack [9] and AWESIME [12], [13]. In this Appendix, we provide an overview of these two simulation libraries.

2.7.1. SimPack

SimPack is a simulation package or toolkit made up of a collection of C and C++ libraries. It supports several different simulation approaches, including discrete-event simulation, continuous simulation, and combined or multimodel simulation. The toolkit aims at providing the user with a basic set of utilities to produce a working simulation from a model description. The toolkit includes examples to show how several special-purpose simulation programming languages can be constructed using language translation software within the SimPack utilities.

SimPack was created with certain issues in mind. The important issues are outlined below.

1. Variety of Model Types. Since different models are suitable for different problems, the creators of SimPack felt that a simulation package must provide a set of tools that allow translation from unique graphing approaches (e.g., Petri nets for resource graphs and queueing graphs for queueing problems) into callable routines. SimPack arose out of these ideas, and hence provides many varieties of model types when compared to other packages.

2. Creation of Template Algorithms. The creators of SimPack found that, in most cases, users find it difficult to know exactly where to begin when creating a simulation for a particular application. To make it easier for users, SimPack provides a set of template algorithms so that the users can see how to solve a simple problem of a specific type and develop their simulations based on these templates.

3. No Special Language Syntax to Be Learned. As in the case of CSIM and SMPL, the aim of SimPack was to make sure that any C or C++ programmer would be able to write simulations, without having to learn a new language.

4. Event- and Process-Oriented Discrete-Event Simulation. SimPack was also designed to show the relationship between Event- and Process-Oriented Discrete-Event Simulation. SimPack views process-oriented simulation as one level higher than that of event orientation. Users interested in programming at a process level can use a SimPack tool such as MiniGPSS which compiles process code into event code. Hence, event orientation provides a base level in SimPack, and process orientation is achieved by building software that hides this level.

SimPack is available free of charge to anyone who wants to build any of a wide range of simulation models. SimPack Version 2.22 is available for anonymous ftp from ftp.cis.ufl.edu (cd to pub/simdigest/tools, specify "binary" and get simpack-2.22.tar.Z and simpack-2.1++.tar.Z).

Some of the model types supported by SimPack are as follows:

1. Declarative Models. These emphasize explicit state-to-state changes as found in finite-state automata and Markov models.

2. Functional Models. These deal with functions or procedures as in queueing networks, block models, pulse processes, and stochastic Petri nets.

3. Constraint Models. These focus on differential and difference equations.

4. Multimodels. These deal with conglomerates of more than one model connected in a graph or network to solve combined simulation problems at multiple abstraction levels.

Some of the components of SimPack of particular interest to us are the following:

1. SimPack Queueing Library. The queueing library includes a set of functionally complete routines, similar to the SMPL routine library by M. H. MacDougall. The SMPL library was used as a base, and Sim-Pack added several routines and extended options. The event list can be made of any one of the following types: HEAP, CALENDAR, or LINKED. SimPack also includes the code necessary to implement nine data structures for use in the SimPack Queueing Library. To use them, a call to initialize is needed with any one of the following nine data structures: HEAP, LINKED, CALENDAR, HENRIK, BINOMIAL, LEFIST, PAGODA, PAIR, SKEWDN, SKEWUP, SPLAY, or TWOLIST.

2. MiniGPSS Compiler. A subset of the GPSS Simulation Programming Language, MiniGPSS, has been built using YACC and LEX. This

makes it very easy to construct a simulation language for any other purpose using this compiler. Given a GPSS model description, the MiniGPSS
compiler compiles it into C code. The generated C code also allows the
user to see the manner in which the simulation is implemented.

2.7.2. AWESIME

AWESIME is short for A Widely Extensible Simulation Environment. It
is an object-oriented library for parallel programming and for process-
oriented simulation on computers with a shared address space. AWESIME
is written in C++. Its features go beyond that of other similar packages in
that AWESIME has a group of C++ classes that can manipulate or specify different aspects of a parallel programming environment. Classes can
simply be added to these classes to build more complex process-oriented
simulations. In this added functionality, AWESIME takes after the CSIM
simulation package.

At present, AWESIME has been ported and configured on the following architectures: Sun SPARC, Motorola 680x0, Intel i386, the
Motorola 88K family, the National Semiconductor NS32K family, and
the MIPS R2000/R3000 machines. Just like SimPack, AWESIME is
free and is available for anonymous ftp from ftp.cs.colorado.edu (cd
to /pub/distribs/Awesime and get Awesime-12-21-93.tar.gz and users-
guide.ps.Z).

AWESIME consists of a library of C++ classes, built into a Class
Hierarchy. The classes provided include container classes (e.g., for queues
and priority queues), classes for random variates, classes for statistics collection and analysis (including a subclass for histograms), and a variety of
classes to support process-oriented simulation. The latter are of particular
interest to us, so we will discuss them further.

Threads

Threads represent the lowest level of concurrency in AWESIME. User-
defined threads (threads in any application) must be declared as a subclass
of this class, and threads must only be created using the function new. Note
that defining threads statically at the main level is not allowed, and although
possible within routines, it is not recommended. The class Threads includes
a few class instance variables that are used to record details of the calling
environment. The thread constructor is used to provide this information
to the class. The destructor is just to clean up the class variable. When a
thread is executed for the first time, it must be scheduled, and a series of

other actions result. One of these is a call to routine main(). An absence of main() is reported as an error.

Thread Container Class

A thread container is something into which a thread is placed. The threadContainer class by itself is an abstract one, and only its subclasses are of interest to us. A few of the methods in this class are: 1) add a thread, 2) remove a thread, 3) return the size of the container (number of threads in it), and 4) test for emptiness of the thread container.

Some important subclasses of this class are the following:

1. CPU. The abstract processor which executes the AWESIME program. The CPU class includes several subclasses that implement CPU multiplexing (CPU switching between threads when a synchronization constraint delays a specific thread).

2. FifoScheduler. As the name suggests, this provides first-in first-out thread schedulers.

3. HeapScheduler. This provides priority thread schedulers.

Synchronization Classes

Synchronization is done by two levels of locking. One is at the CPU level, and the other is at the Thread level. CPU Level Locking is done using the SpinLock class. The reserve and release members perform the functions to reserve and release the entire CPU, and not just the thread currently using the CPU. SpinLocks are efficient, and use in-line functions for reserve and release to reduce function call overhead. Thread Level Locking can be accomplished by a variety of specialized classes: Monitor, Barrier Synchronization, EventSequence, Condition, Join, Semaphore, Facility, and Owned Facility.

References

[1] O. Balci and R. E. Nance, "Simulation model development environments: A research prototype," *J. Oper. Res. Soc.*, vol. 38, no. 8, 1987, pp. 753–763.

[2] G. Birtwistle et al., *SIMULA Begin*. Studentlitertur and Auerbach Publishers, 1973.

[3] G. Birtwistle, *DEMOS: A System for Discrete Event Modelling on SIMULA*. New York: Springer-Verlag, 1987.

[4] CACI, *MODSIM II: The Language for Object-Oriented Simulation*, Los Angeles, CA, Jan. 1990.

[5] M. A. Centeno and C. R. Standridge, "Databases: Designing and developing integrated simulation modeling environments," in *Proc. 1993 Winter Simulation Conf.*, Los Angeles, CA, 1993, pp. 526–534.

[6] P. Chen, "The entity-relationship model—Toward a unified view of data," *ACM Trans. Database Syst.*, vol. 1, Mar. 1976.

[7] A. Cornelio and S. B. Navathe, "Applying active database models for simulation," in *Proc. 1993 Winter Simulation Conf.*, Los Angeles, CA, 1993, pp. 535–543.

[8] L. M. L. Delcambre and L. F. Pollacia, "The object flow model for data-based simulation," in *Proc. 1993 Winter Simulation Conf.*, Los Angeles, CA, 1993, pp. 519–525.

[9] P. A. Fishwick, "SimPack: Getting started with simulation programming in C and C++," in *Proc. 1992 Winter Simulation Conf.*, Arlington, VA, Dec. 1992, pp. 154–162.

[10] M. S. Fox et al., "Knowledge-based simulation: An artificial intelligence approach to system modeling and automating the simulation life cycle," in *Artificial Intelligence, Simulation and Modeling*, L. E. Widman, K. A. Loparo, and N. R. Nielsen, Eds. New York: Wiley Interscience, 1989.

[11] A. Goldfine, *Information Resource Dictionary System Requirements Specification Standing Document*, NIST, Feb. 1993.

[12] D. C. Grunwald, *A User's Guide to AWESIME: An Object Oriented Parallel Programming and Simulation System*, Tech. Rep., Univ. Colorado, Boulder, 1991.

[13] D. C. Grunwald, *User's Guide to AWESIME-II: A Widely Extensible Simulation Environment*, Tech. Rep., Univ. Colorado, Boulder, 1992.

[14] M. Hitz, H. Werthner, and T. Oren, "Employing databases for large scale reuse of simulation models," in *Proc. 1993 Winter Simulation Conf.*, Los Angeles, CA, 1993, pp. 544–551.

[15] L. Hobbs and K. England, *Digital's CDD/Repository*. Digital Press, 1993.

[16] R. E. Hodges, *Repository Context, Information Resource Dictionary System (IRDS)*, Reference Model Tech. Rep., NIST, Sept. 1992.

[17] R. Hull and R. King, "Semantic database modeling: Survey, applications, and research issues," *ACM Computing Surveys*, vol. 19, Sept. 1987.

[18] K. J. Kochut, J. A. Miller, and W. D. Potter, "Design of a CLOS version of Active KDL: A knowledge/data base system capable of query driven simulation," in *Proc. 1991 AI and Simulation Conf.*, New Orleans, LA, Apr. 1991, pp. 139–145.

[19] M. H. Law, *Guide to Information Resource Dictionary System Applications: General Concepts and Strategic Systems Planning*, NBS Special Publ. 500-152, 1988. (NBS is now NIST.)

[20] D. Lea, *User's Guide to the GNU C++ Library*. Boston, MA: Free Software Foundation, Inc., 1992.

[21] M. Lenard, "A prototype implementation of a model management system for discrete-event models," in *Proc. 1993 Winter Simulation Conf.*, Los Angeles, CA, 1993, pp. 560–568.

[22] D. McArthur, P. Klahr, and S. Narain, *The ROSS Language Manual*, The RAND Corp., N-1854-1-AF, Sept. 1985.

[23] J. A. Miller and O. R. Weyrich, Jr., "Query driven simulation using SIMO-DULA," in *Proc. 22nd Annu. Simulation Symp.*, Tampa, FL, Mar. 1989, pp. 167–181.

[24] J. A. Miller et al., "Model instantiation for query driven simulation in Active KDL," in *Proc. 23rd Annu. Simulation Symp.*, Nashville, TN, Apr. 1990, pp. 15–32.

[25] J. A. Miller and N. D. Griffeth, "Performance modeling of database and simulation protocols: Design choices for query driven simulation," in *Proc. 24th Annu. Simulation Symp.*, New Orleans, LA, Apr. 1991, pp. 205–216.

[26] J. A. Miller et al., "Query-driven simulation using Active KDL: A functional object-oriented database system," *Int. J. Comput. Simulation*, vol. 1, no. 1, 1991, pp. 1–30.

[27] J. A. Miller et al., "The Active KDL object-oriented database system and its application to simulation support," *J. Object-Oriented Programming* (Special Issue on Databases), vol. 4, July–Aug. 1991, pp. 30–45.

[28] J. A. Miller, W. D. Potter, and K. J. Kochut, "Knowledge, data, and models: Taking an objective orientation on integrating these three," *IEEE Potentials*, vol. 11, Dec. 1992, pp. 13–17.

[29] J. A. Miller et al., *Design of a WSRC Repository with an End-User Emphasis*, Tech. Rep., Westinghouse Savannah River Co. (WSRC), Aiken, SC, Jan. 1994.

[30] J. A. Miller, W. D. Potter, and K. J. Kochut, "Repository design with an end-user emphasis," in *Proc. 5th Int. Users Group Conf.: Repository/Architecture/Development*, Chicago, IL, Nov. 1994.

[31] J. A. Miller, Guest Ed., *Int. J. Comput. Simulation* (Special Issue on Object-Oriented Simulation and Simulation Support), vol. 5, no. 4, 1995.

[32] W. D. Potter and L. Kerschberg, "A unified approach to modeling knowledge and data," in *Proc. IFIP TC2 Conf. Knowledge and Data (DS-2)*, Algarve, Portugal, Nov. 1986. [Published by North-Holland as *Data and Knowledge DS-2* (1988).]

[33] W. D. Potter and R. P. Trueblood, "Traditional, semantic and hyper-semantic approaches to data modeling," *IEEE Computer*, vol. 21, June 1988, pp. 53–63.

[34] W. D. Potter, R. P. Trueblood, and C. M. Eastman, "Hyper-semantic data modeling," *Data & Knowledge Eng.*, vol. 4, 1989, pp. 69–90.

[35] W. D. Potter et al., "Supporting an intelligent simulation/modeling environment using the Active KDL object-oriented database programming language," in *Proc. 21st Annu. Pittsburgh Conf. Modeling and Simulation*, vol. 21, part 4, Pittsburgh, PA, May 1990, pp. 1895–1900.

[36] W. D. Potter et al., "Extending decision support systems: The integration of data, knowledge, and model management," *Annals Oper. Res.* (Special Issue on Model Management), vol. 38, 1992, pp. 501–527.

[37] W. D. Potter et al., "The evolution of the knowledge/data model," *Int. J. Expert Syst.* (Special Issue on Artificial Intelligence and Databases), vol. 6, no. 1, 1993, pp. 39–81.

[38] W. D. Potter, J. A. Miller, and K. J. Kochut, "A hyper-semantic approach to intelligent information systems," *Integrated Comput.-Aided Eng.* (Special Issue on Intelligent Information Systems), 1993.

[39] Y. V. Reddy et al., "The knowledge-based simulation system," *IEEE Software*, Mar. 1986.

[40] M. Rovira, D. Spooner, and J. Haddock, "The concept of views in simulation," in *Proc. 1993 Winter Simulation Conf.*, Los Angeles, CA, 1993, pp. 552–559.

[41] J. Rumbaugh et al., *Object-Oriented Modeling and Design*. Englewood Cliffs, NJ: Prentice-Hall, 1991.

[42] A. R. Simon, *The Integrated CASE Tools Handbook*. New York: Van Nostrand Reinhold, 1993.

[43] C. Standridge and A. Pritsker, *TESS: The Extended Simulation Support System*. New York: Halstead Press, 1987.

[44] B. Stroustrup, *The C++ Programming Language*, 2nd ed. Reading, MA: Addison-Wesley, 1991.

[45] A. Tannenbaum, *Implementing a Corporate Repository: The Models Meet Reality*. New York: Wiley, 1994.

[46] A. K. Thompson, "CASE data integration: The emerging international standards," *ICL Tech. J.*, May 1992, pp. 54–66.

[47] G. Thompson, "The need for CASE integration," Tech. Rep., R&O, Inc., Apr. 1993.

[48] G. Wilkie, *Object-Oriented Software Engineering: The Professional Developer's Guide*. Reading, MA: Addison-Wesley, 1993.

[49] G. Zhang and B. P. Zeigler, "The system entity structure: Knowledge representation for simulation modeling and design," in *Artificial Intelligence, Simulation and Modeling*, L. E. Widman, K. A. Loparo, and N. R. Nielsen, Eds. New York: Wiley Interscience, 1989.

[50] B. P. Zeigler, "Hierarchical, modular discrete event modelling in an object oriented environment," *Simulation*, vol. 49, no. 5, Nov. 1987, pp. 218–230.

[51] B. P. Zeigler, *Object-Oriented Simulation with Hierarchical, Modular Models: Intelligent Agents and Endomorphic Systems*. Boston, MA: Academic Press, 1990.

Chapter 3

The Object Flow Model
for Object-Oriented Simulation
and Database Application Modeling

Lissa F. Pollacia   *Department of Mathematical*
                           and Physical Sciences
                           Northwestern State University
                           Natchitoches, Louisiana, USA

Lois M. L. Delcambre   *Department of Computer Science*
                           and Engineering
                           Oregon Graduate Institute
                           Portland, Oregon, USA

Editor's Introduction ─────────────────────────────────────

Now, let us get back to looking at other simulation languages—in this case, a higher order language that can be used to describe the dynamic, as well as structural aspects of a simulation application. The need for dynamic modeling has led to the development of languages and methodologies called "conceptual modeling languages" for integrating the specification of structure and dynamics into a single conceptual model. By adopting some conceptual modeling formalism, the designer may concentrate on the semantics of the application domain rather than the implementation details of the delivered system.

The Object Flow Model (OFM) is the conceptual modeling language examined in this chapter. The modeling of dynamics includes both of the methods associated with object-oriented models, as well as an active component for event- and data-driven invocation of processing steps. For the simulation community, this represents a shift in emphasis from procedural coding to a more object-oriented approach. The specification of system dynamics using OFM consists of developing more Object Flow Diagrams. Object Flow Diagrams are closely related to an extended Petri net formalism called the

Predicate Transition Net model. Object Flow Diagrams provide an object-oriented framework for modeling the flow of objects through processes. The Object Flow Diagram serves as a model for discrete-event simulation. This chapter investigates the contribution of the OFM to simulation and to the conceptual modeling of database applications.

Key Words

Conceptual modeling, Discrete-event simulation, Object-oriented modeling, Petri net, Predicate transition net.

3.1.   INTRODUCTION

For many years, designers of complex software systems have recognized the need to construct an abstract model of the system prior to its actual implementation [45]. This recognition stems from the fact that many development and maintenance problems are a direct result of improper modeling of the system during the early phases of development [43]. To aid designers in modeling during these early phases, many tools, techniques, languages, methodologies, etc., have emerged from various fields including software development, database application development, and simulation modeling. This research is motivated by these three areas, and contributes an object-oriented conceptual modeling language that is suitable for simulation as well as database application modeling. The focus of this chapter is on the detailed presentation of the model, with examples from both the simulation and database areas.

The software engineering community responded to the modeling problem with a plethora of tools, techniques, and languages [66], [78] which target the requirements analysis and specification phase [21], [79]. The most well-known approaches used by industry were developed in the 1970s, e.g., SASD [24], SADT [69], and JSD [36]. More recently, a variety of Computer-Assisted Software Engineering (CASE) tools have been developed that emphasize the front end, or requirements analysis and specification phase [46]. Some representative CASE tools include TARA [28], IEF [49], IEW/ADW [40], MetaEdit [74], and RAMATIC [8].

The database community also responded to the modeling problem, and determined that the classical data models, i.e., the hierarchical, network, and relational models, were too low-level and inflexible for modeling large database applications [34]. This lack of *semantic expressiveness* [9] resulted in the development of a new class of data models called *semantic data models* [34], [56]. These models are characterized by a set of richer, more flexible modeling constructs than available with the classical data models. This process is often termed *conceptual modeling* because of the natural and intuitive constructs provided by semantic data models.

In recent years, more emphasis has been placed on the importance of describing the dynamic, as well as structural, aspects of a database application. These dynamic aspects include primitive object operations (e.g., methods), database transactions, and other application processes. The need for dynamic modeling has led to the development of languages and methodologies, called *conceptual modeling languages*, for integrating the specification of structure and dynamics into a single conceptual model. Conceptual modeling is a natural and effective way of abstracting and understanding the particulars of a system without concern for the implementation details. Models that are created in this way may be mapped to machine-level models quite easily and efficiently. Many conceptual modeling languages use a semantic data model for specifying structure, and build on some other formalism, e.g., Petri nets [25] or directed graphs [3], for the specification of dynamics. Interest in conceptual modeling has also been expressed by linguists, cognitive psychologists, and researchers in the fields of business administration and management [44]. More recently, a number of object-oriented modeling techniques have been proposed [35], [68]. The goal of an object-oriented model is to provide for the development of a conceptual model with integrated, encapsulated structure and behavior.

The benefits of a conceptual model are equally important in simulation. It has been argued that, given the complexities and problems of constructing a discrete-event simulation model, the challenges and benefits of conceptual modeling of discrete simulations may be even more significant than in many other areas of software development [17]. The importance of conceptual modeling for simulation is illustrated by a diagram of the simulation methodology, given in [55], and shown in Figure 3.1. First, the problem must be defined and objectives decided, after which a conceptual model, existing primarily within the developer's mind, arises. To make this model of the system more formal and concrete, a *communicative model* is constructed, which is nontechnical and easily understood by all persons involved. This communicative model corresponds to our conceptual model of the application to be simulated. From this communicative model, the actual system, or programmed model, is constructed. The aim of the communicative (conceptual) model is to eliminate errors and inconsistencies while they are easier to correct, i.e., before the system is programmed. Thus, conceptual modeling languages and methods for discrete-event simulation are part of the larger family of conceptual modeling languages and methods used in other areas of software development.

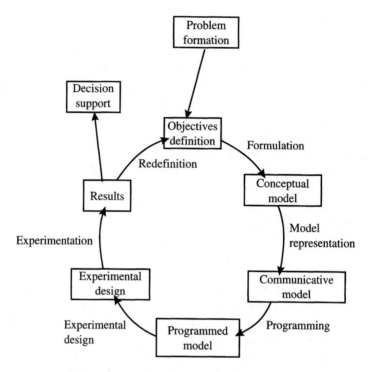

Figure 3.1 Methodological cycle for simulation.

This chapter presents the OFM as a language for the construction of conceptual models of database applications [60] and discrete-event simulation systems [62], [61], [23]. The development of the OFM was influenced by semantic and object-oriented database models and discrete-event simulation models. The OFM consists of two main components: the object model (which describes the structure of object classes and the encapsulated methods to manipulate objects) and the Object Flow Diagram (OFD). The object model of OFM is similar to other object models, particularly the model defined by the Object Database Management Group (ODMG) [4], although it was developed independently [59]. The major contribution of the OFM is the OFD, a visual formalism [33] that complements the object model by describing how objects invoke processing steps. The OFD was strongly influenced by network-based, process-oriented, discrete-event simulation languages and models, in part, because such models provide a graphical and intuitive description of the application processing. The formal semantics of an OFD was derived from rule-based query languages in the database field [2], and ultimately based on predicate transition nets [29], a form of Petri nets [58].

Section 3.2 presents background and related research. The third section presents a detailed description of the OFM, including a running example. Section 3.4 illustrates the use of the OFM for simulation. Section 3.5 evaluates the OFM by comparing it to related efforts, and the chapter concludes with a description of current and future work in Section 3.6.

3.2.   BACKGROUND AND RELATED WORK

The development of the OFM and the associated modeling approach is related to work in the following areas: semantic and object-oriented data models, discrete-event simulation models, and conceptual modeling languages for database applications.

3.2.1. Semantic and Object-Oriented Data Models

The object model of the OFM is a synthesis of various modeling features from prominent object-oriented databases, e.g., O_2 [53] and ObjectStore [42], and is quite similar to although less expressive than the ODMG object model [4], particularly with regard to collection types. The structural aspects of these models were introduced as part of semantic data models [1], [11], [12], [32], [48], [51]. The Entity-Relationship (ER) Model [18], one of the first semantic models, has become one of the most widely used approaches for the conceptual design of databases and information systems [30], and has been extended in various ways [6], [26].

3.2.2. Discrete-Event Simulation Models

The dynamic modeling components of the OFM, i.e., OFDs, are similar to the various languages and methods proposed for conceptual modeling of discrete-event simulation. Some of these languages provide an abstract, high-level representation of the system. Pooley [63] reviews several process-oriented diagramming languages and models, and proposes one such language for process-based models in [64]. Ceric [17] surveys and classifies conceptual modeling languages for simulation, and in particular, those which utilize a diagrammatic representation.

One such category of languages is called "simulation strategy neutral" by Ceric, and includes those languages and methods that do not adhere to a specific simulation strategy or language. Many of these methods are based on Petri nets [58], with which it is assumed the reader has some familiarity. *Augmented Petri nets* [27] extend original Petri nets by allowing multiple tokens at a place, individuality of tokens, control arcs that are associated with a predicate, and time delays at transitions. *Simulation nets* [77] also provide extensions, such as queues, test arcs, and interrupt arcs, to Petri nets.

Function nets [71] are another extended Petri net modeling language/method. Transitions, called *agencies*, have an associated activity, which may have a delay and an optional selective input/output specification. The notion of a token has been extended to represent individual entities, which may have an associated message that can be interpreted and manipulated by an adjacent agency when that agency is firing. Several other extensions include: multiple tokens that may be queued at a place, optional initialization of places with tokens, and the choice between "copy reading" and "destructive reading" of tokens when the agency fires. Copy reading of a token leaves a copy of it in the respective input places, whereas destructive reading represents the normal case; the firing of an agency removes the token from the input place.

Some simulation languages provide a diagrammatic equivalent of the textual code, where each symbol in the diagram corresponds to one or more statements of the language. GPSS [72] block diagrams and SLAM II networks [65] are examples of what Ceric terms "simulation language oriented methods." Other such languages include: SIMAN [57], SIMF [75], INSIGHT [67], SIMNET [76], and VSIM [16]. These languages are surveyed in [59], and compared with the OFM in [61] and [23]. Although these languages contain a diagramming network, they are not what we consider "conceptual modeling languages" in that a model constructed with one of these languages, even in diagrammatic form, is essentially an implementation of the system.

3.2.3. Conceptual Modeling Languages for Database Applications

Like semantic data models, conceptual modeling languages for database applications claim to capture more of the *semantics* of the application in a concise and understandable manner. Unlike most semantic data models, they attempt to capture the *dynamics* of the application as well.

A number of languages have been proposed in this area; three categories may be distinguished, based on the level of specification provided by the language [14]. *Action-level* conceptual modeling languages are limited to the specification of primitive database actions, such as insert, delete, and modify, and any other operation that involves only one type of object. One such language is Gambit [13], which provides a diagramming tool for modeling actions and the update propagations that are a result of those actions.

The *transaction-level* languages address issues involving the design of database transactions. A *transaction* is a related group of operations, either actions or other transactions, that form a single logical unit of computation. In a database situation, a transaction may involve the primitive actions of multiple object types, or may include the invocation of other transactions. The ACM/PCM methodology [15] was one of the first conceptual modeling languages for database dynamics, and models transactions by adding operation labels to the schema of objects affected by those transactions. An extension to ACM/PCM, transaction schema [52], emphasizes the specification of transactions, along with their actions and other transaction invocations, prior to schema design. After transaction specification, the schema is automatically formulated using these specifications.

The *flow level* of specification deals with modeling the processes of an application and how objects participate in those processes. Thus, in addition to transaction modeling, the interconnections or communication between processes are shown. This level is more abstract than the transaction level, and is designed to show the gross dynamic properties of an application by defining the flow of objects through many actions and transactions. The *design schema* of the Event Model [39] is one such flow-level modeling language, and is based on the concept of a dataflow diagram. The nodes represent activities of the application, and the arcs indicate the flow of data between activities. After the design schema is complete, a more detailed conceptual schema is constructed, with additional information from the user. Another flow-level language is the Behavior Network Model [41], which provides diagrammatic representations for process and interface modeling, and for modeling at the transaction level. The semantics of these are adaptations of the Petri net formalism, with extensions, for token movement and firing. A complete modeling methodology is defined as well.

Object Behavior Diagrams [38] and modeling transition [31] are also flow-level conceptual modeling languages. Object Behavior Diagrams model various levels of an individual class's life cycle, from an abstract, high-level representation to implementation details. Transition modeling emphasizes the structural schema of an application, and the incremental refinement of the schema to include arcs that represent the movement of objects between classes of the schema.

A variety of object-oriented models are reviewed by Hutt [35]. The Object Modeling Technique (OMT) [70] was one of the first. OMT provides three related models for the structural, dynamic, and functional views of a system. OMT focuses on the dynamic behavior of individual objects, and thus promotes the design of methods to manipulate individual objects. OMT has a particularly rich object model, much like semantic data models, with graphical notation for all aspects of the object model. A more detailed comparison of the OFM with a number of these models appears below (in Section 3.5).

3.3.   THE OBJECT FLOW MODEL (OFM)

This section describes the two main components of the OFM, which are an object model for the specification of structural information and method signatures, and the OFD for the description of behavioral characteristics of the system. One benefit of the OFM is its flexibility in carrying out the modeling process. The modeler may choose to first define the structural characteristics of the objects, i.e., the object model, after which one or more OFDs are constructed to model system behavior. Alternatively, the modeler may first define behavior (the simulation) followed by the structural definition. As a third alternative, the structural and behavioral modeling may proceed in an integrated fashion, with refinements taking place as the model is constructed.

3.3.1. Structural Modeling Concepts

This section describes the structural modeling features of the OFM, which are inherent to object-oriented databases and semantic data models. One of the fundamental features is *classification*, i.e., the objects of a system are classified, or grouped into semantically meaningful sets of classes. The OFM supports three types of classes: 1) *simple classes*, e.g., integer, which represent atomic entities; 2) *abstract classes*, e.g., person, which represent abstract entities that correspond to real or conceptual entities of the application domain; and 3) *event classes*, e.g., request arrival, which represent happenings in the real world. The notion of objects in the OFM is the same as that in an object-oriented database system, i.e., they are active entities in that they may have associated *actions* (methods) that specify their behavior. Abstract objects have their own *identity*, that is, their existence is not dependent upon any identifier. Graphically, simple classes are represented by rectangles, abstract and event classes are shown as ellipses. For example, in the Resort Reservation object model (given in the Appendix), *HotelType* is a simple class, *Person* is an abstract class, and *CustomerEvent* is an event class. The set of graphical object model components of the OFM are shown in Figure 3.2.

Another fundamental component of the OFM is the representation of *relationships*, also called *properties*, which are essentially functions between objects of two classes. For example, *HasHotels* is a relationship between a resort and the set of hotels that are located at that resort (Figure 3.15). The range of a property, called its *value class*, may be any class specified in the object model. The value of a property is an object of the value class. The property may be *single-valued* where the value is a single object, or *multivalued* where the value is a set of objects. For example, *HName* is a single-valued property and *HasRooms* is a multivalued property

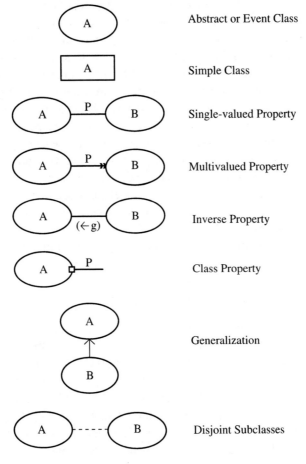

Figure 3.2 Graphical components of the OFM object model.

of the class *Hotel*. Graphically, single-valued properties are specified by undirected named arcs that relate the domain class to the range class. A multivalued property is represented by a named, doubled-headed arc pointing to the value class. For each property, there exists an implicit *inverse property*, which may be explicitly named if the modeler so desires, e.g., *IsIn* between *Hotel* and *Resort*. This inverse property specifies in which resort any given hotel is a member. A *class property* is a property of a class as a whole, and not to individual objects of the class, e.g., *AveAge* of a class *Person*, which contains the average age of all persons represented as objects in *Person*. These properties are represented in the graphical object model by an arc connected to the class by a small box.

The second fundamental abstraction of semantic database design is *generalization* of classes, which is the subset, or *ISA* relationship, between a class and another class. Generalization is represented by a directed arc pointing from a class (the subclass) to a more general class (the superclass). Each subclass strictly inherits all properties of its superclasses, and its members form a subset of the superclass objects. As an example, *Guest* and *Customer* are subclasses of *Person*. A subclass may have local properties in addition to inherited properties, e.g., *IsOccupying of Guest*, which indicates which room the guest is currently occupying. Without restrictions, the object sets in sibling subclasses may overlap. The modeler may, however, specify that certain subclasses are *disjoint*, i.e., nonoverlapping. This is represented by a dashed line between the disjoint classes.

All user-defined classes in an object model are subclasses of the generic class called *Class*, which has three class properties: *Count*, *Max*, and *Initial_No*. These properties contain the current count of objects in the class, the maximum number of objects that may reside in a class, and the initial number of objects placed in a class, respectively.

3.3.2. The Object Definition Language

The OFM graphical object model representation is intended to specify the gross structural properties of an application. A corresponding textual language, the OFM Object Definition Language (ODL), is designed to provide the structural details that are not graphically expressed, or to serve as an alternative to the graphical object model. The OFM ODL is an extension of the data definition language of the *Class Model* [22]. Although the OFM ODL has the same name as the Object Definition Language of the ODMG model [4], these two languages are distinct and were developed independently.

Methods may be specified with classes to define the behavior of the objects of that class. The OFM adheres to the object-oriented approach to object manipulation, i.e., encapsulation of data and methods. Instances of a class may only be manipulated using the methods associated with this class. Methods are associated with a class by including them as part of the method clause of the OFM ODL class definition.

The specification of methods in the OFM ODL corresponds to action-level specification in other CMLs, e.g., ACM/PCM, DATAID. As a specification language, the OFM is not concerned with the implementation of a method, but with its effect on the object to which it is applied. Thus, the OFM ODL adopts a declarative approach to specification of methods where each method is specified by its name and signature, i.e., a list of its input and output arguments and their types. For example, the following method, *ReduceAvailability*, is associated with class *Room* to adjust a room's availability dates whenever it is reserved by a customer.

```
Method ReduceAvailability (IN: StartDate:Date, EndDate:Date)
```

Once defined with a class, a method may be invoked within the definition of a process to manipulate objects of the associated class. The OFM also provides some predefined methods for data manipulation, e.g., create a new object of a class, delete a specified object from a class extension, add an object to a class extension, retrieve the value of a property, etc. Whenever a class is defined in the object model, these methods are considered to be automatically generated, and available for use in specifying the details of a process, i.e., within the process definition.

3.3.3. Dynamic Modeling Component of the OFM

One of the major contributions of the OFM lies in the formalism defined for the modeling of the dynamics of an application. This formalism, called an OFD, depicts classes of objects and the progression or flow of objects through the activities that comprise a process. As is the case for the structural modeling component, a corresponding textual language, the Process Flow Language (PFL), is defined in order to specify more details of the process behavior.

Object Flow Diagrams

An OFD is a directed graph that shows the flow of objects through a single process of the application domain. A *process* is an abstraction of some real-world procedure or activity; what constitutes a process within a domain is subjective, and is based on the goals and requirements of the modeler. Note that capturing the requirements specification of an application is beyond the scope of this research.

An OFD references *objects* and events from the object model. The purpose of the OFD is to describe how the arrival of objects and the occurrence of events can trigger or initiate *processes* that represent activities in which objects engage. The objects flow through the OFD, triggering processes, participating in classes, and undergoing data transformations.

An OFD may contain two types of nodes: *class nodes* and *process nodes*. A class node, represented by an ellipse, contains the name of an abstract object or event class from the object model. A process node, represented by a rectangle, corresponds to some processing step, such as scheduling or filling of an order. Each process node has an optional *time delay* associated with it, and an optional *guard* that imposes constraints on input objects. The guard is a predicate that specifies selection criteria for objects from input classes and optional ordering criteria for input objects. The guard may also indicate matching criteria for objects from two or more input classes. The *edges* of the OFD are directed arcs, and may be solid, indicating the input/output of objects between class nodes and process nodes, or may be dotted arcs, indicating objects that are only referenced by a process node. OFD constructs are shown in Figure 3.3.

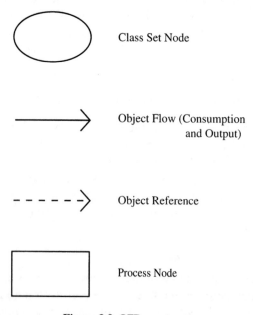

Figure 3.3 OFD constructs.

As an example of an OFD, consider the *MakeReservation* process node shown in Figure 3.4. This process node is to be executed whenever a request arrives, indicating that a person wants to make a reservation at a particular resort and hotel.

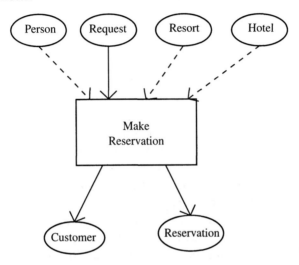

Figure 3.4 OFD for *MakeReservation* process node.

The class nodes of this OFD are *Person, Request, Resort, Hotel, Customer*, and *Reservation*; the process node is *MakeReservation*. The solid edge from *Request* to *MakeReservation* indicates that an object from *Request* will be *consumed*, i.e., removed from the class node, by the process node. The dotted edges from *Person, Resort*, and *Hotel* to *MakeReservation* indicate that an object from each of these three class nodes is *referenced*, but not consumed, by the process node. The edges leading from *MakeReservation* to *Customer* and *Reservation* are output edges, indicating that a single object will be placed in each of these nodes upon completion of the process node. An edge may connect a class node to a process node and vice versa. That is, an OFD is a bipartite graph on the two sets: class nodes and process nodes. Reference edges must be input edges.

The semantics of OFDs are based on those of extended Petri nets; thus, the dynamics of an OFD basically consist of the triggering of processes and the movement of objects to and from class nodes. The arrival of one object from each of the input classes that collectively satisfy the guard and timing delay of a process node *triggers* the process node or causes it to *fire*. When this occurs, the statements that comprise the behavior of the process node are executed. Upon firing, an object is produced in each of the subsequent class nodes (the *output* nodes). The output nodes of a process node may be input to another process node; thus, the production of an object may trigger the next process node, and so on. Process node firing is determined by the availability of objects in the input class nodes, and process nodes fire independently and asynchronously.

Class Nodes

A class node represents a class of objects or events that participate in the process being specified by the OFD. The name of a class node must be that of a class defined in the object model of the application. A class node is considered a repository of objects, i.e., all objects of that class residing in the database at the current time. These objects are called the *extension* of the class node, and correspond to the extension of the class in the database. Note that this is one of the ways in which the OFM is simpler than the ODMG model [4]; the ODMG model allows any number of persistent collections of objects of a given type.

Within a single OFD, each class node is unique and represents all objects in the class extension. However, for clarity and notational convenience, the modeler may place more than one class node with the same class name within an OFD. For example, the two OFDs shown in Figure 3.5(a) and (b) are equivalent. The two nodes labeled C1 in (b) actually represent the same class.

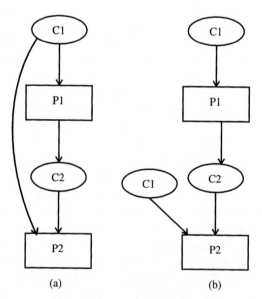

Figure 3.5 Equivalent OFDs.

A class node may also represent complex objects formed by the aggregation of two or more objects. In an OFD, a class node containing two or more class nodes indicates object aggregation. For example, Figure 3.6 shows the aggregation of worker and machine objects to form a single workstation object composed of one worker and one machine.

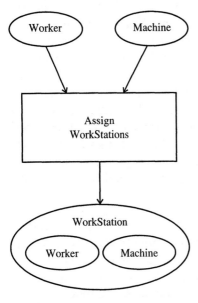

Figure 3.6 Aggregation of objects.

This allows for the explicit and conceptually natural representation of aggregation in a dynamic fashion. A similar OFD process node with an aggregate object class as input and component object classes as output may be used to specify the deaggregation of a composite object into its components.

Object Flows

An *object flow*, represented by a directed edge in an OFD, symbolizes the communication of objects between processes. An object flow extends the notion of a *data path* in dataflow diagrams by associating additional semantics with the edges, i.e., the semantics of object consumption, manipulation, and creation.

As stated in the previous section, an OFD is a bipartite graph on the two sets **C** = {class nodes} and **P** = {process nodes}. Thus, an object flow is either an *input flow* (from a node of **C** to a node of **P**), or an *output flow* (from a node of **P** to a node of **C**). The terms object flow and edge are used interchangeably.

The OFM defines two types of input edges: 1) a solid edge representing object consumption, and 2) a dotted edge representing object *reference*.

When an object is consumed by a process node, it means that the object is removed from the extension of the input class node and any other classes to which it may belong at the moment the process node begins execution. The object, with its properties and methods, is available to the process node during execution, but the object is no longer a member of the input class. When the edge indicates object reference, then the object is available for reference or property update, but the object remains a member of the input class, i.e., it is not consumed. An edge from a process node to a class node represents an *output object flow*, and indicates that an object is placed in the extension of the class node upon completion of the process node firing.

Note that it is not strictly necessary to delete an object from an input class and then insert it into an output class. The delete semantics for input objects, as just described, corresponds to the formally defined, primitive actions of the OFD. Research in progress is defining higher level (macro) constructs of OFDs to indicate that an object is moving from one subclass to another, from a subclass to a superclass, or vice versa within a process node.

Process Nodes

The process nodes of an OFD represent the tasks or subprocesses that make up the application being modeled by the OFD. Figure 3.7 shows the general representation of a process node within an OFD. The name of the process node is required. The process node may optionally contain an *order criterion*, which indicates the order in which eligible objects (one from each input class) will proceed to the process node, and a *process guard*, which imposes selection criteria on the objects of the input class nodes.

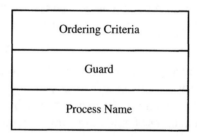

| Ordering Criteria |
| Guard |
| Process Name |

Figure 3.7 OFD process node.

A process node may fire whenever an object is present in each of the input class nodes that collectively satisfy the conditions of the guard. When a process node fires, the objects selected by the guard to trigger the process node are removed from the input class nodes, except for input objects on reference edges. That is, one object is removed and input to the process node for each consumption edge, and one object input to the process node for each reference edge.

A process node is used to signify a major activity or processing step of the system. Each process node may have an associated *process behavior* that contains details of the dynamics of the process node. The process node behavior consists largely of the invocation of methods associated with the input and output classes. After the behavior is executed, an object is placed in each of the output class nodes.

OFD Construction

OFD components may be legally combined in the following manner. Each input class node is connected by a solid or dotted edge to one or more process nodes, i.e., there is a directed edge from a class node to a process node. A process node may be connected by a solid edge to one or more output class nodes. These connections are illustrated in Figure 3.8(a). A class node may not be directly connected to another class node, i.e., a directed edge between two class nodes is not allowed. An output class node of one process node may be an input class node for a subsequent process node, as seen in Figure 3.8(b). Edges that directly connect process nodes are also not allowed.

A process or class node with no incoming edges must have at least one outgoing edge and vice versa, i.e., the OFD must be connected. A class node may be input to more than one process node, and a class node may be the output of multiple processes. These situations are illustrated in Figure 3.8(c) and (d), respectively. The interested reader can find the formal definition of an OFD and its construction in [59].

Textual Specification of Object Flow Diagrams

The OFM provides a textual specification language that supplements the graphical OFD representation, allowing the modeler to specify more details of a process node. The envisioned use of the dynamic modeling constructs (the OFDs and their corresponding textual specification) of the OFM is as follows:

1. The modeler constructs one or more OFDs corresponding to the processes of the application. These OFDs show the gross dynamics of classes and object flow.

2. The modeler refines each process node of the OFDs by specifying a corresponding textual process definition for each process node.

The textual language provides a complete specification of the dynamics, except for the method bodies. The OFD contains two embedded languages: the Process Guard Language (PGL) for defining the guard and the Process Flow Language (PFL) for defining the process behavior.

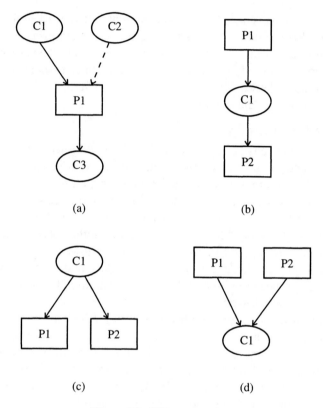

Figure 3.8 OFD construction.

Process Node Definition

The textual specification of an OFD consists of a nonempty set of process node definitions. A process node definition consists of: the process node name, the process node guard, written in the PGL, and the process node behavior, written in the PFL. For example, consider the following process node definition for the *GuestCharging* process node of the Resort Object model.

```
Process      GuestCharging

Guard        GuestService.ForRoom = Guest.IsOccupying

Behavior     CONS (GS : GuestService)
             REF (G : Guest)
             OUT( CH : ChargeItem)
             CH.ChargeItem := GS.TypeOfService
```

```
CH.ChargeDate := TodaysDate
CH.ChargeAmt := USER
G.HotelBill.Charges +Set(CH)
```

The process node name, in this example *GuestCharging*, is an identifier. The optional guard specifies selection criteria for objects from input sets, ordering criteria on those sets, and join conditions. In this example, the join condition in the guard states that a charge to a particular room (*Guest-Service.ForRoom*) and the room number for the guest (*Guest.IsOccupying*) must match. This ensures that when a charge for a service occurs, it is charged to the appropriate room.

The guard may be viewed as a database query to objects of input class nodes. That is, the guard selects objects from the input classes (the database) that satisfy the stated criteria (the query). The term *guard* is used to indicate that the predicate "guards" the process node by allowing only the proper objects to flow through and trigger the process node. The guard language is similar to a relational algebra with select and join operators, with the semantics extended to accommodate object-oriented navigation through relationships. Like a relational query language, the PGL is a set-level language. Its statements operate on set of objects, i.e., objects of the input class nodes, and can produce a set of objects as its result, i.e., the set of process-triggering objects. Stated another way, the answer to the "query" represented by the guard returns all combinations of objects that satisfy the guard. Each tuple in the answer represents a set of objects (one from each input class) that can trigger the process node.

The process node behavior specifies the manipulation of a single set of input objects (one for each input arc) to produce a single set of output objects. As the guard defines *which* set of objects will flow through the process node, the process node behavior describes *what changes* occur to these objects within the process node.

The process node behavior specification consists of a signature followed by zero or more object manipulation statements, expressed in the PFL. The signature is a list of parameters that are passed to the process node as input (consumption and reference) or produced by the process node as output. In the above example, there is one consumption parameter, *GS* of type *GuestService*, there is one reference parameter, *G* of type *Guest*, and one output parameter, *CH* of type *ChargeItem*. The signature specifies which objects are accessible to the process node during its execution. When a class appears in the signature, then the objects of that class (that satisfy the guard) and any methods associated with those objects are available to the process node. That is, the process node may invoke any of that object's methods to manipulate that object.

The Process Guard Language

The Process Guard Language (PGL) is provided to specify the selection and/or ordering of objects from the input class nodes. The guard is a conjunction of selection and/or join clauses. Each input class has at most one selection clause, and may appear in zero or more join clauses. A selection clause is used to select objects with certain property values, e.g., Customer.Name = 'Jones', or to impose an ordering on input objects, e.g., Order by RequestDate. A join clause specifies a join of two classes based on a certain property. The join may be *value-based*, e.g., Customer.SSN = Request.CustSSN, or *connection-based*, e.g., *HasReservation* between the two classes *Customer* and *Reservation*.

Each selection or join clause may reference property names of input class nodes. A property name may be *qualified*, e.g., *Customer.Address*, or when there is no ambiguity, *unqualified*, e.g., *Address*. When the value class of a property is an abstract or event object, it may be referenced using dot notation, e.g., *Customer.Address.City*. Thus, explicitly or implicitly, there is a reference to a class, say C, to which the clause will be applied. The objects that are presented, i.e., *instantiated* [5], to the process node are the instances of C which satisfy the clause(s) that refer to C.

A single selection clause may be a Boolean combination of selections, which may involve single-valued or multivalued properties. For example,

```
(Customer.Name = 'Jones') AND (Customer.Age < 35 OR

NOT(Customer.MStatus = 'Married'))
```

selects the objects from *Customer* whose *Name* property is "Jones" and who are younger than 35 or not married. Each of the three predicates involves single-valued properties. The selection clause

```
Room.Availability AT LEAST(1)

(RoomAV.StartDate _ Request.StartDate AND

RoomAV.EndDate _ Request.EndDate)
```

is a selection on the multivalued property *Availability of Room*. This clause ensures that a room has an availability within the requested dates before that room is reserved.

A join clause returns tuples of objects from two or more input classes that are related by specified property values (value-based) or by properties (connection-based). For example, the join clause

```
Hotel.HType = Request.ReqHotel
```

returns *Hotel, Request* pairs that match on the value of *HType*. The value class of *HType* and *ReqHotel* are both *HotelType*. This value-based join is similar to a relational join, except that tuples of objects instead of concatenated tuples are returned.

A connection-based join expresses the situation that arises when an object has a property whose value class is an abstract or event class. The property represents a connection, or link, between an object and one or more objects of the value class, e.g., the property *ForHotel* between the classes *Reservation* and *Hotel*. This type of join returns tuples of objects that are connected via this property. A connection-based join is specified by placing the property name within brackets, e.g., [ForHotel]. The clause [ForHotel] returns *Reservation, Hotel* pairs, say (R,H), where the value of *ForHotel* for R is H.

In addition to select and join clauses, a guard may contain ordering expressions that impose a linear ordering on input flows. There may be an ordering specified for:

1. a selected set of objects (those that result from a class's selection clause)

2. all the objects in a class (no selection clause is present for that class)

3. a set of ordered tuples of objects (the result of a join clause).

Only the final output from the guard, viewed as a query, can be ordered. Thus, options 1 and 2 for ordering are appropriate only when there is no join clause. The ordering may be expressed according to a class property, e.g., *Order by DateOfPlacement*, or according to a user-defined method, e.g., *Order by SelectPromisingEmployee*.

In addition to ordering specification, a class name may be given an *alias*, or alternative identifier, to be used in a selection, join, and/or ordering clauses. The alias may be used for abbreviation purposes, or may be used when a class is to be joined with itself. For example, the following guard specifies a join of Customer with itself to produce a pair of customers located in the same city.

```
Guard

Alias  Customer C1, Customer C2

((C1.Addr.City = C2.Addr.City) AND

   (C1.SSN <> C2.SSN))
```

The PGL essentially provides for select-join queries, expressible in both relational and object-oriented terms. The relational operator *project*, which returns a subset of an entity's properties, is not supported by the OFM as the intent of the language is to model the flow of entire objects, not projected "pieces" of those objects.

With respect to object-oriented query languages, the PGL has adopted some common features of a query language, e.g., multivalued selection and connection-based join. In general, the PGL guard can be expressed in a relational, object-relational [50], or object-oriented [4] query language because it corresponds to simple select-join queries. We believe that additional object-oriented query capabilities may be included in the PGL, but we currently focus on the manipulation of individual objects.

Effect of Consumption Semantics on the Guard

The set of query answers for the guard (where each answer consists of a set of objects which can trigger the process node) varies, depending on the type of input flow, i.e., reference or consumption. This variation is due to the difference between object reference (normal query) and object consumption (extended Petri net) semantics.

To illustrate the effect of consumption on guard results, consider the object model excerpt, class extensions, and OFD shown in Figure 3.9. The notation Sur. represents the surrogate, or internal identifier, of an object.

The guard of the process node *ScheduleWorkstation* establishes a condition that must be met by an *AvailableEmployee* and an *AvailableMachine*, i.e., that they are connected by the *CanWorkOn* property. As both input edges are consumption edges, after an employee and machine are scheduled, they are removed from the AvailableEmployee and AvailableMachine sets so that they will not be considered for scheduling thereafter. Thus, one set of pairs of objects that would trigger the process node is (E1, M1), (E2, M3), and (E3, M2). Other sets of pairs of objects could also trigger the process node, depending on the ordering criteria specified for the input. If both of the input edges were reference edges, however, the set of pairs of

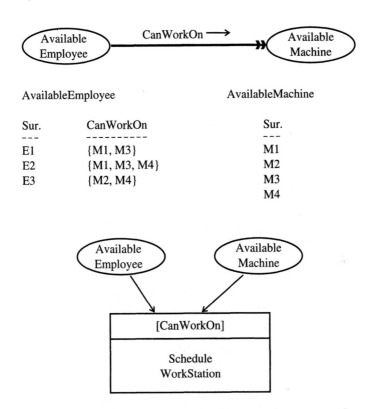

AvailableEmployee   AvailableMachine

Sur.	CanWorkOn	Sur.
E1	{M1, M3}	M1
E2	{M1, M3, M4}	M2
E3	{M2, M4}	M3
		M4

Figure 3.9 Employee/machine example.

triggering objects would be the same as an equi-join, i.e., (E1, M1), (E1, M3), (E2, M1), (E2, M3), (E2, M4), (E3, M2), (E3, M4). Consumption arcs (i.e., Datalog with negation) result in nondeterministic rule programs where there can be more than one final answer for a query.

The Process Flow Language

The Process Flow Language (PFL) is an embedded specification language expressing the transformation of objects as they participate in a process node. A behavioral specification expressed in the PFL describes the changes that occur to one set of objects that trigger the process node. The goals of the PFL are:

1. to provide a conceptually natural, high-level language for the modeling of process dynamics

2. to utilize object-oriented concepts, i.e., message-passing and methods, within the language

3. to model the progress of input objects as they participate in a process, and to model how the output objects are produced, i.e., object
transformation and manipulation.

The PFL is not intended to be a computationally complete programming
language, and does not address programming language issues in general.
The complete specification of methods (beyond the signature) is outside the
scope of the OFM, and is assumed to be done in an object-oriented language.
ODMG has defined both a C++ binding as well as a Smalltalk binding
which provides concrete syntax for defining method bodies, among other
things [4]. The main purpose of the PFL is to describe object transformation
and manipulation by a process. Thus, the constructs of the PFL concentrate
on the access to input objects and creation of output objects that occur in
the execution of a process.

PFL Syntax.   The basic PFL construct is the *message* which can
be sent to objects defined in the object model. This causes a corresponding
method to be applied to the object. A message is of the form

<ReceiverObject> <Message> (<Arguments>)

where <ReceiverObject> identifies the object to which the message is sent,
<Message> is the name of the method or a symbol representing a method,
and <Arguments> is the list of arguments passed to the corresponding
method. If there are no arguments, the set of parentheses is omitted. The
receiver object must be an instance of the class to which the method is
associated. For some methods, the receiver object is a class (an instance
of a metaclass); for others, it is a member of the extension of a class. A
method returns a result to which another method may be applied. As in the
majority of object-oriented systems, method application in PFL is from left
to right. For example, the following PFL expression

Customer **NEW** ObtainMailingInfo

means to apply the method **NEW** to create a new instance of the class
Customer and to apply the method *ObtainMailingInfo* to that new instance.

PFL Statements.   The behavior specification of a process node
definition consists of zero or more PFL expressions/statements. As an example, again consider the *GuestCharging* process node definition of the
Resort Reservation system. The PFL statements are labeled (a)–(d).

```
Process     GuestCharging

Guard       GuestService.ForRoom = Guest.IsOccupying
```

```
Behavior      CONS(GS:GuestService)
              REF(G:Guest)
              OUT(CH:ChargeItem)

              (a) CH.ChargeType := GS.TypeOfService
              (b) CH.ChargeDate := TodaysDate
              (c) CH.ChargeAmt  := USER
              (d) G.HotelBill.Charges +Set(CH)
```

The statements (a), (b), and (c) specify the assignment of values to the properties of the output object, CH. In (d), the object bound to CH is to be added to the set of *Charges* associated with the guest who incurred the charge.

The modeler may express process node behavior, i.e., object transformation, using one or more of the following:

1. object-returning expressions

2. set-returning expressions

3. class-returning expressions

4. assignment statements

5. For statements.

Any object-returning expression and any set-returning expression may include messages (i.e., method calls) as long as they deliver objects of the appropriate type. Note that the PFL (like the OFM ODL) was defined independently [59] of the ODMG model and other object-oriented database languages. The PFL could be modified to use OQL of the ODMG model or other object-oriented database languages. Each of the five PFL expression types is described below.

1. Object-returning expressions are expressions that return a single object. An object-returning expression is usually embedded within a method or PFL statement, and is used to represent some object within the process node. An object-returning expression may be one of the following:

- *An object variable.* This is an identifier that represents a single object, e.g., Person1.

- *A single-valued property variable.* This is an identifier that represents a single-valued property of an object, e.g., Person1.Name. Property variables are formed by concatenating an object variable with a dot followed by a property name.

- *A create method*. This method specifies the creation of a new object of a class, e.g., Customer **NEW**.

- *A literal, arithmetic, or aggregate expression*. These are expressions involving literals, variables, arithmetic operators, and/or aggregate operators, e.g., 'Sally', (X + 15.00) * Y.HourlyWage, **AVG**(Emp.MonthlySalary). A single object of a simple class is returned by each of these expressions.

- *A message that invokes a method* that returns a single object.

2. Set-returning expressions represent a set of objects. Some of these expressions may be used independently as a single statement, and some may be embedded within other PFL statements. A set-returning expression may be one of the following:

- *A multivalued property variable*. This is a property variable that represents the set of objects that comprise the range value of a multivalued property. For example, Person1.Friends would be a multivalued property variable representing the set of objects associated with the property *Friends* for the object bound to the object variable Person1.

- *Methods to add (remove) objects from sets*. These methods specify the addition (removal) of an object from the range value of a multivalued property. For example,

        Person1.Friends +**Set** (P2) (Person1.Friends −**Set** (P2)).

Specify that the object P2 is to be added (removed) from the set *Person1.Friends*.

- *Set of object-returning expressions*. This is a set of object-returning expressions explicitly listed by the modeler, e.g., (P1.Salary, M1.HourlyRate, 30.2). This set may be assigned to a multivalued property variable or may specify objects to be added or removed from a set.

- *A message that invokes a method* that returns a set of objects.

3. Class-returning expressions may be one of the following:

- Guest +**Class** (P1)
- Guest −**Class** (P1).

These methods specify that the object P1 is to be added (removed) from the class *Guest*. It is also possible for a message to invoke a method that returns a class.

4. The assignment statement is similar to the assignment statement found in most programming languages, and has the syntax

<Identifier> := <Expression>.

This means that the expression on the right-hand side is to be evaluated, and this value bound to the identifier on the left-hand side.

The PFL assignment statement may be used for two purposes: 1) to assign a value to an object's properties, or 2) to assign a specified object to an identifier. The left-hand side may be a property or object variable. When the right-hand side expression is evaluated, the type of the result must be compatible with the type of the property or object variable given on the left-hand side of the statement.

When the assignment statement is used for property value assignment, one or more property variables may be specified, along with the range value expression to be assigned. The right-hand side expression may consist of any compatible expression or the predefined term *User*.

For example, consider the class *Request*, with properties *ReqNo*, *Req-From*, and *Wait*, and R1, an object variable of type *Request*. Then the properties of R1 may be updated by the following PFL statements:

```
R1.ReqNo := 308
R1.ReqFrom := Person1
R1.Wait := User.
```

The first statement assigns the integer value 308 to the property *ReqNo* (Request Number) of R1. The second statement is an example of assigning another object variable as the value of a property, i.e., the current request is from person *Person1*. The expression of the last assignment statement is *User*, meaning that this value will be supplied by the user. This allows the designer to model the situation in which a value is to be supplied by means outside of the stored database. The left-hand side of the assignment may also be a multivalued property variable, e.g., Stu1.TestScores := (90,86,79).

When more than one property is to be assigned the same value, they may be grouped together in a shorthand notation. In the following example, each of the three properties *ReqNo*, *ReqFrom*, and *Wait* of object R2 will be supplied its value from the user:

(R2.ReqNo, R2.ReqFrom, R2.Wait) := User.

5. The For statement allows the modeler to specify iteration over a set of objects. This set of objects, called a *multivalued selection set*, consists of objects of the range value of a multivalued property that satisfy selection criteria of the guard.

For example, the object model of Figure 3.10 shows the class *Person* with the multivalued property *HasPets*, whose image is a set of *Pet* objects.

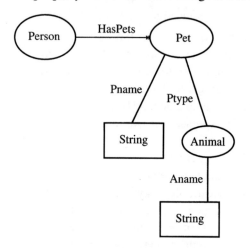

Figure 3.10 Person/Pet object model.

Consider the OFD segment for this object model (Figure 3.11):

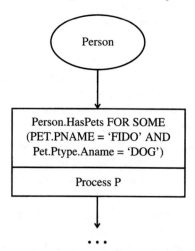

Figure 3.11 Person/Pet OFD.

The guard of the process node returns the set of *Person* objects that satisfy this condition, namely, that the person has at least one dog named Fido. In many applications, however, it is useful for the modeler to access those objects of *HasPets* that satisfy the portion of the guard dealing with that property. That is, in addition to having access to each *Person* object that satisfies the guard, the For construct provides access to those *Pet* objects that are dogs named Fido for each *Person* object that flows through the process node. This set of pets, denoted by !P.HasPets!, is the set of objects of *HasPets* for the person P that satisfies the guard condition.

The For statement allows one or more PFL statements/methods to be performed on one or more objects of the multivalued selection set. For example,

```
For X = ALL of !P.HasPets! do
        (X.PName := 'Murphy')
```

would change the range value of *PName* for each object of !P.HasPets! from 'Fido' to 'Murphy'. The modeler may specify all, one, or any number of objects from the multivalued selection set as part of the For statement.

3.4.   OBJECT FLOW MODEL FOR SIMULATION

As an example of using the OFM for discrete simulation, consider a "workstations in series" problem, which is stated in [65]:

> A facility performs two operations on units that need maintenance. The operations must be performed in series, i.e., operation 1 followed by operation 2. The facility only has space for four units prior to operation 1, and space for two units prior to operation 2. A unit not gaining access to the in-house facility is sent to a subcontractor. If the queue to workstation 2 (that performs operation 2) is full, the first operation is blocked and a unit cannot leave that station. A blocked station cannot serve other units.

This example is also presented in [62].

As shown in Figure 3.12, the classes *Unit* and *Workstation* are subclasses of *Class*, and thus inherit the standard properties, *Count*, *Max*, and *Initial_No*. The subclasses of the class *Unit* are *Zero_Ops_Completed*, *One_Op_Completed*, *Maintained_Unit*, and *Sub_Contract_Unit*, which define specializations, or different states, of *Unit*. Each class has an associated *extension*, i.e., all objects that are instances of that class; thus, every class is essentially a queue. Technically, the class extension is a set. But the ordering criterion of a process node guard allows the input class to function as a (sorted) list or (sorted) queue. Note that Figure 3.12 is one possible object model for this problem. A simpler model, with no specialized subclasses of *Unit*, could suffice. Alternatively, a more detailed object model could be constructed. For example, properties such as *Efficiency*, *SerialNo*, etc., could be added to *Workstation*, providing more structural detail about the workstations.

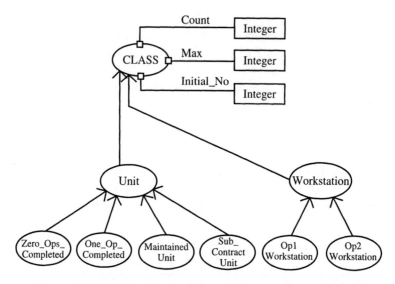

Figure 3.12 OFM object model for the workstation in series problem.

The OFD, shown in Figure 3.13, begins its execution when an object is placed in the class *Unit*. One of the two process nodes, *Send Unit to Subcontractor* or *Enter Unit in Line*, will fire. The guard of *Enter Unit in Line* states that there must be fewer than four units already residing in *Zero_Ops_Completed*. If *Zero_Ops_Completed* contains four objects, then the units are sent to the subcontractor, and the triggering *Unit* object becomes a *Sub_Contract Unit* object. *Operation 1* requires both a *Zero_Ops_Completed* object and an *Op 1 Workstation* in order to fire, and requires t_1 time units. In addition, the class *One_Op_Completed* must have space to receive the unit after *Operation 1* is complete; thus, the guard for *Operation 1* specifies that the count (current number in the extension) for *One_Op_Completed* is less than two.

The consumption of an *Op 1 Workstation* object by the *Operation 1* process node and its subsequent replacement by the completion of *Operation 1* illustrates the modeling of a server class of objects. That is, consumption of an object by *Operation 1* removes one object from the class *Op 1 Workstation*, thus reducing the available pool of these workstations by one. The insertion of an object as output from *Operation 1* increases the number of available *Op 1 Workstations* by one. The cycle to and from the class *Op 2 Workstations* also represents consumption and replacement in a server class.

The rest of the OFD illustrates the continued maintenance of a unit in *Operation 2*, as an object residing in *One_Op_Completed* becomes a

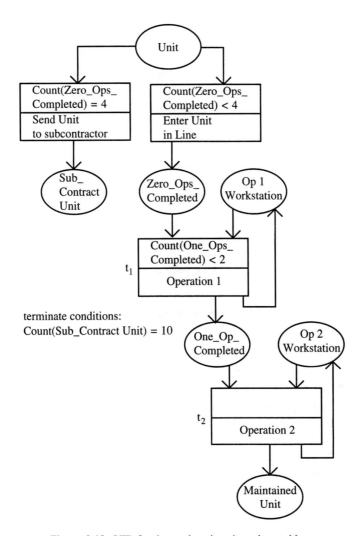

Figure 3.13 OFD for the workstations in series problem.

Maintained Unit. Operation 2 requires time t_2. The modeler may use any convenient notation for the expression of time delays associated with process nodes. The subclasses of *Unit* essentially represent the states of the unit during the entire maintenance.

The SLAM network model for the workstations in series problem is shown in Figure 3.14. It demonstrates that the OFM can describe a simulation model. Some of the differences between the two are the explicit class nodes and guards of the OFD in Figure 3.13.

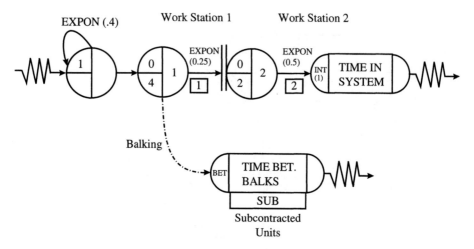

Figure 3.14 SLAM model for the workstations in series problem.

3.5.   RELATIONSHIP OF THE OFM TO OTHER WORK

When compared to other discrete-event simulation modeling languages, the OFM is most closely related to what Ceric terms "simulation strategy neutral" methods. Thus, the OFM provides a strategy-neutral, abstract modeling language/method, and closely resembles augmented Petri nets and simulation nets. In particular, the OFD component of the OFM has been formalized as a Predicate Transition Net, which extends Petri nets by modeling individuals and their changing properties and relationships. A transition may contain a logical formula, or predicate, which must be satisfied by the individuals of the input places in order for the transition to fire.

With respect to conceptual modeling languages designed for database applications, the OFM provides constructs that address all three levels of modeling: the action level, the transaction level, and the flow level. Action-level specification with the OFM is given with the specification of the object model, and is similar to Gambit in this respect. The OFM models the actions of an object by specifying the local methods associated with the object class. The OFM provides for transaction-level modeling by specifying the complete details of the process node associated with that transaction. The OFM was developed to address the flow level of specification. An OFD explicitly models the interaction and state change of multiple objects that may invoke a process node.

When compared with various object-oriented models for analysis and design [35], the OFM, through the OFD, has a rather singular focus on process node invocation (based on the availability of input objects that satisfy the guard). We believe that the OFM is complementary to other object-oriented models. Some techniques encourage good software engineering [10], [37] and promote object-oriented thinking [7], [80]. Some models focus on modeling information systems [19], [20], [47]. Both Rumbaugh [70] and Jacobson [37] provide an interaction diagram to graphically model various objects and their pattern of communication. But their models have informal semantics, and serve (only) to guide the object-oriented code construction rather than formally specify how process node invocation will take place. Finally, the state diagrams of Shlaer and Mellor [73] resemble the OFM process model, but they describe only one object at a time. This makes it difficult to describe a transition enabled by the presence of two or more objects. We feel that the OFM provides process invocation semantics beyond a single method call, and that it is useful in many applications, and especially for simulation modeling.

3.6.   CONCLUSIONS AND FUTURE WORK

This chapter described the OFM as an object-oriented framework for the conceptual modeling of database applications and discrete-event simulation. The OFM provides a conceptually natural notation for the expression of simulation models, and provides rich modeling constructs for describing structural features. These modeling constructs include abstractions for classification, generalization (ISA), and properties, as defined for object-oriented databases. Strengths of the OFD include the use of a guard language (to express constraints on the objects that can fire a process node) with formal semantics that directly allows the specification of access and manipulation of objects from multiple input classes by a single process node. The OFM can be viewed as integrating technology from the two areas of object-oriented database systems and discrete-event simulation.

To conceptual modeling of discrete-event simulation, the OFM contributes a richer and more diverse set of features for structural modeling than is generally found in other languages and methods. Another contribution is the intuitive constructs for modeling process node invocation through the OFD, fully integrated with the object model of the OFM.

The OFM has been formally defined in [59] as a conceptual modeling language for database applications [60]. The influence of discrete-event simulation languages is quite apparent in the structure and semantics of Object Flow Diagrams. The OFM also served as the basis for implementing a simulator for an apparel manufacturing shop floor, a discrete manufacturing environment. The use of the OFM as a simulation model has been published, along with the experience gained from implementing the simulator [23]. One interesting aspect of the implementation is its reliance on a combination of the event list technique (commonly used in discrete-event simulation) with join processing techniques for materialized views (commonly used in database query processing).

Work in progress is focusing on several areas. The use of OFDs as a workflow language is underway with flexible modeling for resources and the flow of tasks. From a methodology point of view, the use of "dynamic abstraction" for the construction of OFDs is being developed to ease the use of the OFM and to explore the synergy between the structural model and the OFD definition. This includes the definition of "macros" for the OFD to describe the movement of objects from one class to another.

3.7.   APPENDIX: WORKED EXAMPLE—RESORT RESERVATION SYSTEM

3.7.1. Problem Statement

This example is a restatement of that in [54], and concerns a reservation system for hotel rooms in ski resorts.

An individual or travel agency may request a reservation. Each request is characterized by the name, address, and telephone number of the person who makes the request, the resort requested, the hotel category, the number of rooms, and the period that the person requests.

A request can be accepted if there is suitable space available in a hotel of the requested category, in the right resort, and for the right period. If these conditions are not satisfied, the request can be wait-listed if the person so desires, and processed by the system as soon as possible.

When a request has been accepted, the system is required to send an acknowledgment to the customer confirming the reservation, namely, the name, address, and telephone number of the hotel, the period of the reservation, the number of rooms reserved, and the price (tariff) per day.

The tariff for the room depends on the type of season, hotel, and room. The definition of each season is standardized for all hotels and all resorts.

The main aim of the system is to manage requests and reservations. It must also be possible to take into account any modification resulting from a cancellation. The system must also be able to manage the customers, that is to say, the persons who have an existing reservation or have had a reservation in the past. This includes the details of each person's stay in a hotel, the associated check-in, check-out, miscellaneous charges, and final invoice.

3.7.2. Structural Component: The Resort System Object Model

Graphical Object Model for the Resort System

The classes of the Resort System fall into four main categories: 1) Resort/Hotel Resources, 2) Requests and Confirmations, 3) Reservations and Billing, and 4) System Events, as shown in Figures 3.15 to 3.18. The graphical object model for each of these is as follows.

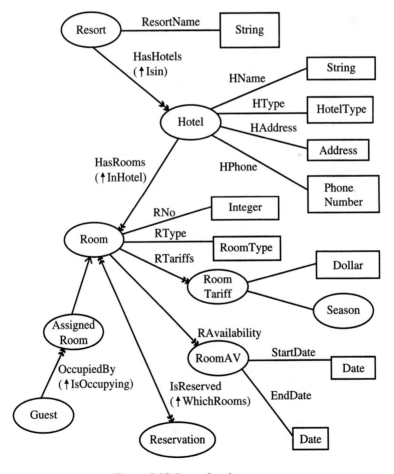

Figure 3.15 Resort/hotel resources.

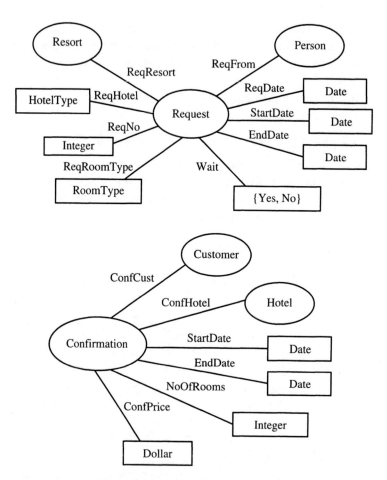

Figure 3.16 Requests and confirmation.

Object Definition Language Specification of the Resort Object Model

Object Schema ResortSystem
    SimpleClass Dollar   {All two-decimal real numbers}
    SimpleClass HotelType   {FiveStar, FourStar, ThreeStar, TwoStar}
    SimpleClass RoomType   {Single, Double, King, Suite, Honeymoon}
    SimpleClass SocSecNum   Integer (000000000..999999999)
    SimpleClass String50   {All strings of length 50 chars or less}
    SimpleClass String20   {All strings of length 20 chars or less}
    SimpleClass ChargeItemType   {Food, Drink, Gratuity, Laundry, Phone}

    AbstractClass Resort BaseClass
      Property ResortName Range String50   Cardinality {(1,1)}

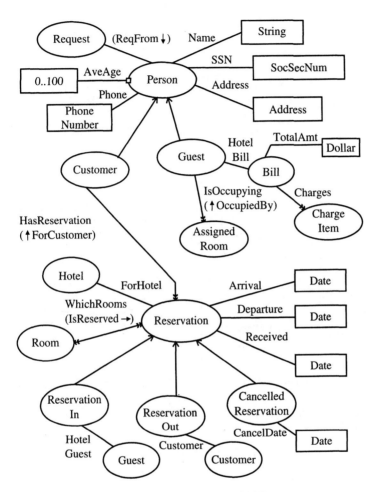

Figure 3.17 Reservations and billing.

Property HasHotels Range Hotel   Cardinality {(1,M)}
                                   Inverse IsIn

AbstractClass Hotel BaseClass
    Property HName Range String50   Cardinality {(1,1)}
    Property HType Range HotelType   Cardinality {(1,1)}
    Property HAddress Range Address   Cardinality {(1,1)}
    Property HPhone Range PhoneNumber   Cardinality {(1,1)}
    Property HasRooms Range Room   Cardinality {(1,M)}
                                          Inverse InHotel

    Property IsIn Range Resort   Cardinality {(1,1)}
                                          Inverse HasHotels

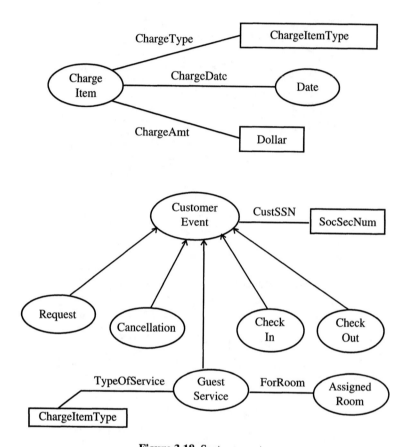

Figure 3.18 System events.

AbstractClass Room BaseClass
    Property Rno Range Integer   Cardinality {(1,1)}
    Property RType Range RoomType   Cardinality {(1,1)}
    Property RTariffs Range RoomTariff   Cardinality {(1,M)}
    Property RAvailability Range RoomAV Cardinality {(1,M)}
    Property IsReserved Range Reservation Cardinality {(1,M)}
                                     Inverse WhichRooms
    Property InHotel Range Hotel   Cardinality {(1,1)}
                                     Inverse HasRooms
    Method ReduceAvailability   (IN StartDate:Date, EndDate:Date)
    Method RestoreAvailability   (IN StartDate:Date, EndDate:Date)

AbstractClass RoomTariff BaseClass
    Property Price Range Dollar   Cardinality {(1,1)}
    Property ForSeason Range Season   Cardinality {(1,1)}

AbstractClass RoomAV BaseClass
   Property StartDate Range Date   Cardinality {(1,1)}
   Property EndDate Range Date   Cardinality {(1,1)}

AbstractClass AssignedRoom
   ConstrainedBy Room
   Property OccupiedBy Range Guest   Cardinality {(1,1)}
                                       Inverse IsOccupying

   Method UnassignRoom

AbstractClass Request BaseClass
   Property ReqResort Range Resort   Cardinality {(0,1)}
   Property ReqHotel Range HotelType   Cardinality {(0,1)}
   Property ReqNo Range Integer   Cardinality {(0,1)}
   Property ReqRoomType Range RoomType   Cardinality {(0,1)}
   Property ReqFrom Range Person   Cardinality {(1,1)}
   Property ReqDate Range Date   Cardinality {(1,1)}
   Property StartDate Range Date   Cardinality {(1,1)}
   Property EndDate Range Date   Cardinality {(1,1)}
   Property Wait Range {Yes,No}   Cardinality {(1,1)}

AbstractClass Confirmation BaseClass
   Property ConfCust Range Customer   Cardinality {(1,1)}
   Property ConfHotel Range Hotel   Cardinality {(1,1)}
   Property StartDate Range Date   Cardinality {(1,1)}
   Property EndDate Range Date   Cardinality {(1,1)}
   Property NoOfRooms Range Integer   Cardinality {(1,1)}
   Property ConfPrice Range Dollar   Cardinality {(1,1)}

AbstractClass Person BaseClass
   Property Name Range String50   Cardinality {(1,1)}
   Property SSN Range SocSecNum   Cardinality {(1,1)}
   Property Address Range Address   Cardinality {(1,1)}
   Property Phone Range PhoneNumber   Cardinality {(0,1)}
   ClassProperty AveAge Range Integer (0..100)   Cardinality {(0,1)}

AbstractClass Customer
   ConstrainedBy Person
   Property HasReservation Range Reservation   Cardinality {(1,M)}
                                         Inverse ForCustomer

AbstractClass Guest
   ConstrainedBy Person
   Property HotelBill Range Bill   Cardinality {(1,1)}
   Property IsOccupying Range AssignedRoom   Cardinality {(1,M)}
                                       Inverse OccupiedBy

AbstractClass Bill BaseClass
    Property Charges Range ChargeItem   Cardinality {(1,M)}
    Property TotalAmt Range Dollar   Cardinality {(0,1)}
    Method AddTaxes

AbstractClass Reservation BaseClass
    Property Arrival Range Date   Cardinality {(1,1)}
    Property Departure Range Date   Cardinality {(1,1)}
    Property Received Range Date   Cardinality {(1,1)}
    Property ForHotel Range Hotel   Cardinality {(1,1)}
    Property WhichRooms Range Room   Cardinality {(1,M)}
                                     Inverse IsReserved
    Property ForCustomer Range Customer   Cardinality {(1,1)}

AbstractClass ReservationIn
    ConstrainedBy Reservation
    Property HotelGuest Range Guest   Cardinality {(1,1)}

AbstractClass ReservationOut
    ConstrainedBy Reservation
    Property Cust Range Customer   Cardinality {(1,1)}

AbstractClass CancelledReservation
    ConstrainedBy Reservation
    Property CancelDate Range Date   Cardinality {(1,1)}

AbstractClass PhoneNumber BaseClass
    Property AreaCode Range Integer   Cardinality {(1,1)}
    Property Local Range Integer   Cardinality {(1,1)}

AbstractClass Address BaseClass
    Property Street Range String50   Cardinality {(1,1)}
    Property City Range String50   Cardinality {(1,1)}
    Property State Range String20   Cardinality {(1,1)}
    Property Zip Range String20   Cardinality {(1,1)}

AbstractClass Season BaseClass
    Property StartDate Range Date   Cardinality {(1,1)}
    Property EndDate Range Date   Cardinality {(1,1)}

AbstractClass ChargeItem BaseClass
    Property ChargeType Range ChargeItemType   Cardinality {(1,1)}
    Property ChargeDate Range Date   Cardinality {(1,1)}
    Property ChargeAmt Range Dollar   Cardinality {(1,1)}

AbstractClass Date BaseClass
    Property Month Range Integer (1..12)   Cardinality {(1,1)}

Property Day Range Integer (1..31)   Cardinality {(1,1)}
Property Year Range Integer (1950..2000)   Cardinality {(1,1)}

EventClass CustomerEvent BaseClass
  Property CustSSN Range SocSecNum   Cardinality {(1,1)}

EventClass RequestArrival
  ConstrainedBy CustomerEvent

EventClass Cancellation
  ConstrainedBy CustomerEvent

EventClass CheckIn
  ConstrainedBy CustomerEvent

EventClass CheckOut
  ConstrainedBy CustomerEvent

EventClass GuestService
  ConstrainedBy CustomerEvent
  Property TypeOfService Range ChargeItemType Cardinality {(1,1)}
  Property ForRoom Range AssignedRoom   Cardinality {(1,1)}

End ResortSystem.

3.7.3. Dynamic Component: The Resort System
Object Flow Diagrams

Textural Description of Dynamic Component

The dynamic behavior of the Resort System is composed of three main categories of processes and events: (1) Request Management, (2) Reservation Management, and (3) Guest Billing Management, as illustrated in Figures 3.19 to 3.21.

Request Management is responsible for handling a person's request that a reservation be made. When a request arrives, a reservation is generated and all necessary information is obtained from the user. If all of the conditions are satisfied, i.e., the desired resort, hotel type, and room type are available for the requested dates, then the request becomes a reservation. Otherwise, if the person so desires, the request remains pending until the conditions are favorable. Requests are prioritized according to the date they are received; thus, older, pending requests are given priority over incoming requests. If the person does not wish to keep the request pending, it is cancelled. After a reservation is made, a confirmation is created to be sent to the person who made the request. The confirmation contains information such as the hotel, arrival and departure dates, and the price per room.

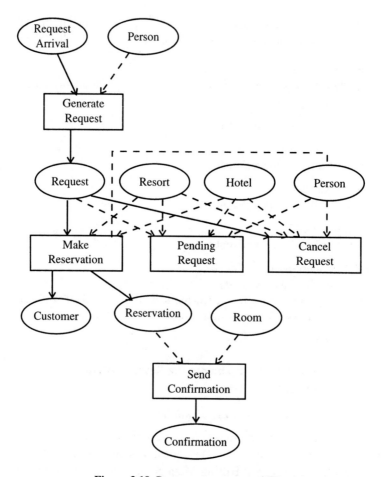

Figure 3.19 Request management OFD.

When a reservation is made, one or more rooms are reserved for the person who makes the request. To reserve a room, its availability is reduced, i.e., the database reflects the fact that the room is no longer available for the reserved dates. It is assumed that there are system constants, e.g., Todays-Date that returns the current date, and operators, e.g. $=$, $\leq$, etc., defined for dates.

Reservation Management handles a customer's reservation, the check-in process, the check-out process, and the cancellation of a reservation. When a customer arrives to check in, the customer becomes a guest, is assigned the one or more rooms that have been reserved for him/her, and the reservation becomes a reservation-in. When a guest checks out, that guest becomes a customer, the rooms are unassigned, and the reserva-

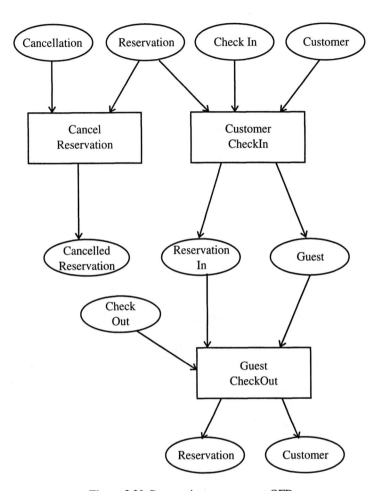

Figure 3.20 Reservation management OFD.

tion becomes a reservation-out. When a reservation is cancelled, the reservation becomes a cancelled-reservation. The availability of the rooms that have been reserved is restored to reflect that fact that these rooms are again available. The system maintains information on guests and customers and the details of their associated reservations.

Guest Billing Management is responsible for handling the charges incurred by guests during their stay in a hotel. The bill must be calculated and paid by the guest whenever he or she checks out. Charges include the room tariff, as specified by the guest's confirmation, as well as other items that are charged to the room. Each charge item is of a given type and is charged to the guest occupying the room on a given date.

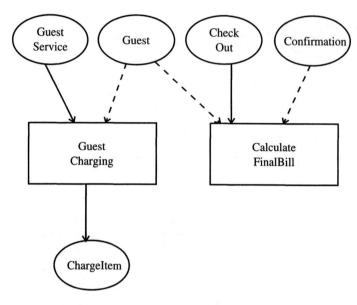

Figure 3.21 Guest billing management OFD.

The processes that have been identified for these three categories of dynamics are the following:

1. Request Management
   Request Creation
   Person Identification
   Request Acceptance
      Reservation Choices
      Room Availability Update
   Pending Request Management
   Request Cancellation
   Confirmation Creation

2. Reservation Management
   Reservation Cancellation
      Room Availability Update
   Customer Check-In
      Occupation Adjustment
   Customer Check-Out
      Room Availability Update

3. Guest Billing Management
   Guest Charging
   Guest Billing

Object Flow Diagram Specification of Resort System

The OFD specification of the Resort System consists of three main OFDs corresponding to Request Management, Reservation Management, and Guest Billing Management, respectively. The processes of these OFDs correspond to the processes identified above. The textual specification of the OFDs, i.e., the process definitions, are found in [59].

References

[1] S. Abiteboul and R. Hull, "IFO: A formal semantic database model," *ACM Trans. Database Syst.*, vol. 12, Dec. 1987, pp. 525–565.

[2] S. Abiteboul and E. Simon, "Fundamental properties of deterministic and nondeterministic extensions of datalog," *J. Theoretical Comput. Sci.*, 1990.

[3] T. L. Anderson, "Modeling events and processes at the conceptual level," in *Proc. 2nd Int. Conf. Databases*, S. M. Deen and P. Hammersley, Eds., Cambridge, Sept. 1983, pp. 151–168.

[4] T. Atwood et al., *The Object Database Standard: ODMG-94*. Los Altos, CA: Morgan Kaufmann, 1994.

[5] J. Banerjee, W. Kim, and K. Kim, "Queries in object-oriented databases," in *Proc. 1988 Int. Conf. Data Eng.*, pp. 31–38.

[6] C. Batini, S. Ceri, and S. Navathe, *Conceptual Database Design: An Entity-Relationship Approach*. New York: Benjamin Cummings, 1992.

[7] K. Beck and W. Cunningham, "A laboratory for teaching object-oriented thinking," in *Proc. Conf. Object-Oriented Programming Syst. Languages and Appl. (OOPSLA)*, 1989, pp. 1–6.

[8] P. Bergsten et al., "RAMATIC—A CASE shell for implementation of specific CASE tools," TEMPORA T6.1, SISU, Stockholm, Sweden, 1989.

[9] L. Bic and J. P. Gilbert, "Learning from AI: New trends in database technology," *IEEE Computer*, vol. 19, no. 3, 1986, pp. 44–54.

[10] G. Booch, *Object-Oriented Analysis and Design*, 2nd ed. Redwood City, CA: Benjamin Cummings, 1994.

[11] A. Borgida, "Features of languages for the development of information systems at the conceptual level," *IEEE Software*, Jan. 1985, pp. 63–72.

[12] A. Borgida, "Conceptual modeling of information systems," in *On Knowledge Base Management Systems*, M. L. Brodie and J. Mylopoulos, Eds. New York: Springer-Verlag, 1986, pp. 461–469.

[13] R. P. Braegger et al., "Gambit: An interaction database design tool for data structures, integrity constraints, and transactions," *IEEE Trans. Software Eng.*, vol. SE-11, July 1985, pp. 574–582.

[14] M. L. Brodie, J. Mylopoulos, and J. W. Schmidt, Eds., *On Conceptual Modeling: Perspectives from Artificial Intelligence, Databases, and Programming Languages*. New York: Springer-Verlag, 1984.

[15] M. L. Brodie and D. Ridjanovic, "On the design and specification of database transactions," in M. L. Brodie, J. Mylopoulos, and J. W. Schmidt, Eds., *On Conceptual Modeling: Perspectives from Artificial Intelligence, Databases, and Programming Languages*. New York: Springer-Verlag, 1984, pp. 277–306.

[16] J. Calhoun and E. Kortright, "VSIM: A graphics based model engineering tool," in *Proc. 6th Annu. Modeling and Simulation Conf.*, San Diego, CA, Jan. 1987.

[17] V. Ceric and R. J. Paul, "Diagrammatic representations of the conceptual simulation model for discrete event systems," *Math. and Comput. in Simulation*, vol. 34, 1992, pp. 317–324.

[18] P. Chen, "The entity-relationship model—Towards a unified view of data," *ACM Trans. Database Syst.*, vol. 1, Mar. 1976, pp. 9–36.

[19] P. Coad and E. Yourdon, *Object-Oriented Analysis*. 2nd ed. Englewood Cliffs, NJ: Prentice-Hall, 1992.

[20] P. Coad and E. Yourdon, *Object-Oriented Design*. Englewood Cliffs, NJ: Prentice-Hall, 1991.

[21] *IEEE Computer*, Special Issue on "Requirements Engineering," Apr. 1985.

[22] K. C. Davis, "A formal foundation for object-oriented, algebraic query processing," Ph.D. dissertation, Univ. Southwestern Louisiana, Lafayette, Apr. 1990.

[23] L. M. L. Delcambre, J. Narayanswamy, and L. F. Pollacia, "Simulation of the object flow model: A conceptual modeling language for object-oriented applications," in *Proc. 26th Annu. Simulation Symp.*, Washington, DC, Mar. 1993, pp. 216–225.

[24] T. De Marco, *Structured Analysis and System Specification*. New York: Yourdon Press, 1978.

[25] J. Eder, "BIER—The behavior integrated entity-relationship approach," in *Proc. 5th Int. Conf. Entity-Relationship Approach*, S. Spaccapietra, Ed. Amsterdam: North-Holland, 1986.

[26] *Proc. 12th Int. Conf. Entity-Relationship Approach*, Arlington, TX, Dec. 1993.

[27] J. B. Evans, *Structures of Discrete Event Simulation*. Chichester: Ellis Horwood, 1988.

[28] A. Finkelstein and J. Kramer, TARA: "Tool assisted requirements analysis," in P. Loucopoulos and R. Zicari, *Conceptual Modeling, Databases, and CASE*. New York: Wiley, 1992.

[29] H. J. Genrich and K. Lautenbach, "System modeling with high-level Petri nets," *Theoretical Comput. Sci.*, vol. 13, Jan. 1981, pp. 109–136.

[30] M. Gogolla et al., "Integrating the ER approach in an OO environment," in *Proc. 12th Int. Conf. Entity-Relationship Approach*, Arlington, TX, Dec. 1993.

[31] G. Hall and R. Gupta, "Modeling transition," in *Proc. 1991 Data Eng. Conf.*, Kobe, Japan, pp. 540–549.

[32] M. Hammer and D. McLeod, "Database description with SDM: A semantic database model," *ACM Trans. Database Syst.*, vol. 6, Sept. 1981, pp. 351–386.

[33] D. Harel, "On visual formalisms," *Commun. ACM*, vol. 31, May 1988, pp. 514–529.

[34] R. Hull and R. King, "Semantic database modeling: Survey, applications, and research issues," *ACM Computing Surveys*, vol. 19, Sept. 1987, pp. 201–260.

[35] A. T. F. Hutt, *Object Analysis and Design, Description of Methods*. New York: Wiley, 1994.

[36] M. A. Jackson, *System Development*. London: Prentice-Hall, 1983.

[37] I. Jacobson, M. Christenson, P. Jonsson, and G. Overgaard, *Object-Oriented Software Engineering, A Use Case-Driven Approach*, rev. 4th printing. New York: Addison-Wesley, 1994.

[38] G. Kappel and M. Schrefl, "Object/behavior diagrams," in *Proc. 1991 Data Eng. Conf.*, Kobe, Japan, pp. 530–539.

[39] R. King and D. McLeod, "A unified model and methodology for conceptual database design," in M. L. Brodie, J. Mylopoulos, and J. W. Schmidt, Eds., *On Conceptual Modeling: Perspectives from Artificial Intelligence, Databases, and Programming Languages*. New York: Springer-Verlag, 1984, pp. 313–327.

[40] Knowledgeware-Inc., IEW/The Information Engineering Workbench, 1985.

[41] D. C. Kung, "The behavior network model for conceptual information modeling," *Inform. Syst.*, vol. 18, no. 1, 1993, pp. 1–21.

[42] C. Lamb et al., "The ObjectStore database system," *Commun. ACM*, vol. 34, Oct. 1991, pp. 50–63.

[43] B. P. Lientz, "Issues in software maintenance," *ACM Computing Surveys*, vol. 15, Sept. 1983, pp. 271–278.

[44] P. Loucopoulos and R. Zicari, *Conceptual Modeling, Databases, and CASE*. New York: Wiley, 1992.

[45] P. Loucopoulos and B. Theodoulidis, "CASE—Methods and support tools: An introduction," in P. Loucopoulos and R. Zicari, *Conceptual Modeling, Databases, and CASE*. New York: Wiley, 1992, pp. 373–388.

[46] J. Martin and C. McClure, *Structured Techniques: The Basis for CASE*. Englewood Cliffs, NJ: Prentice-Hall, 1988.

[47] J. Martin and J. Odell, *Object-Oriented Analysis and Design*. Englewood Cliffs, NJ: Prentice-Hall, 1993.

[48] D. McLeod and J. M. Smith, "Abstraction in databases," in *Proc. ACM Workshop on Data Abstraction, Databases, and Conceptual Modeling, ACM SIGMOD Rec.*, Jan. 1981, pp. 19–25.

[49] I. G. McDonald, *Information Engineering. Information System Design Methodologies: Improving the Practice*. Amsterdam: Elsevier Science Publishers B.V., North-Holland, 1986.

[50] J. Melton, "Object technology and SQL: Adding objects to a relational language," *Bull. Tech. Committee on Data Eng.*, IEEE Computer Society, vol. 17, Dec. 1994.

[51] J. Mylopoulos, P. A. Bernstein, and H. K. T. Wong, "A language facility for designing database-intensive applications," *ACM Trans. Database Syst.*, vol. 5, June 1980, pp. 185–207.

[52] A. H. H. Ngu, "Transaction modeling," in *Proc. 5th Int. Conf. Data Eng.*, 1989, pp. 234–241.

[53] O. Deux et al., "The O_2 system," *Commun. ACM*, vol. 34, pp. 34–48, Oct. 1991.

[54] T. W. Olle et al., *Information Systems Methodologies*. Workingham, England: Addison-Wesley, 1988.

[55] C. M. Overstreet and R. E. Nance, "A specification language to assist in analysis of discrete event simulation models," *Commun. ACM*, vol. 28, no. 2, 1985, pp. 190–201.

[56] J. Peckham and F. Maryanski, "Semantic data models," *ACM Computing Surveys*, vol. 20, Sept. 1988, pp. 153–189.

[57] C. D. Pegden, "Introduction to SIMAN," in *Proc. 1986 Winter Simulation Conf.*, pp. 95–103.

[58] J. L. Peterson, *Petri Net Theory and the Modeling of Systems*. Englewood Cliffs, NJ: Prentice-Hall, 1986.

[59] L. F. Pollacia, "The object flow model: A conceptual modeling language for object-driven software," Ph.D. dissertation, Univ. Southwestern Louisiana, Lafayette, May 1991.

[60] L. F. Pollacia and L. M. L. Delcambre, "The object flow model: A formal framework for describing the dynamic construction, destruction and interaction of complex objects," in *Proc. 12th Int. Conf. Entity-Relationship Approach*, Arlington, TX, Dec. 1993, pp. 1–12.

[61] L. F. Pollacia and L. M. L. Delcambre, "The object flow model for discrete event simulation," *Int. J. Comput. Simulation* (Special Issue on Object-Oriented Simulation), G. W. Zobrist, ed., Norwood, NJ: Ablex Publ. Corp., 1995.

[62] L. F. Pollacia and L. M. L. Delcambre, "Object-oriented conceptual modeling of discrete event systems," in *Proc. Object-Oriented Simulation Conf. (OOS'94)*, Tempe, AZ, Jan. 1994.

[63] R. J. Pooley, "Towards a standard for hierarchical process oriented discrete event simulation diagrams," *Trans. Soc. for Comput. Simulation*, vol. 8, Mar. 1991, pp. 1–20.

[64] R. J. Pooley, "Part II: The suggested approach to flat models," *Trans. Soc. for Comput. Simulation*, vol. 8, Mar. 1991, pp. 21–31.

[65] A. A. B. Pritsker, *Introduction to Simulation and SLAM II*, 2nd ed. New York: Wiley, 1984.

[66] C. V. Ramamoorthy et al., "Software engineering problems and perspectives," *IEEE Computer*, vol. 17, Oct. 1984, pp. 191–209.

[67] P. Robertson, "A rule based expert simulation environment," in *Proc. SCS Conf. Intelligent Simulation Environments*, Jan. 1986, pp. 9–15.

[68] C. Rolland and C. Cauvet, "Trends and perspectives in conceptual modeling," in P. Loucopoulos and R. Zicari, *Conceptual Modeling, Databases, and CASE*. New York: Wiley, 1992.

[69] D. T. Ross and K. E. Schoman, "Structured analysis for requirements definition," *IEEE Trans. Software Eng.*, vol. SE-3, no. 1, 1977.

[70] J. Rumbaugh et al., *Object-Oriented Modeling and Design*. Englewood Cliffs, NJ: Prentice-Hall, 1991.

[71] G. Schiffner and H. Godvbersen, "Function nets: A comfortable tool for simulating database system architectures," *Simulation*, vol. 46, May 1986, pp. 201–210.

[72] J. J. Schriber, *Simulation Using GPSS*. New York: Wiley, 1974.

[73] S. Shlaer and S. Mellor, *Object Lifecycles: Modeling the World in States*. NJ: Yourdon Press, 1992.

[74] K. Smolander et al., "MetaEdit—A flexible graphical environment for methodology modeling," in *Proc. CAiSE 91 Conf.*, Trondheim, Norway, May 1991, pp. 168–193.

[75] K. L. Stanwood, L. N. Waller, and G. C Marr, "System iconic modeling facility," in *Proc. 1986 Winter Simulation Conf.*, pp. 531–536.

[76] H. A. Taha, "SIMNET simulation language," in *Proc. 1987 Winter Simulation Conf.*, pp. 222–229.

[77] A. A. Torn, "Simulation nets, A simulation modeling and validation tool," *Simulation*, vol. 45, Aug. 1985, pp. 71–75.

[78] *IEEE Trans. Software Eng.* (Special Issue on Requirements Specification), vol. SE-3, no. 1, 1977.

[79] *IEEE Trans. Software Eng.* (Special Section on Requirements Engineering), vol. 17, no. 3, 1991.

[80] R. Wirfs-Brock, B. Wilkerson, and L. Wiener, *Designing Object-Oriented Software*. Englewood Cliffs, NJ: Prentice-Hall, 1990.

Chapter 4

Reusable Simulation Models in an Object-Oriented Framework

Tag Gon Kim
Myung Soo Ahn

Department of Electrical Engineering
Korea Advanced Institutes of Science
and Technology
Taejon, Korea

Editor's Introduction ————————————————————

Let us shift gears and look into discrete-event simulation. This chapter describes a methodology for developing reusable simulation models in an object-oriented framework. It also provides models for microcomputer systems/communications networks to exemplify the technique.

Discrete-event simulation has, for a long time, employed the object-oriented framework in a model development life cycle. Such a framework offers a basis for developing reusable simulation models, thereby improving the productivity of model development and quality in modeling engineering.

The DEVS (Discrete-Event System Specification) formalism supports the specification of discrete-event models in hierarchical, modular form. Such hierarchical, modular specifications make it possible to develop reusable models which can be saved in an organized library called the model base.

Defining two model types, the DEVS formalism is known as being compatible with the object-oriented modeling/simulation environment which realized the DEVS formalism and associated hierarchical simulation algorithms in C++. Thus, DEVSim++ supports formalism and the object-oriented framework.

4.1. INTRODUCTION

Software reuse is the reapplication of a variety of knowledge about one system to other similar systems. From the technological viewpoint, composition and generation are the two major technologies that are important in achieving software reusability. We classify these technologies based on the nature of parts being reused [3]. The objective of software reuse is to reduce efforts in the development and maintenance of software systems, thereby improving the productivity and quality of the software development process. An excellent review in software reuse can be found in [15].

Modeling for computer simulation is the software development process in that models eventually are to be implemented as executable programs. In this sense, model specification is software specification and model verification/validation is software testing. As recognized in [8], simulation has for a long time employed concepts of software reusability in the model development life cycle. Uses of a discrete-event simulation language and a library of components in models construction are examples of generation-based reuse and composition-based reuse, respectively.

Hierarchical modeling provides a basis for reusability of simulation models [10]. It exploits composition-based reusability. In hierarchical modeling, lower level models are included in a higher level model as components. The higher level one may then be reused as a component of yet higher level models, and so on. Thus, the structure of such a hierarchical model is a tree. Although hierarchical modeling seems to be natural, none of the major discrete-event simulation languages provides the modeling capacity [17].

We employ Zeigler's DEVS (Discrete-Event Systems Specification) formalism for composition-based reusability of discrete-event simulation models. The DEVS formalism specifies discrete-event models in a hierarchical manner based on the "closure under coupling" concept [5]. The DEVS formalism specifies discrete-event models in two classes: atomic and coupled models. An atomic DEVS model is one that cannot be decomposed into components, while a coupled one can be decomposed into component models. An atomic DEVS model is specified in terms of timed state transition. A coupled DEVS model is specified in terms of component DEVSs and connections between components and the coupled one. Thus, the formalism provides a theoretical basis for composition-based reusability.

The discrete-event system's world view considers a system as a collection of entities and relationships between entities. Such a world view is recognized as being compatible with the object-oriented world view. In fact, the object-oriented programming paradigm was originated from the discrete-event simulation language SIMULA [7]. The object-oriented programming enhances software quality by supporting maintainability, extensibility, and reusability [6].

DEVSim++ is an object-oriented environment for discrete-event simulation, which implements the DEVS formalism in the object-oriented environment of C++ [19]. Thus, the environment supports the development of reusable simulation models using the DEVS formalism in C++. This chapter describes a framework for reusability in simulation models within the DEVSim++ environment. An object-oriented, hierarchical composition methodology, the framework achieves model reusability in two dimensions, one through inheritance in the object-oriented environment of C++, and the other through hierarchical composition by the DEVS formalism.

After a brief discussion of software reuse in general, Section 4.2 proposes a framework for simulation model reuse. Section 4.3 discusses the DEVS theory as a basis for the proposed framework, which includes the DEVS formalism, associated hierarchical simulation algorithms, and model base concepts. In Section 4.4, DEVSim++, a realization of the DEVS theory in C++, is described. Examples of the development of hierarchical reusable models within the framework are given in Section 4.5. Section 4.6 concludes our discussion of reusable simulation models.

4.2.   FRAMEWORK FOR SIMULATION MODEL REUSE

Viewing modeling as the software development process, this section discusses the reusability of simulation models in the software reuse perspective. The section first describes the general principle of software reuse technologies. It then proposes a framework for reusability technology in simulation modeling, called the object-oriented, hierarchical composition methodology.

4.2.1. Principle of Software Reusability Technologies

Software developers have been reusing software components in system development. Such reuse saves time and effort by requiring fewer lines of code and spending less time in the development of systems. It is widely believed that reusability plays a key role in improving the productivity and quality in software development.

Reusability can be considered from a variety of facets. Here, we address reusability from the technology viewpoint. In that viewpoint, there are two groups of technologies to be applied for software reusability, depending on the nature of components being reused [3]. One is composition technologies, and the other is generation technologies. Reuse of component libraries and reuse of application generators are typical examples of the composition technology and the generation technology, respectively.

Composition technologies reuse building blocks to construct complex programs by applying composition principles. Ideally, the reused blocks are to be unchanged in the course of their reuse. The blocks act as passive elements that can be activated only by an external agent. In that case, construction requires an interface between one program's output and another program's inputs.

Generation technologies reuse patterns of code or patterns with transformation rules. Application generators reuse patterns of code, and transformation systems reuse patterns with transformation rules. A system may employ both an application generator and transformation rules.

4.2.2. Reusability in Simulation Modeling

The principle of reusability for simulation models focuses more on composition technologies than generation technologies. We consider five kinds of reusability in model development that contribute to modeling productivity.

1. Functions may be reused in the development of models.
2. Data may be reused in the development of models.
3. Models may be reused in the construction of composite models, which in turn are reused as components of higher level composite models.
4. Models may be reused in the development of new models that are slightly different from old ones.
5. Models may be reused in a variety of applications.

The principle applied in reusability 1 above is function abstraction. It is widely used in the specification of transition functions of a discrete-event system, which represents the dynamics of the system in terms of a sequence of state transitions. By applying different arguments to the functions so defined, they may be reused in developing models with similar behaviors.

The principle applied in reusability 2 above is data abstraction. In data abstraction, data are reused by a family of admissible functions applied to them. In the modeling context, a set of state variables is an example of such data. The principle applied to reusability 3 is composition. A complex model can be constructed by the composition of less complex component models. Then, the complex model can be reused to construct more complex models, which in turn are reused as components, and so on. By using such a composition technique, a modeler can develop a simulation model in a hierarchical structure.

In reusability 4, we assume that reused models remain in the course of their reuse. Then, the principle applied to reusability 4 is inheritance as used in the object-oriented paradigm. Inheritance in the paradigm allows modelers to develop a new class of models based on an old class. Finally, reusability 5 is related to how frequently models are used in applications. Although reusability 5 concerns library technology, we will not discuss that aspect in this chapter.

4.2.3. Object-Oriented, Hierarchical Composition Framework

We base our reusability framework on the composition technologies of reusability 1–reusability 4 discussed in the previous subsection. We call our framework the object-oriented, hierarchical composition methodology. The framework exploits the reusability of simulation models by means of the hierarchical composition methodology in an object-oriented environment. To realize the framework, the DEVSim++ environment was developed by implementing the hierarchical, modular DEVS formalism and associated abstract simulators in C++. The environment will be described in the next section.

To clarify the concepts of hierarchical composition, we explain the difference between (nonhierarchical) composition and hierarchical composition in simulation modeling. Simulation models can be developed by reusing existing modules in a library. Composition techniques reuse such models as components in the development of more complex models. A simulation model so developed has the structure of a directed graph of component models.

In hierarchical composition, higher level models include low-level models as components. Such higher level models can be reused as components of yet higher level models. A simulation model developed by the hierarchical composition methodology is a tree structure. The DEVS formalism is a framework for such hierarchical specification of discrete-event models based on the principle of "closure under coupling" [5]. Figure 4.1 shows two composition technologies in simulation modeling.

Note that in a hierarchical model, lower level components within a higher level model are not visible outside the higher level model. Thus, direct access to a lower level component model from the outside world is not allowed. The access can be done through the higher level one. The

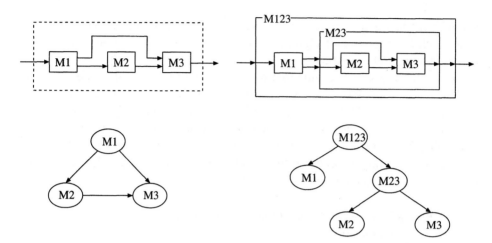

Figure 4.1 Nonhierarchical model (left) versus hierarchical model (right).

advantage of the methodology is that reusability of simulation models can be achieved at any level of hierarchy in a tree. For such hierarchical reuse, the DEVSim++ environment supports the concepts of model base in model development.

4.3.   DEVS THEORY IN HIERARCHICAL MODELING/SIMULATION

This section describes the DEVS theory in hierarchical modeling and simulation, which has been developed by Zeigler since the 1970s [21]–[23]. Included in the theory are the DEVS formalism, the hierarchical abstract simulators algorithm, and the model base concepts.

4.3.1. DEVS Formalism

A set-theoretic formalism, the DEVS formalism, specifies discrete-event models in a hierarchical, modular form. Within the formalism, one must specify: 1) the basic models from which larger ones are built, and 2) how these models are connected together in a hierarchical fashion. A basic model, called an *atomic model* (or *atomic DEVS*), has the specification for dynamics of the model. An atomic model M is specified by a 7-tuple [22]:

$$AM = < X, S, Y, \delta_{int}, \delta_{ext}, \lambda, ta >$$

X: input events set
S: sequential states set
Y: output events set

δ_{int}: $S \rightarrow S$: internal transition function
δ_{ext}: $Q \times X \rightarrow S$: external transition function
λ: $S \rightarrow Y$: output function
ta: $S \rightarrow Real$: time advance function
where $Q = \{(s, e) \mid s \in S, 0 \leq e \leq ta(s)\}$: total state of AM.

We call the four functions in the tuple, namely, internal transition function, external transition function, time advance function, and output function, the DEVS characteristic functions. Note that the formalism specifies a discrete-event system in the system-theoretic viewpoint. That is, the first three elements in the 7-tuple are system's input, system's state set, and system's output, respectively, and the next four elements give constraints among the three. Thus, when developing an atomic DEVS model, modelers can specify the characteristic functions independently. As we shall see later, such separated specification exploits the reusability of the characteristic functions through inheritance in our object-oriented simulation environment of DEVSim++.

The second form of the model, called a *coupled model* (or *coupled DEVS*), defines how to couple (connect) several component models together to form a new model. This latter model can itself be employed as a component in a larger coupled model, thus giving rise to construction of complex models in hierarchical fashion. A coupled model DN is defined as [22].

$$CM = < X, Y, M, EIC, EOC, IC, SELECT >$$

X: input events set
Y: output events set
M: DEVS components set
$EIC \subseteq CM.IN \times M.IN$: external input coupling relation
$EOC \subseteq M.OUT \times CM.OUT$: external output coupling relation
$IC \subseteq M.OUT \times M.IN$: internal coupling relation
$SELECT$: $2^M - \emptyset \rightarrow M$: tie-breaking selector
where the extensions .IN and .OUT represent the input ports set and output ports set of respective DEVS models.

The three coupling relations, namely, EIC, EOC, and IC, specify input/output connections between component models and the coupled model. The coupling scheme (CS) of a coupled model is defined as a collection of the three relations, (EIC, EOC, IC). The coupling scheme plays the main role in the hierarchical construction of DEVS models.

EIC is the relation of the input ports of the coupled model DN to those of the component models M. It indicates how the input ports of the composite model are connected to the input ports of the components. For example, a coupling relation (DN.in, M1.in) in EIC indicates that the input port "in" of the coupled model DN is connected to the input port "in" of the component model M1.

EOC is the relation of the output ports of the coupled model to those of the component models. It represents how the output ports of the composite model are connected to the output ports of the component models. Finally, IC is the relationship between the output ports of the components and the input ports of other components. It specifies how the components inside the coupled model are interconnected by indicating how the output ports of some components are connected to input ports of other components.

Detailed descriptions for the definitions of the atomic and coupled DEVS can be found in [22].

4.3.2. Abstract Simulators: Hierarchical Simulation Algorithms

The *abstract simulator* introduced in [22] is a conceptual device capable of interpreting the dynamics of DEVS models. Two classes of the abstract simulator have been defined: one for the *atomic DEVS*, and the other for the *coupled DEVS*. As will be seen in Section 4.4, within DEVSim++, a pair of a model and an abstract simulator is created, and the association of the two is made for simulation.

The job of an abstract simulator for an atomic model is to schedule the next event time and execute the model's transition functions and output function in a timely manner as simulation proceeds. The responsibilities of the abstract simulator for a *coupled DEVS* model are to *synchronize* the component abstract simulators for scheduling the next event time and to route external event messages to component simulators. The complete algorithms for both abstract simulators and the proof for the correctness of the algorithms can be found in [5]. The architectures and performance of distributed simulation systems, derived from the abstract simulator concept, have been intensively studied in [2], and some were implemented by multiprocessor computer systems [4], [20], [18].

4.3.3. Model Base Concepts

An atomic DEVS model in a modular form is like a circuit component, and a coupled DEVS model in hierarchical, modular form is like a circuit board in reusability. A model base, which exploits the principle of closure under coupling in DEVS theory, is an organized library of such reusable models. Models in a model base can be either atomic or coupled ones. New models can be saved in, and saved models can be retrieved from, the model base. Models so retrieved may be reused to construct a hierarchical model which can be reused as a component model in the construction of yet more complex, hierarchical models. Again, the complex, hierarchical model is saved in the model base, and can be reused later, and so on.

Figure 4.2 shows the fundamental concepts of model base. Assume that three atomic models, BUFF(buffer), MRCV(message processor), and MGEN(message generator), are developed and saved in the model base of Figure 4.2(a). If these model descriptions are in a proper modular form, we can create a new model PROC (processing element) by assembling

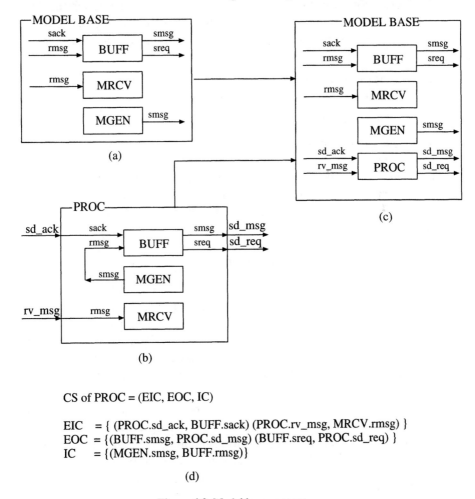

CS of PROC = (EIC, EOC, IC)

EIC = { (PROC.sd_ack, BUFF.sack) (PROC.rv_msg, MRCV.rmsg) }
EOC = {(BUFF.smsg, PROC.sd_msg) (BUFF.sreq, PROC.sd_req) }
IC   = {(MGEN.smsg, BUFF.rmsg)}

(d)

Figure 4.2 Model base concept.

BUFF, MRCV, and MGEN by means of an operation called coupling. The resulting model PROC, shown in Figure 4.2(b), is a coupled model, which is once again in modular form. As can be seen, the term modularity, as used here, means the description of a model in such a way that it has recognized input and output ports through which all interaction with the external world is mediated.

Note that in the coupled model, PROC, BUFF, and MGEN do not know how they are coupled; only PROC knows the coupling information of its components. Representing coupling information in such a way allows modelers to construct a complex model in a hierarchical manner. Once placed in the model base in Figure 4.2(c), PROC can itself be employed to construct yet larger models in the same manner used with its component models. Note that the coupling scheme CS of PROC is specified in three coupling relations, namely, EIC, EOC, and IC, defined in the DEVS formalism.

4.4. DEVSim++: OBJECT-ORIENTED, HIERARCHICAL COMPOSITION FRAMEWORK

The DEVSim++ environment allows modelers to develop discrete-event models using the hierarchical composition methodology in an object-oriented framework. The environment is a result of the combination of two powerful frameworks for systems development: the DEVS formalism and the object-oriented paradigm. This section describes the DEVSim++ environment.

4.4.1. Implementation Strategy

Given the DEVS formalism and associated abstract simulators, there may be different ways to develop an object-oriented environment to support simulation modeling within the DEVS formalism. Our question is: Which one is the best to support our object-oriented, hierarchical composition methodology for model reusability? To answer the question, we refer to the ideal case for software parts reuse through composition technologies in software development.

In the ideal case, components should be passive ones which are operated on by an external agent. As explained in the previous subsection, the simulation sequence of DEVS models is controlled by abstract simulators associated with models. Models have no executing thread of simulation control that determines the order for models to be executed. In the control scheme shown in Figure 4.3, a DEVS model is activated only when the associated simulator requests it to do so. Simulation proceeds by means of the message passing among abstract simulators, not among DEVS models.

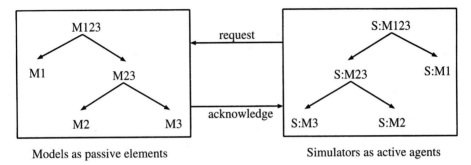

Figure 4.3 Passive models and active simulators.

Thus, we identify DEVS models as passive components, and associated abstract simulators as external active agents. If so separated, a model and the associated simulator should be able to exchange information for simulation. Of course, while the specification of a model is a modeler's responsibility, the creation of an associated simulator and its pairing must be managed by the simulation environment implicitly. Moreover, the environment should be such that a modeler develops subclasses of models based on existing classes without defining new abstract simulator classes to be associated with the model subclasses. The development of new model classes in such a way allows modelers to evolve the simulation environment by developing hierarchical classes within it [12].

4.4.2. Overview of DEVSim++

Following the strategy discussed earlier, some implementations are already in place [9], [22], [23], [13]. One such implementation, DEVSim++, defines classes for modeling and those for simulation separately, as shown in Figure 4.4. For modeling, DEVSim++ provides modelers with classes, the definitions of which are based on the DEVS semantics. Classes for simulation are transparent to modelers, which realize abstract simulators instrumented with hierarchical scheduling algorithms.

The development of an atomic model or a coupled model in DEVSim++ is to specify instance variables of the *Atomic_models* class or

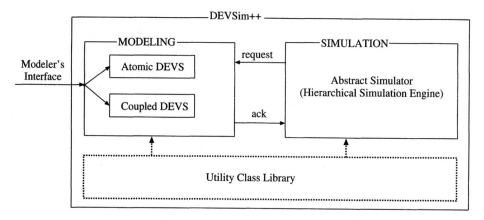

Figure 4.4 DEVSim++ architecture overview.

the *Coupled_models* class defined in DEVSim++, respectively. Instance variables of *Atomic_models* include input/output ports, state variables, and four characteristic functions. Those for *Coupled_models* include input/output ports, component models, coupling relations, and the select function.

DEVSim++ reuses a set of classes in the NIH class library (NIHCL) [14] with some modification. The classes include the NIH root class, the container class, and some basic data type classes such as integer, float, and string. Figure 4.5 shows the class hierarchy in DEVSim++.

The class *Object*, the root class of NIHCL, supports general facilities for operations and queries on objects, including class name, class description, class comparison, and others. An element of any container class in DEVSim++ is assumed to be an instance of a subclass of the root class. The container classes are for manipulating a collection of entities, which includes the *Collection* class and its subclasses.

The class *State_vars* manages the state variables and associated values. Two general functions are visible to the modelers. One is to refer to the values, and the other is to modify them. The class *Messages* is defined to provide a means of transmission of events between models. It supports a facility to direct an event to the specified output port. See Section 4.5 for the usage of the *State_vars* and *Messages* classes.

The class *Entities* is the universal class for models and associated simulators in DEVSim++. The inheritance mechanism in C++ ensures that general facilities shared for all classes need only be defined in the two classes once and for all. *Entities* defines the name of an entity, and provides such methods as naming objects and referencing the name. The class

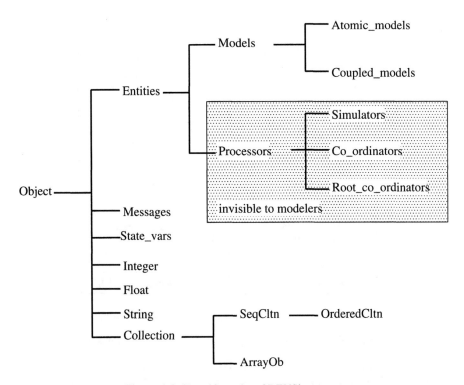

Figure 4.5 Class hierarchy of DEVSim++.

Models, one of the main subclasses of DEVSim++, provides the basic constructs needed for modeling. The class is further specialized into the major classes *Atomic_models* and *Coupled_models* that realize atomic DEVS and coupled DEVS, respectively. The class *Models* defines instance variables and member functions for specifying the input and output ports of all classes of models.

The class *Atomic_models* realizes the atomic level of the DEVS formalism. It has instance variables corresponding to each element in the 7-tuple for the formalism and associated methods operating on them. The class *Coupled_models* is the realization of the coupled models definition in the DEVS formalism which embodies the hierarchical construction of modular models. The definition of a coupled DEVS model includes specification of its component models (called its children) and a coupling scheme. Accordingly, *Coupled_models* provides methods to specify component models and their coupling scheme. Figure 4.6 shows class definitions for *Atomic_models* and *Coupled_models* in DEVSim++.

The simulation of DEVS models developed in DEVSim++ is managed by means of communication among the three subclasses of *Proces-*

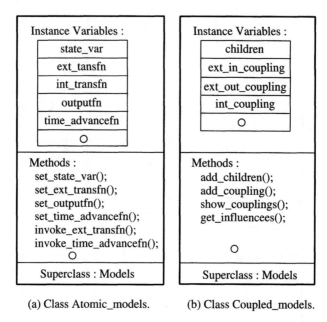

(a) Class Atomic_models.   (b) Class Coupled_models.

Figure 4.6 Definitions for Atomic_models and Coupled_models.

sors: *Simulators*, *Co_ordinators*, and *Root_co_ordinators*. Such subclasses realize the abstract simulator principles in the DEVS theory. *Simulators* and *Co_ordinators* are assigned to *Atomic_models* and *Coupled_models* in a one-to-one manner. DEVSim++ automatically records such model-processor pairing in instance variables of Models and Processors. Finally, *Root_co_ordinators* is linked to a *Co_ordinator* of the outmost coupled model to manage the overall simulation. For details of implementation, see [1].

4.4.3. Model Reusability in DEVSim++

We now describe the reusability of simulation models using our framework of the DEVSim++ environment. Figure 4.7 shows the reusability of simulation models in two dimensions. The reusability in the horizontal axis is achieved by means of the object-oriented environment of C++. Inheritance is the principle of such reusability. It is applied to develop a new class of models as a subclass of *Atomic_models* or *Coupled_models* classes. Recall that within the DEVSim++ environment, modelers can develop new model subclasses without developing associated abstract simulators for the new models.

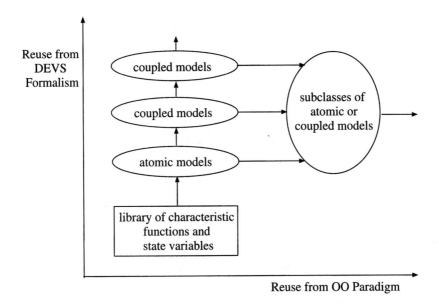

Figure 4.7 Reusability of simulation models in two dimensions.

The reusability in the vertical axis is achieved by means of the hierarchical DEVS formalism. The principles of such reusability are function abstraction, data abstraction, and the closure under coupling property of the DEVS formalism. The reusable components at the lowest level in the axis are the DEVS characteristic functions and the state variables set for atomic DEVSs. The reusable ones at the highest level in the axis are coupled DEVSs. Note that such hierarchical reusability in model development may not be achieved only by exploiting the object-oriented paradigm.

4.5. REUSABLE MODEL DEVELOPMENT IN DEVSim++

This section shows the development of hierarchical reusable models in DEVSim++ using the object-oriented, hierarchical composition framework. Exemplified is the development of a simulation model for evaluation of various message-routing policies in a hypercube computer.

4.5.1. Informal Description of Problem

Due to the increasing demands on computing capability for complex real-time control systems, distributed or multiprocessor systems are used for real-time applications [16]. When a set of node computers in a multiprocessor system cooperates for a real-time task, the messages to be transmitted between cooperating node computers are also time-constrained, depending on the deadline of the task. In this case, the timely delivery of the messages is important since the late arrival of a message may delay the completion time of a task and cause it to miss its deadline.

When a sequence of messages needs to be routed through a single link at a node, channel conflict occurs since only one message can be transmitted over the link at any instant. To resolve such channel conflicts, the order in which messages are transmitted is determined. In general-purpose applications, First-Come First-Routed (FCFR) is generally used as a conflict-resolving policy, but it may not be the best in the real-time environment. Some alternatives to be considered are as follows [24]:

Method 1. *Minimum Deadline First (MDF)*
   Sends the message with the earliest deadline first.

Method 2. *Minimum Laxity First (MLF)*
   Sends the message with the smallest laxity time first.

Method 3. *Most Farthest First (MFF)*
   Sends the message with the farthest distance to destination first.

Other policies or combinations of the above policies can also be considered. It is very difficult, and sometimes impossible, to analytically predict the performance of the routing policies when message distributions in the system are dynamically changing. Thus, we describe the discrete-event modeling of hypercube computers to evaluate such routing policies.

4.5.2. Overview of Model Development

The primary focus in the modeling of a system should be the behavior of the system. Thus, modeling work is a process to reflect the behavior of a system to be observed into a computational model. To do this modeling work, an appropriate abstraction of the behavior of a system is essential. Since we are interested in routing mechanisms in hypercube computers, simulation models should specify time-constrained message transmissions between node computers.

To develop a hypercube model in a modular, hierarchical manner using the DEVS methodology, we first develop six atomic DEVS models as the components of a node computer. The six models are: MGEN for a message generator, MRCV for a message processor in a processing module,

BUFFER for a message buffer in a processing module, RINPUT for input buffers of a router, ROUT for a router, and ROUTPUT for output buffers of a router. For developing reusable models for the various routing policies, two kinds of reusability described in Section 4.2.2, namely, functions reuse (reusability 1) and data reuse (reusability 2), are applied. Also, the inheritance (reusability 4) is applied to atomic model development.

After developing the atomic models, we construct two DEVS coupled models: a processing module (PROC) and a communication module (COMM) for a node computer. The coupling of PROC and COMM results in a coupled model NODE for a node computer. Figure 4.8 shows a simulation model for the node computer. Finally, we construct a hypercube computer model by coupling the NODE models in a hypercube topology. With slight modification of the router model (ROUT) and the communication module (COMM), we can construct node computers for different multiprocessor topologies, such as mesh, ring, and bus.

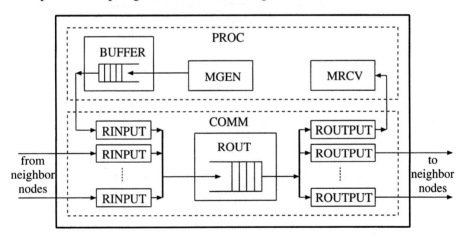

Figure 4.8 Model of a node computer.

4.5.3. Atomic Model Development

To explain atomic model development in DEVSim++, we first develop the atomic model BUFFER as a subclass of *Atomic_models* in DEVSim++. We then develop three subclasses of BUFFER, specific to three message-routing policies mentioned previously. Let us describe the function of BUFFER informally. BUFFER controls the flow of messages from the processing module to the communication module. Figure 4.9(a) shows the I/O structure and the state variables of the model.

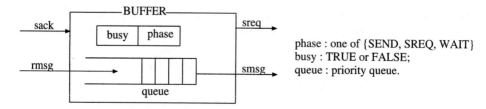

(a) I/O Ports and State Variables.

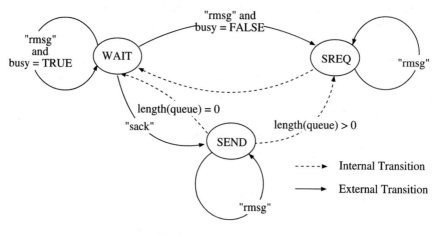

(b) Phase Transitions Diagram.

Figure 4.9 Atomic model BUFFER.

When BUFFER receives a message packet from the message generator MGEN, it inserts the packet into a priority queue. Whenever the queue
is not empty, BUFFER repeats the message transmission operation. The
operation begins by sending a request to the communication module. Upon
receiving an acknowledge signal, BUFFER transmits a packet to the communication module based on the channel conflict method chosen. These
phase transitions of BUFFER are shown in Figure 4.9(b). The BUFFER
model can be specialized, depending on three routing policies.

To find some common operations among three buffer models, let us
relate the DEVS characteristic functions above to the well-known operations on a buffer, namely, insert, delete, send. As shown in Figure 4.10, the
external transition function is related to the insert operation, the internal
transition function to the delete operation, and the output function to the
send operation. If the insert operation inserts a message into the priority
queue according to the priorities of waiting messages, the delete operations

```
// External Transition Function //
when receive an input(x,t)
    case input port of :
        "sack"
            phase := SEND;
        "rmsg" :
            insert(x,queue);
            if (phase = WAIT and busy = FALSE) phase := SREQ;
            else continue;

// Internal Transition Function //
case phase of :
    "SEND" :
        delete(first,queue);
        busy := FALSE;
        if (length(queue) = 0) phase := WAIT;
        else phase := SREQ;
    "SREQ" :
        phase := WAIT;
        busy := TRUE;

// Output Function //
case phase of:
    "SREQ" :  sreq := 1;
    "SEND" :  smsg := first(queue);

// Time Advance Function //
case phase of:
    "SREQ" :  ta(s) := ReqTime;
    "SEND" :  ta(s) := mem_access_time(first(queue));
    "WAIT" :  ta(s) := INFINITY
```

Figure 4.10 BUFFER pseudocode in DEVS formalism.

of the three buffers are the same: deletion of the first message in the waiting queue. Also, the send operations for the buffers are the same. Thus, the internal transition functions and output functions are the same for all classes. Note that the time advance functions of the buffer models do not depend on the resolving policies, and are the same for the three subclasses. We shall define such functions in the class BUFFER which can be reused for the classes MDF, MLF, and MFF through inheritance. Based on the discussion above, we define BUFFER as a subclass of *Atomic_models* in DEVSim++, as shown in Figure 4.11. By reusing the class BUFFER, let us now develop three classes, MDF, MLF, MFF, as subclasses of BUFFER.

The three classes inherit the internal transition function, the output function, and the time advance function from the superclass BUFFER, which we need not specify. However, we need to define the external transition functions specific to MDF, MLF, and MFF that were not defined in the class BUFFER. DEVSim++ codes for the MDF model are shown in Figure 4.12.

```
// define new class for atomic model BUFFER
class BUFFER : public Atomic_models {
public :
    BUFFER(const char* name) :  Atomic_models(name) {
        // define I/O ports and state variables//
        add_inports(2,"rmsg","sack");
        add_outports(2,"smsg","sreq");
        set_state_var(3,"busy","phase","queue");

        // initialize the state variables//
        set_state_value("phase",WAIT);
        set_state_value("busy",FALSE);
        set_state_value("queue",new msgq());

        // set characteristic functions //
        set_int_transfn(BUFFER_int_transfn);
        set_outputfn(BUFFER_outputfn);
        set_time_advancefn(BUFFER_time_advancefn);
    }
};

// internal transition function //
void BUFFER_int_transfn(State_vars& s)
{
    if (s.get_value("phase") == SEND) {
        s.set_value("busy",FALSE);
        s.get_value("queue") -> delete_msg();
        if (s.get_value("queue")->isEmpty())
            s.set_value("phase",WAIT);
        else
            s.set_value("phase",SREQ);
    } else if (s.get_value("phase") == SREQ) {
        s.set_value("phase",WAIT);
        s.set_value("busy",TRUE);
    }
}

// output function //
void BUFFER_outputfn(const State_vars& s)
{
    if (s.get_value("phase") == SREQ)
        message.set("sreq",TRUE);
    else if (s.get_value("phase") == SEND)
        message.set("smsg",s.get_value("queue")->get_msg());
}

// time advance function //
timeType BUFFER_time_advancefn(const State_vars& s)
{
    if (s.get_value("phase") == SEND)
        return s.get_value("queue") -> mem_access_time();
    else if (s.get_value("phase") == SREQ)
        return ReqTime;
    else
        return INFINITY;
}
```

Figure 4.11 DEVSim++ code for atomic model BUFFER.

```
// define new class for atomic model BUFFER
class MDF : public BUFFERS {
public :
    MDF(const char* name) :  BUFFER(name) {
        set_ext_transfn(MDF_ext_transfn);
    }
};

// external transition function //
void MDF_ext_transfn(State_vars& s, const timeType& e, const Messages& message)
{
    if (messge.get_port() == "sack")
        s.set_value("phase",SEND);
    else if(messge.get_port() == "rmsg") {
        s.get_value("queue") -> InsWithDeadline(message.get_value());
        if (s.get_value("phase") == WAIT && s.get_value("busy") == FALSE)
            s.set_value("phase",SREQ);
        else
            CONTINUE();
    }
}
```

Figure 4.12 DEVSim++ code for atomic model MDF.

The procedure explained above can be recursively applied to the development of subclasses of MDF or MLF, if needed. For example, a class of priority queues can be defined as a subclass of MDF. In such a case, we only need to define DEVS characteristic functions for the subclass that are different from those defined for MDF. The functions defined in the subclass can override the ones defined in its superclass.

We can develop the rest of the atomic models in a similar manner. The approach to developing atomic models shown above is novel. The combination of the object-oriented paradigm and the DEVS semantics makes it possible to support the approach. Once atomic models are developed based on the approach above, such models can be saved in the model base for later reuse in the development of coupled DEVS models. The following section describes how such models are to be reused as independent objects.

4.5.4. Coupled Model Development

In coupled model development, model reusability is achieved by exploiting hierarchical composition technologies supported by the DEVS formalism. Since object models in the model base are self-contained, it is possible to take them out from the model base and reuse them as components. This subsection explains such reusability in the development of coupled models.

A coupled DEVS model can be developed by specializing the class *Coupled_models* defined in DEVSim++. *Coupled_models* is the major class which embodies the hierarchical model composition of the DEVS formalism. Depending on coupling schemes being used, *Coupled_models* is specialized into two subclasses: *Digraph_models* for nonuniform coupling, and *Kernel_models* for uniform coupling.

A digraph model is composed of a finite set of explicitly specified children and an explicit coupling scheme connecting them. We use the *Digraph_models* for two component modules, COMM and PROC, of a node computer and for the node computer itself. Due to the uniform connection structure of the hypercube topology, it is easier to use the *Kernel_models* to couple node computers in the hypercube topology.

The coupled model PROC, which employs the MDF routing policy, can be represented in DEVS semantics as follows:

$$DNPROC = < X, Y, M, EIC, EOC, IC, SELECT >$$

$X = \{rv\_msg, sd\_ack\}$
$Y = \{sd\_msg, sd\_req\}$
$M = \{MGEN, MDF, MRCV\}$
$EIC = \{(PROC.rv\_msg, MRCV.rmsg), (PROC.sd\_ack, MDF.sack)\}$
$EOC = \{(MDF.smsg, PROC.sd\_msg), (MDF.sreq, PROC.sd\_req)\}$
$IC = \{(MGEN.smsg, MDF.rmsg)\}.$

The method *add_children* of the class *Coupled_models* is used for specifying the children of the components of a coupled model. The children are atomic models developed in the previous subsection. The method *add_coupling* of *Digraph_models* is applied for specifying the explicit couplings connecting components. Figure 4.13 shows DEVSim++ code implementing the coupled model PROC. The developed coupled models, COMM and PROC, are saved in the model base for later reuse.

```
Digraph_models PROC = *(new Digraph_models("PROC"));

// define components models and I/O ports //
PROC.add_children(3,mgen,mrcv,mdf);
PROC.add_inports(2,"rv_msg","sd_ack");
PROC.add_outports(2,"sd_msg","sd_req");

// external input and output couplings //
PROC.add_coupling(PROC,"rv_msg",mrcv,"rmsg");
PROC.add_coupling(PROC,"sd_ack",mdf,"sack");
PROC.add_coupling(mdf,"smsg",PROC,"sd_msg");
PROC.add_coupling(mdf,"sreq",PROC,"sd_req");

// internal couplings between component models //
PROC.add_coupling(mgen,"smsg",mdf,"rmsg");
```

Figure 4.13 DEVSim++ code for coupled model PROC.

A hypercube model is completed by coupling the coupled model NODEs, each of which consists of COMM and PROC. For hypercube coupling, we specialize the class *Kernel_models* to the class *Hypercube_model*. Since the hypercube topology employs a uniform connection structure, the kernel model does not keep explicit coupling between components.

For example, consider the three-dimensional hypercube model shown in Figure 4.14. The *out-in-coup* table of the model contains the following coupling information:

$$(0, smsg0, rmsg0), (0, sreq0, rreq0), (0, rack0, sack0)$$
$$(1, smsg1, rmsg1), (1, sreq1, rreq1), (1, rack1, sack1)$$
$$(2, smsg2, rmsg2), (2, sreq2, rreq2), (2, rack2, sack2).$$

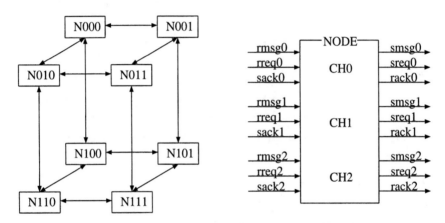

Figure 4.14 Three-dimensional hypercube and channel interface.

The 3-tuple (0, smsg0, rmsg0) in the table means that the port *smsg0* of the origin node is connected to the port *rmsg0* of its first neighbor. The 3-tuple (1, smsg1, rsmg1) indicates that the port *smsg1* of a node is connected to the port *rmsg1* of its second neighbor. If the node with address 111 sends a message to the port *smsg0*, the hypercube model can compute the influences, the node 110, and a receiving port, *rmsg0*, by looking up the out-in-coup table. The DEVSim++ code for the hypercube model is shown in Figure 4.15.

```
Hypercube_models CUBE = *(new Hypercube_models("CUBE"));
// define components models;//
CUBE.make_member(8,node);

// channel interface between node computers //
CUBE.set_channel("smsg","rmsg");
CUBE.set_channel("rack","sack");
CUBE.set_channel("sreq","rreq");
```

Figure 4.15 DEVSim++ code for hypercube model CUBE.

As a summary of class development in the modeling of a hypercube computer, Figure 4.16 shows the modeler-defined model classes being subclasses of *Atomic_models* and *Coupled_models* of DEVSim++.

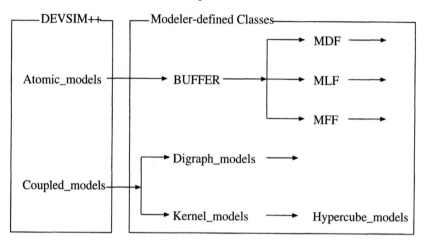

Figure 4.16 Modeler-defined classes for modeling of a hypercube computer.

4.6.   CONCLUSIONS

The hierarchical DEVS formalism provides a theoretical basis for developing highly reusable simulation models which are saved in a model base. An atomic DEVS model in the model base is like a circuit component, and a coupled DEVS model is like a circuit board in its reusability. The reuse of such models in the model base markedly enhances the productivity and quality of modeling engineering. Viewing modeling as a software development process, we have proposed a framework for model reusability called the object-oriented, hierarchical composition methodology. We have discussed the reusability of simulation models within the framework.

The DEVSim++ environment supports the development of highly reusable simulation models within the framework. DEVSim++ is a result of the combination of two powerful methodologies: the hierarchical, modular DEVS formalism, and the object-oriented programming. Such a combination has achieved model reusability in two dimensions: one through inheritance and encapsulation from the object-oriented paradigm, and the other through hierarchical composition technologies from the DEVS formalism.

DEVSim++ has separated definitions for model classes from those for abstract simulator classes. For simulation management, it implicitly creates simulators and associates them with corresponding models. Hierarchical simulation algorithms instrumented in abstract simulators allow the modeler to develop new model classes without developing associated simulator classes. Thus, the DEVSim++ environment can be evolved as new classes of models are developed in the modeling engineering process.

References

[1] M. S. Ahn and T. G. Kim, "The DEVSim++ Simulation Environment," in preparation, 1994.

[2] D. K. Baik, "Performance evaluation and optimal decomposition of hierarchical distributed simulation," Ph.D. dissertation, Dep. Comput. Sci., Wayne State Univ., Detroit, MI, 1985.

[3] R. J. Biggerstaff and C. Richter, "Reusability framework, assessment, and directions," *IEEE Software*, vol. 4, Mar. 1987.

[4] A. I. Concepcion, "The implementation of the hierarchical abstract simulator on the HEP computer," in *Proc. Winter Simulation Conf.*, San Francisco, CA, Dec. 1985, pp. 428–434.

[5] A. I. Concepcion and B. P. Zeigler, "DEVS formalism: A framework for hierarchical model development," *IEEE Trans. Software Eng.*, vol. 14, Feb. 1988, pp. 228–241.

[6] B. J. Cox, *Object Oriented Programming: An Evolutionary Approach*. Reading, MA: Addison-Wesley, 1986.

[7] O. Dahl and K. Nygaard, "SIMULA—An ALGOL-based simulation language," *Commun. ACM*, vol. 9, no. 9, 1966, pp. 671–678.

[8] E. Horowitz and J. B. Munson, "An expansive view of reuseable software," *IEEE Trans. Software Eng.*, vol. SE-10, Sept. 1984.

[9] T. G. Kim and B. P. Zeigler, "The DEVS formalism: Hierarchical, modular system specification in an object oriented framework," in *Proc. 1987 Winter Comput. Simulation Conf.*, Atlanta, GA, Dec. 1987, pp. 559–566.

[10] T. G. Kim, "A knowledge-based environment for hierarchical modelling and simulation," Ph.D. dissertation, Dep. Elec. and Comput. Eng., Univ. Arizona, Tucson, 1988.

[11] T. G. Kim and B. P. Zeigler, "The DEVS-scheme simulation modeling environment," in *Knowledge Based Simulation: Methodology and Applications*, P. A. Fishwick and R. B. Modjestki, Eds. New York: Springer-Verlag, 1990, ch. 2.

[12] T. G. Kim, "Hierarchical development of model classes in the DEVS-scheme simulation environment," *Expert Syst. Appl.*, vol. 3, no. 3, 1991, pp. 343–351.

[13] T. G. Kim and S. B. Park, "The DEVS formalism: Hierarchical modular systems specification in C++," in *Proc. 1992 European Simulation Multiconf.*, York, England, 1992, pp. 152–156.

[14] K. E. Gorlen, S. M. Orlow, and P. S. Plexico, *Data Abstraction and Object-Oriented Programming in C++*. Reading, MA: Addison-Wesley, 1990.

[15] C. Krueger, "Software reuse," *ACM Computing Surveys*, vol. 21, no. 2, 1992, pp. 131–183.

[16] P. Ramanathan and K.G. Shin, "Delivery of time-critical messages using a multiple copy approach," *ACM Trans. Comput. Syst.*, vol. 10, no. 2, 1992, pp. 144–166.

[17] R. G. Sargent, "Hierarchical modeling for discrete event simulation (panel)," in *Proc. WSC'94*, Los Angeles, CA, Dec. 1993, pp. 569–572.

[18] Y. R. Seong et al., "Parallel simulation of hierarchical modular DEVS models," *Int. J. Comput. Simulation*, accepted for publication, 1994.

[19] B. Stroustrup, *The C++ Programming Language*. Reading, MA: Addison-Wesley, 1987.

[20] Y. Wang, "Discrete-event simulation in a massively parallel computer," Ph.D. dissertation, Dep. Elec. Eng., Univ. Arizona, Tucson, 1992.

[21] B. P. Zeigler, *Theory of Modelling and Simulation*. New York: Wiley, 1976 (reissued by Krieger Publ., Malabar, FL, 1985).

[22] B. P. Zeigler, *Multifacetted Modeling and Discrete Event Simulation*. Orlando, FL: Academic, 1984.

[23] B. P. Zeigler, *Object-Oriented Simulation with Hierarchical Modular Models*. Boston, MA: Academic, 1990.

[24] W. Zhao and K. Ramamritham, "Virtual time CSMA protocols for hard real-time communication," *IEEE Trans. Software Eng.*, vol. SE-13, no. 8, 1987, pp. 938–952.

Chapter 5

Object-Oriented Frameworks for Multilevel Simulation Modeling

Douglas A. Popken   *Department of MIS and Decision Sciences*
Atish P. Sinha   *University of Dayton*
                     Dayton, Ohio, USA

Editor's Introduction

Now that we have some good basics under our belt and have seen some specifics, let us get into a little bit of abstract methodology or, as I sometimes call it, cosmic thinking.

Object-oriented modeling approaches provide the simulationist with new opportunities to simplify model development and improve software engineering practices. These opportunities result in large part from the ability to effect a more direct mapping of components from the physical system, to the conceptual model, and then to its software implementation. This ability is enhanced when the simulationist can vary the fidelity of the model. The simulationist would often like to have the capability to select either a detailed model, or a consistent yet more abstract model of a system, depending on the time available, the data available, and the study objectives. This chapter discusses the issues involved in attempting to provide a multilevel simulation modeling capacity within object-oriented frameworks. Examples are provided of two implementations of multilevel simulation modeling, one in Smalltalk-80 and the other in C++, which we just examined in the previous chapter.

5.1. INTRODUCTION

Multilevel models incorporate model components at multiple levels of resolution. The components reside in an integrated hierarchical framework that allows model builders and model users a choice of the appropriate level(s) of detail for a given simulation study. A typical simulation study involves modeling components of greatest interest at higher levels of detail (base components), and components of lesser interest at lower levels of detail (abstract components). Therefore, the multilevel modeling approach generally relies on the ability to transform base components or processes to more abstract model components that are simpler and often very useful for studying higher level behaviors.

This chapter has several objectives. The first is to provide motivations for a multilevel modeling approach. The second is to demonstrate alternative approaches to multilevel simulation, using object-oriented programming languages such as Smalltalk-80 and C++. The demonstrations are preceded by a discussion relating the approaches to existing simulation time management approaches and world views. The demonstrations serve to illustrate the strengths and limitations of existing object-oriented languages and techniques currently available for multilevel simulation models. A final objective is to illustrate, using demonstrations, how object-oriented analysis and design techniques can enhance the development of multilevel simulation models.

5.2.   MOTIVATIONS FOR MULTILEVEL MODELING TECHNIQUES

5.2.1. Aggregation and Abstraction

The transformation of a model component to a more abstract model component has been variously referred to as either *abstraction* or *aggregation*, with several definitions being applied to either category. It would therefore be useful to first clarify terms. We will remain consistent with the definitions found in [11]. We consider aggregation, a "lumping together" of model components, as only one aspect of abstraction.

A multilevel framework can contain both concrete and abstract model components. There are a number of potential advantages to using an abstract model component:

Enhanced reusability. The abstract model component may be applicable to a wider variety of modeling situations with possibly only minor modifications.

Computational efficiency. An abstract model component is usually less computationally complex.

Comprehensibility. The abstract model component may be easier to understand. This could facilitate better communication between members of a study team by providing a common level of understanding.

Selective outputs. An abstract model component could be more selective in recording or transmitting model outputs.

Security. The abstract model component may conceal proprietary or classified model details.

System design tracking. Model specializations, beginning with abstract model components, can provide the evolutionary path of the current system design.

This is not to say that abstract model components are always preferable. Clearly, a tradeoff will always exist between complexity and data sufficiency.

The categories of abstraction relevant to multilevel modeling of discrete systems are:

Abstraction by representation. This is sometimes referred to as *structural* abstraction. The representations of model components are abstracted, but not the behaviors. In practice, the model user need only see or refer to a single component, but the actual underlying computer model could consist of multiple connected components. This type of abstraction can provide greater comprehensibility through modularity, but not greater computational efficiency.

Cerebral abstraction. This type of abstraction does not necessarily involve a mapping or mathematical transformation of the base model component(s). Two methods of cerebral abstraction are *system dynamics* and *qualitative modeling* [4]. These types of modeling generally involve creating intuitive models that conform to the modeler's notion of system behavioral trends and state dependencies without necessarily assigning specific numerical values to results. Computational efficiency and comprehensibility may be greater with these forms of abstract model components, but validation is more problematic.

Abstraction by induction. The abstract behaviors of base model components are approximated via inductive inference. For example, statistically based methods such as regression, formation of empirical simulation distributions [22], or neural networks [21] could be applied to base model component input/output data sets to generate approximate abstract behaviors. The required sample data are obtained by recording inputs, and the corresponding outputs are generated by repeated runs of the base model. The advantage of this approach over, say, a cerebral abstraction is that levels of confidence in matching the input/output relationships of the abstract model component to those of the base component(s) can be directly calculated using statistical methods.

System morphism. A morphism is a verifiably correct algorithm that maps base model components to abstract-level components. A complete one-to-one mapping between levels is a *total* system morphism, while a mapping of only some base model components, without necessarily preserving all relations and behaviors, is a *partial* system morphism. Examples of partial system morphisms would include techniques for the aggregation of queueing networks [7] such as numerical techniques or analytical techniques for product form networks. Theoretical principles of system morphisms are discussed at length in [28].

Multilevel modeling provides an approach to incorporating the various types of abstraction in the modeling process. A typical multilevel model could integrate submodels developed at various levels of abstraction, using different categories of abstraction techniques.

5.2.2. Distinct High-Level Behaviors

In model abstraction, high-level components represent or substitute for base model component(s). However, the behavior of high-level objects (corporations, multimember research groups, automated manufacturing systems) cannot always be easily specified in terms of the behavior of their components, leading to situations where it is desirable to model high-level components with behaviors distinct from those of any base model components. This is most often true when the system being modeled implies a need for base model components "controlled" by high-level components. Potential applications include command and control systems, organizational or "enterprise" models, and manufacturing control systems. To illustrate the latter case (developed as a complete example below), a manufacturing cell can be modeled as a group of workstations augmented with cell level production control logic. Similarly, one could model a manufacturing shop as a group of manufacturing cells augmented with shop level production control logic. This approach could be described as a *structural* abstraction augmented with high-level behaviors. Because this "augmented structural abstraction" is strictly internal to the high-level component, interaction with other model components would be unaffected.

5.2.3. Hierarchical and Heterarchical Frameworks

A specification of recursively applied abstraction relationships (perhaps with augmentation) forms the basis for a multilevel framework of model components. The specific form of the hierarchy is determined by the number of levels and the types of communication allowed between components at a given level in the hierarchy. Four forms of hierarchical architectures are defined in [10] in the context of control models for automated manufacturing systems, but these definitions serve well in other application contexts (Figure 5.1). A *centralized* control architecture is one where all other components communicate only with a single high-level component. A *proper hierarchical* control architecture is one that only allows communication between parent and child components. A *modified hierarchical* control architecture is one that also allows communication between intermediate level components, in addition to parent/child communication. A *heterarchical* control architecture is similar to the modified hierarchical architecture, except that there is no top-level control component. The C++ multilevel modeling example given later in this chapter is in proper hierarchical form in terms of both communication (message-passing) and assembly (part–whole) structures. However, real-world organizational and system structures increasingly emphasize horizontal communication and cooperation between components, that is, more heterarchical struc-

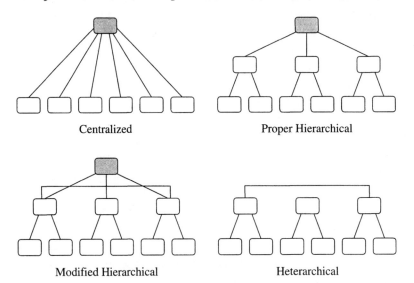

Centralized   Proper Hierarchical

Modified Hierarchical   Heterarchical

Figure 5.1 Four forms of hierarchical architecture.

tures. Examples include distributed computing systems (with ring, broadcast, or bus configurations), "flattened" organizational structures, and emerging forms of "cooperating" control systems for automated manufacturing [19]. Depending on the application, the advantages of a more heterarchical architecture could include reduced complexity, better fault tolerance, greater flexibility, and quicker reaction. Multilevel modeling has no restrictions on the form of the structures within the model framework.

5.2.4. Contributions/Limitations of Object Orientation

Object-oriented analysis [8], design [5], and programming [27] have provided more direct means of implementing multilevel models than were previously available. The advantages of object-oriented approaches that are relevant to our purposes are *encapsulation, inheritance*, and *polymorphism.* Through *encapsulation*, we are able to design and implement models as software modules with localized *state* and *behavior*, and that interact with other modules only through well-defined message interfaces. Through *inheritance*, we are able to automate much of the process of defining new modules as specializations of existing modules. Through *polymorphism*, we ensure a transparent module interface in that generalized messages trigger a response appropriate to a module specialization, without having to know the nature of that specialization. The importance of this to multilevel modeling is that abstract model components must maintain the same external messaging protocol as the base level model components.

Object-oriented programming does not automatically give us everything we would desire for robust and generalized multilevel modeling. For instance, while inheritance relationships (class–subclass) between objects are directly supported by object-oriented languages, part–whole relationships are not. There is no ready mechanism in object-oriented programming languages for encapsulating combinations of objects to create large-scale components [26], a necessity in creating structural abstractions. In the software implementation, this must instead be done "manually" through the use of some form of pointers. This solution is still not completely satisfactory because there is no automatic way to keep other objects from accessing the "contained" objects. Again, a "manual" solution is required where the developer must add his own access enforcement mechanisms for each case. In summary, it is still up to the individual developer/modeler to provide multilevel modeling mechanisms that conform to "best practice" software engineering standards.

5.3.   SIMULATION TIME MANAGEMENT
AND WORLD VIEWS

Before demonstrating specific approaches to multilevel modeling, it is useful to provide an overview of existing simulation time management schemes and world views. This provides a context for categorizing the demonstrated approaches within the broader area of simulation modeling.

In simulation models, an *event* represents an instantaneous change of state. The sequencing of these events can be managed via either event-driven or time-driven approaches. However, event-driven time management is generally the best choice for simulating discrete-event systems. In *time-driven simulation*, the global simulation clock increments according to a predetermined fixed increment (tick). All objects are given the opportunity to take action (update state and pass messages) at each tick. The clock will not continue until all appropriate actions are completed. In *event-driven simulation*, the global simulation clock increments from one event time to the next. Event-driven simulation is often more efficient as there may be many ticks during which no events occur. On the other hand, if the system being modeled is essentially continuous, but is being approximated in discrete time steps, time-driven approaches can be more appropriate. (One can view time-driven simulation as a special type of event-driven simulation.)

In most event-driven simulations, events are processed from a time-ordered global event list. The simulation executive program iteratively removes events from the top of the list, advances the global simulation clock to the time of that event, and invokes the software module associated with that event. The specification of the software module depends on which of three "world views"—event scheduling, process interaction, or activity scanning—is used in developing the simulation model. If the model is developed using an *event scheduling* world view, the software modules represent events. An event software module describes the steps that occur at the instant that event takes place. The event scheduling approach is best suited for simulations written in conventional programming languages as it maps more directly to a functional system decomposition of a system than to an object decomposition. However, the event scheduling approach has been used in some object-oriented simulation research efforts such as a New Flavors (LISP)-based model by Boukachour [6], and is one approach available in a set of C/C++ simulation tools called SimPack [12]. If the model is developed using a *process interaction* world view, the software modules represent processes. A process software module describes the actions taken by a model object. An event then corresponds to an entry point in a process software module. The process interaction world view is the one most commonly employed in object-oriented simulation packages (and in conventional simulation languages as well). This may be due to the early influences of Simula [9] and Smalltalk-80 [13], the object focus of process interaction, and the relatively straightforward mapping of simulation processes to methods within simulation objects. The process interaction world view is also used in CSIM++ [24], MODSIM II [3], SIM++ [16], and is one approach available in SimPack. In the *activity scanning* world view, the software modules represent activities. An activity software module describes a collection of actions that will occur when the model reaches a given state. The activity scanning world view is little used in the United States in conventional or object-oriented simulation, but has found wider acceptance in the United Kingdom. It has provided the basis for simulation languages such as DRAFT [17]. (For a detailed discussion of the three modeling world views as implemented in conventional simulation languages, see [20].)

An example of a *time-driven* approach to object-oriented simulation may be found in ERIC [14], which is based on the Common LISP Object System (CLOS). ERIC uses distributed event lists, with each simulation object containing a list of pending events. The global time step is set by the user according to the appropriate level of model granularity.

The Smalltalk-80-based implementation of multilevel modeling described in this chapter augments the process interaction world view of Smalltalk's event-driven simulation framework with "activity networks."

The C++ based implementation of multilevel modeling described in this chapter exemplifies a world view drawing from the DEVS modeling formalism [28], but with an alternative object-oriented decomposition [8]. The DEVS modeling formalism has been implemented using PC-Scheme [29] and C++ [1], [25]. A DEVS-based simulation is event-driven, but there is no global event list; rather, each model component stores the time of its own next event. We shall see that this provides greater modularity, and helps to enable the multilevel modeling framework via a hierarchical time management system.

5.4. MULTILEVEL MODELING IN SMALLTALK-80

The Smalltalk-80 software system is both a programming environment and a general object-oriented programming language. As a programming environment, Smalltalk provides an interactive graphical user interface and a set of graphical tools to build, run, and debug programs that may themselves include graphical user interfaces. As a language, Smalltalk provides a set of primitives (upon which the system is built) and a comprehensive set of classes that provide both system functionality and programmer "templates." Smalltalk supports objects, object classes, single inheritance, object instances, and object methods.

5.4.1. Simulation in Smalltalk-80

Smalltalk's Process Interaction World View

The basic Smalltalk system already provides a complete set of objects to build and run general simulation models. However, a modeler wishing to capitalize on this large set of provided objects must build models that conform with Smalltalk's particular process-interaction-based world view. To begin with, the Smalltalk class, SimulationObject, describes objects that appear in a simulation scenario. Each object will provide a sequence of actions that begin when the object enters the simulation. The general sequence is controlled by sending the messages *startUp*, *tasks*, and *finishup* to the object. In particular, the user-written method, *tasks*, defines the specific sequence of actions that the instances of the particular subclass will carry out. This process interaction approach is further enabled by the SimulationObject's use of the message *holdFor*: aTimeDelay, where the argument aTimeDelay is some amount of simulated time during which the object is to carry out some action. One use of *holdFor* is to model the time either waiting for, or using, some simulation resource.

General Classification Structure

The classification structure of the classes needed to perform multilevel modeling in Smalltalk is depicted in Figure 5.2. Specialized classes are shown in relation to classes provided by Smalltalk. Beginning with the provided simulation related classes, SimulationObject is shown in relation to the top-level class, Object, along with its subclass, EventMonitor. EventMonitor allows the definition of SimulationObjects with their own built-in event tracing capabilities.

The class, Simulation, manages the relationships between simulation objects and schedules events. One instance is created for a simulation run. Resources represent objects acquired by SimulationObjects. They may be either consumable or nonconsumable. When a SimulationObject requests a Resource from a Simulation, the request is stored in a queue as an instance of the class, WaitingSimulationObject. Each time a request is made,

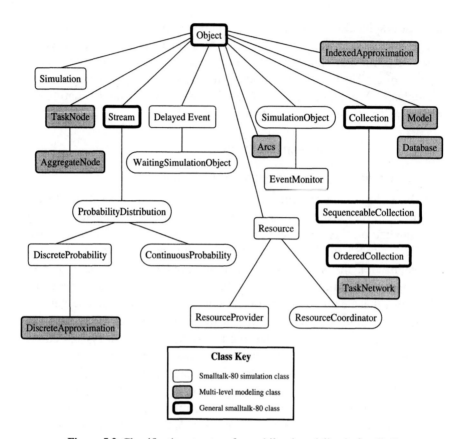

Figure 5.2 Classification structure for multilevel modeling in Smalltalk.

or more resources are produced, or resources in use are released, the appropriate ResourceProvider checks to see if one or more of its pending requests can be satisfied. A ResourceCoordinator is used to coordinate two SimulationObjects whose tasks must be synchronized. Instances of subclasses of ProbabilityDistribution represent random variate generators for the specific probability distribution desired. Typically, the variates they generate are used as arguments in the *holdFor*: message.

5.4.2. Specializations for Multilevel Modeling of Activities

The multilevel modeling capability developed in Smalltalk allows one to model a sequence of actions or activities as a single higher level activity. It illustrates *abstraction by induction* and *abstraction by representation*. However, before describing the abstraction mechanism, we need to first examine the object classes needed to create a generalized hierarchical framework. The classes that provide the structure of the hierarchical activity framework are TaskNetwork, Arcs, and TaskNode. The class, TaskNetwork, enables the sequence of activities invoked by the SimulationObject *tasks* method to include branching based on probabilities or logic conditions. TaskNodes are the focal points for simulated activities. As currently implemented, each node specifies the resource(s) to be used during the activity, the length of time involved, and the possible transitions to succeeding activities. Arcs provide the links to succeeding activities and any associated transition probabilities.

Each TaskNetwork points to the "root node" of a collection of Task-Nodes and Arcs. As shown in Figure 5.2, TaskNetworks are a specialization of the Smalltalk provided class, OrderedCollection, while TaskNodes and Arcs are specializations of the Object class. The main purpose of TaskNet-work is to implement behaviors for network construction, traversal, and information collecting.

To achieve abstraction and multilevel modeling, TaskNodes and TaskNetworks must be used interchangeably by the simulation such that a SimulationObject need not distinguish between the two. If *abstraction by representation* is desired, a TaskNetwork must have the capability to appear to the SimulationObject as a single TaskNode, yet retain all of its structure and behavior. To achieve *abstraction by induction*, a TaskNetwork must be available in an aggregate form as a TaskNode. This is done by creating a specialization of TaskNode called AggregateNode (see Figure 5.2). Normally, SimulationObjects queue for the resource(s) represented by the TaskNode. A TaskNetwork represents a *network* of queues. Because one of these queues contains the SimulationObject, there is no need to queue separately for the network itself. An infinite server queue provides a better model of what actually occurs at the network level. Resources with infi-nite server queues are not provided with Smalltalk, so a special resource type, *dummy*, was created. The infinite server queue effect is achieved by having the simulation create an additional quantity of resource whenever a *dummy* type resource is requested. The specific service time distribution of the aggregate activity is a function of the number of SimulationObjects currently being served (traversing the aggregated network), and can be determined prior to run time using an empirical statistical approach as in [22]. The empirical distributions for each aggregate activity are stored in an instance of Database. The traversal time distribution is provided to the SimulationObject by having the AggregateNode query an instance of In-dexedApproximation. IndexedApproximation determines the current state (number being served) of the aggregate activity, retrieves the appropriate distribution from Database, and passes the distribution to DiscreteApproximation to generate the random deviate. The random deviate is then passed back to the SimulationObject.

Assembly Structures

Figure 5.3 illustrates some of the key part–whole relationships needed to implement multilevel modeling. In the notation of this figure and several following, a link and triangle correspond to a part–whole relationship, with the triangle pointing toward the "whole." For example, Resource objects are a part of a Simulation. The numbers indicate the possible quantities involved, with the notation x,y indicating a feasible range from x to y, and the index m indicating "many." Reading in one direction, a Simulation may contain one-to-many Resource objects. Reading in the other direction, a Resource belongs to exactly one Simulation. The figure shows a one-to-one relationship between a SimulationObject and its (top-level) TaskNetwork. A TaskNetwork contains one "root node" which will be one of either an Aggregate Node, an ordinary TaskNode, or a TaskNetwork. Each "node" will contain zero-to-many outgoing Arcs, with 0 indicating the end of activities for the SimulationObject. Each Arc connects to (contains) either an AggregateNode, a TaskNode, or a TaskNetwork. We can now see the recursive nature of the multilevel modeling framework. Finally, note the one-to-one correspondence between AggregateNodes and IndexedApproximations.

Key Control Methods

An instance of TaskNetwork is created by sending the message *new* to the TaskNetwork class or to a subclass. (In general, a subclass is created for each type of TaskNetwork.) The new TaskNetwork is returned to the message sender. A sample *new* method could be as follows:

```
| aTaskNetwork aNode|
aTaskNetwork←super new.
aNode←TaskA newTaskNode.
aNode taskID: "1."
aTaskNetwork firstTask: aNode.
aNode←TaskB newTaskNode.
aNode taskID: "2."
aTaskNetwork makeArcFrom:  "1" to:  "2" withProb:  0.3.
aNode←TaskC newTaskNode.
aNode taskID: "3."
aTaskNetwork makeArcFrom:  "1" to:  "3" withProb:  0.7.
↑ aTaskNetwork
```

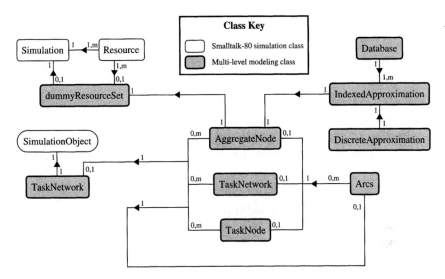

Figure 5.3 Key assembly structures for multilevel modeling in Smalltalk.

This method would return a three-node network that begins with a task of type TaskA, and then branches to either a TaskB or a TaskC with probabilities 0.3 and 0.7, respectively. The method illustrates the use of the message, *newTaskNode*, in creating the required nodes. It also shows how arcs are created and simultaneously linked to nodes by sending the makeArcFrom message to the network under construction.

Network traversal by a SimulationObject identified by objectID is activated by its method, *traverse*, which operates on the subclass specific network identified by its instance variable ClassTaskNetwork:

```
|taskRequest|
ClassTaskNetwork start:  objectID.
currentNode←ClassTaskNetwork current:  objectID.
[currentNode isNil]
whileFalse:  [taskRequest←self acquire:
             1 ofResource:  (currentNode type).
             self holdFor:  (currentNode duration:  self).
             self release:  taskRequest.
             currentNode←ClassTaskNetwork next:  objectID]
```

The *next* method in the final line returns the next TaskNode in the TaskNetwork according to the probabilities of the Arcs emanating from the current TaskNode (currentNode).

The method, *duration: aSimulationObject*, is found in both TaskNodes and TaskNetworks. When this message is received by a TaskNode, the node will return a fixed value or random deviate corresponding to the duration of the corresponding activity:

```
(duration isKindOf:  Number) ifTrue:   (↑duration)
                             ifFalse:  (↑duration next)
```

Note that "aSimulationObject" is a dummy argument when the recipient is a TaskNode rather than a TaskNetwork. However, when the message is received by a TaskNetwork (as when performing abstraction by representation), a simulation process similar to the traverse method is invoked:

```
|taskRequest objectID currentNode|
objectID←aSimulationObject objectID.
self start:  objectID.
currentNode←self current:  objectID.
[currentNode isNil]
whileFalse:[taskRequest←aSimulationObject acquire:
        1 ofResource:  (currentNode type).
        aSimulationObject holdFor:  (currentNode duration:  self).
        aSimulationObject release:  taskRequest.
        currentNode←self next:  objectID]
↑0
```

The method causes aSimulationObject to traverse the receiving TaskNetwork, returning to the higher level of abstraction only after completing the lower level.

The task nodes in the class representing aggregated networks, AggregateNode, have an associated simulation resource of type dummyResource. The *acquire:* and *release:* methods used in Smalltalk to acquire and release simulation resources have been modified to test whether a standard or dummy resource (corresponding to an infinite server) is being affected. In *acquire:*, if a dummy resource is requested, then an additional quantity of resource is produced by the simulation.

```
[Simulation active dummyResourceSet includes:  resourceName]
ifTrue:  [Simulation active produce:  amount of:  resourceName].
↑(Simulation active provideResourceFor:  resourceName)
acquire:  amount withPriority:  0
```

Upon completion of service, the *release:* method will "consume" the dummy resource:

```
[Simulation active dummyResourceSet includes:  aStaticResource]
ifTrue:  [↑aStaticResource consume]
ifFalse:  [↑aStaticResource release]
```

5.4.3. Modeling Application: Airbase Logistics

The objective of airbase logistics is to support the generation of aircraft sorties. The modeling application of this chapter focuses on a critical determinant of sortie generation capability—aircraft maintenance and repair operations. Simulation models are used to evaluate the effects of alternative hardware designs, resource levels, and maintenance procedures on sortie generation capability. The models are probabilistic due to the random failures of aircraft components and associated randomly distributed repair times. Maintenance and repair activities are modeled as task networks as in Figure 5.4. Branchings at an activity node represent the possible outcomes in a fault diagnosis. Aircraft are modeled as a collection of parts. Both aircraft and parts have task networks. All aircraft in the model traverse the following basic activities: land, maintain, refuel, and takeoff. Within "maintain" are all task networks of activities associated with repair and maintenance of aircraft and their component parts.

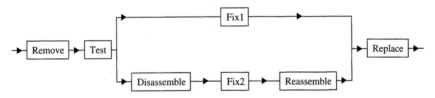

Figure 5.4 Conceptual task network for aircraft maintenance.

Modern combat aircraft are highly complex. Although aircraft subsystems are designed to be fault tolerant, they are subject to high physical stresses and possible battle damage. In practice, this complexity is dealt with through hierarchical and modular hardware design. Aircraft are designed as a tightly integrated collection of subsystems (avionics, airframe, engines, weapons, etc.). Similarly, avionics subsystems are composed of modular units called "line replaceable units" (LRUs). These boxlike units can be repaired on the flight line by "remove and replace" procedures. LRUs are themselves composed of "shop replaceable units" (SRUs). These components can only be repaired at a base or depot repair facility. Because of the hierarchical hardware design and the many possible failure modes, the maintenance and repair task networks tend to be hierarchical, large, and complex. A modeling approach that also incorporates hierarchy motivates the modelers to think like the hardware designers and aircraft maintainers, thus facilitating communication and avoiding needless additional complexity. It also makes it easier to model system and procedural design alternatives without first specifying every task (sub)network in detail.

Classification Structure

The additional classes necessary to model airbase logistics are specializations of classes discussed earlier in this chapter and are shown in Figure 5.5. We begin with the specializations of EventMonitor (itself a specialization of SimulationObject), Aircraft, and Parts. A further specialization exists for each type of aircraft (F-15, F-16, etc.), indexed as Aircraft(y), as maintenance operations differ greatly by aircraft type. Numerous part types also exist, indexed by Part(x). The second-level specializations of TaskNetwork, PartTaskNetwork(i) and PlaneTaskNetwork(i), define sequences of maintenance activities for Parts and Aircraft, respectively. Specializations of TaskNode define the different maintenance activities performed in the various TaskNetworks. The TaskNode specializations, AggregateNode(i), are aggregated (abstract) versions of PartTaskNetwork(i) or PlaneTaskNetwork(i). They have been provided with the state variables and behaviors of TaskNetworks. Conversely, TaskNetworks have been provided with the state variables and behavior of TaskNodes. Thus, a SimulationObject can use TaskNodes and TaskNetworks interchangeably to achieve various levels of abstraction. Note that if Smalltalk supported multiple inheritance, TaskNetworks could inherit the needed behaviors from AggregateNodes.

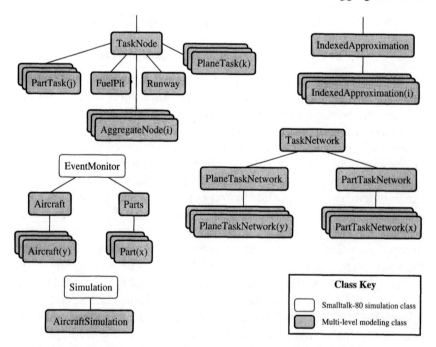

Figure 5.5 Classification structures for multilevel modeling of airbase logistics.

Finally, the specializations, IndexedApproximation(i), provide empirical probability distributions for the AggregateNode(i).

Assembly Structure

The general assembly structure of Figure 5.3 serves as a starting point for the airbase logistics assembly structure in Figure 5.6. The major new element is that an Aircraft will have zero-to-many Part objects, depending on the specific modeling objectives. Both the entire aircraft and its constituent parts will have TaskNetworks associated with them. The TaskNode specializations Runway and FuelPit are shown separately, as each aircraft type in all models must land (Runway) and refuel (FuelPit).

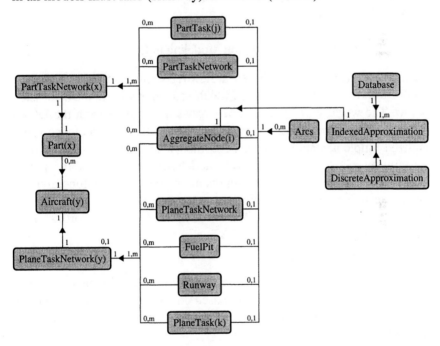

Figure 5.6 Key assembly structures for multilevel modeling of airbase logistics.

5.5.   MULTILEVEL MODELING IN C++

5.5.1. Language Basics/Contrasts with Smalltalk-80

Like Smalltalk, C++ supports objects, object classes, object instances, and object methods. Unlike Smalltalk, C++ supports *multiple* inheritance. C++ is an example of a *strongly typed* language. That is, expressions are guaranteed to be type-consistent at run time, but not necessarily at compile time. Smalltalk supports dynamic binding at message execution time to enhance flexibility. The Smalltalk language actually represents an intermediate point on the scale between structure and flexibility. In contrast, the language CLOS represents an extreme of freedom and flexibility, while C++ is extreme in its choice of structure over flexibility. Structure enhances reliability. Many hold the view that Smalltalk is the best language for rapid prototyping, while C++ should be the language of choice once a software design has stabilized. With respect to language compilation, C++ is more portable because it is based on the widely used C programming language. However, when a C++ application employs a graphical user interface, it becomes less portable.

5.5.2. Multilevel Simulation Modeling in C++

For convenience, the C++ based multilevel simulation framework [23] will be referred to as CMF (C++ Modeling Framework) in the discussion below. The world view used in CMF draws many ideas from the DEVS (Discrete-Event Specification) formalism [28], [30]. DEVS provides a generalized, implementation-independent, theory-based model specification. It begins by specifying "atomic level" models, and then proceeds to specify higher level systems of "multicomponent" models. The multicomponent system specification is hierarchical and recursive. DEVS is clearly one approach to multilevel modeling. Before looking at CMF, it is worthwhile to first provide a brief overview of DEVS.

DEVS World View

DEVS separates the simulator function from the model component. The atomic level model components are based on concepts originating in finite automata theory, with the atomic level model component formally defined as a structure:

$$M = < X, S, Y, \delta, \lambda, \text{ta} >$$

where X is the set of external (input) event types to which the model component will respond;

S is the set of states attainable by the state variables;

Y is the set of possible outputs;

$\delta_{ext}(\delta_{int})$ is a function, the transition specification of how the model component changes state when an input is received (when the time advance function has elapsed). Specifically, δ_{ext} is the external transition function and δ_{int} is the internal transition function.

λ is the output function, generating an external output just before an internal transition takes place;

ta is the time advance function to control the timing of internal events.

The atomic model component specification is most closely identifiable with the process interaction world view, but the DEVS formalism endows it with a modularity property that conventional process-based languages do not support [30].

A *multicomponent* DEVS (in modular form) is defined as a structure:

$$DN =< D, \{M_i\}, \{I_i\}, \{Z_{ij}\}, \ select >$$

where D is a set of component names;

M_i is a component basic model (defined as above);

I_i is the set of influencees of i (those components that receive messages sent by component i);

Z_{ij} is the i-to-j output translation from the state of component i to the input of component j;

select is the tie-breaking selector to choose the most imminent (see "Time Management" below) component of D.

The structure is implemented as a coupled model and its Coordinator. The structure of the coupled model—for example, parallel, series, cellular, etc.—is defined through the I_is and the Z_{ij}s.

DEVS specifies a simulator to be coupled with each atomic model component. In the implementation, the simulator is enabled by the following state variables:

t_N—scheduled time of the next internal event

t_L—time of the last event.

The simulator communicates with its external environment by reporting t_N through an "output port" and by receiving time-stamped messages through an "input port." The time stamp represents the global simulation time. Each simulator may receive two types of messages: external event notices and internal event notices. Upon receipt of either message type, the simulator checks for consistent time synchronization, and then tells the model component to execute the appropriate model state transition. It then updates t_L to the time stamp t, and t_N is advanced using the time advance function.

A multicomponent DEVS model is managed via a "Coordinator," serving as both a message router and a multicomponent simulator. The Coordinator communicates with its external environment the same way as the single component simulator; hence, there is no distinction between the two from an external point of view. This characteristic is critical to the hierarchical and recursive nature of the DEVS formalism. (Those familiar with object-oriented programming will recognize this characteristic as a combination of the object-oriented principles of polymorphism and encapsulation.) The Coordinator routes the internal event notice to the most imminent (one with lowest t_N, subject to the *select* tie breaker) child component simulator. The Coordinator routes external event notices to the appropriate internal component simulator. Finally, the Coordinator sets its t_N variable to the minimum t_N of its child simulator components. Figure 5.7 portrays the functions of the component simulators and the Coordinator required for a two-component DEVS structure.

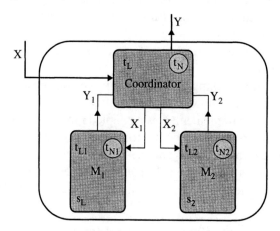

Figure 5.7 Component simulators and coordinator.

Multilevel Modeling

In comparing the CMF to the DEVS, we see both similarities and differences. In both cases, Coordinator components are responsible for maintaining the hierarchical time management scheme described above. However, in the CMF, Coordinators may have state and behavior distinct from those of their child components. Accordingly, CMF Coordinators may also be influences of their child components and vice versa. Both cases rely on the modularity of components to provide encapsulation and on message passing to provide communication and synchronization. However, DEVS is more rigorously modular because of its processor independence and its separation of models and simulators.

Each modeling component (object) of CMF is a specialization of the class, ModelObject. CMF contains two major subclasses of Model-

Objects—Atoms and Coordinators, illustrated in the classification structure of Figure 5.8. Figure 5.8 also illustrates the general assembly structure, showing part–whole relationships between model components. Atoms have no parts, being the lowest level objects in the structure. All ModelObjects except the MasterCoordinator have one or more parent Coordinators. (Allowing more than one parent Coordinator provides a mechanism for sharing resources.) Second-level objects have exactly one Coordinator, the MasterCoordinator. Every Coordinator has one or more children, which may be both Atoms or Coordinators.

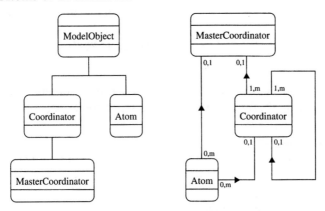

Figure 5.8 (a) Classification structure of CMF. (b) General assembly structure in CMF.

Atoms typically represent physically realizable objects in the modeled system such as machines, robots, queues, and aircraft. Coordinators typically represent higher level conceptual aggregations or abstractions of these objects such as work cells, shops, factories, and squadrons. Regardless of the modeling architecture selected, Atoms may communicate only with a parent Coordinator. Coordinators may communicate with child objects, parent Coordinators, or peer Coordinators, depending on the modeling architecture. Coordinators representing abstract objects may have no children. Coordinators provide the event timing mechanisms necessary to synchronize the behavior of lower level objects in the assembly structure. However, they may also have their own state and behavior.

CMF can be described with the following notation:

t — current global simulation time
s — current state vector
t_L — time of the last event

t_N	— scheduled time of the next internal event
parent	— parent Coordinator object
message-name (x,t)	— an external event message of type message-name with parameter list x arriving at time t
internal-event-notice (t)	— internal event message arriving at time t
output-message-name (y,t)	— output message of type-output message-name with parameter list y sent at time t
ta(s)	— time advance function.

Atoms. An *external* event message results from activities occurring externally to the object. An Atom will react to external event messages as follows:

message-name (x,t):
    if $t_L <= t <= t_N$
        $t_L = t$
        $t_N = t_L + ta(s)$
        update state variables
        send parent *output-message-name* (y,t)
    else
        synchronization error.

An *internal* event, on the other hand, occurs due to activities within an Atom. The internal event message serves as a form of "wake-up call" to let the object know that the global simulation clock has advanced to the scheduled time of its next internal event. A Coordinator may receive an internal event message, but only for relaying it to the appropriate child object. Only Atoms will have internal events. The Atom's time advance function, ta(s), schedules its next internal event. An Atom will react to internal event messages as follows:

internal-event-notice (t)
    if $t = t_N$
        $t_L = t$
        $t_N = t_L + ta(s)$
        update state variables
        send parent *output-message-name* (y,t)
    else
        synchronization error.

Notes: • ta(s) may equal infinity, causing the object to be set to a passive state.

• *output-message-name* may equal null in some cases.

• The statements "send parent..." must occur last as parent Coordinators may query the current state of its children in performing its own processing tasks.

Coordinators. Coordinators may send (receive) external event messages to (from) objects that are above, below, or at the same level to them in the model assembly structure. A Coordinator will react to event messages as follows:

message-name (x,t)
> if $t_L <= t <= t_N$
>> update state variables
>> send each influencee i *output-message-name* (x_i,t)
>> $t_L = t$
>> $t_N = \min tN()$
> else
>> synchronization error

internal-event-notice (t)
> if $t = t_N$
>> find the child objects with minimum t_N
>> SELECT one, send it *internal-event-notice* (t)
>> $t_L = t$
>> $t_N = \min tN$
> else
>> synchronization error.

Notes: • When a "send" statement is encountered, processing halts until the receiver is done.

• mintN() is a function setting t_N to the minimum t_N of the Coordinator's child objects.

• SELECT provides the tie-breaker rule when two or more objects have the same t_N.

5.5.3. Modeling Application: Manufacturing Control Systems

To illustrate CMF, we use an example based on a case study (see [2, pp. 441–446]). The example illustrates *abstraction by representation*. Other forms of abstraction could be implemented by substituting aggregate versions of Coordinators (e.g., Cells). The case, Planar Company Cell Design, describes the operations of a cell containing a drill press and a lathe

(Figure 5.9). Material handling, loading, and unloading operations are performed by a centrally located robot.

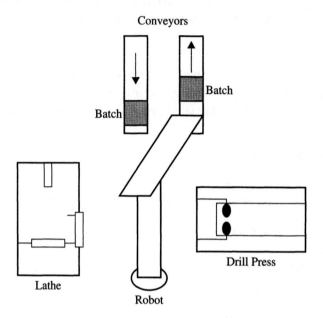

Figure 5.9 Planar Company Cell Design used in CMF application.

We extend the example by assuming that the cell is automated using a hierarchical production control system as proposed by Jones and McLean [15]. The control model contains five levels: Facility, Shop, Cell, Workstation, and Equipment. To simplify the discussion, we consider only the last three levels in the example.

The cell consists of two workstations. The first workstation contains the lathe, and the second contains the drill press. The robot (operator) is shared by the two workstations. Batches of workpieces arrive at the cell, from where they are transferred to the workstations by the robot. Both the cell and the workstations maintain input and output queues (I/O buffers). The cell tries to maintain a given input queue size and a given output queue size for each workstation by placing and removing batches with the help of the robot.

Each machine (lathe or drill press) has a fixed setup time and a fixed processing time. An equipment needs a setup only once at the beginning of the session; the processing time denotes the time to process an individual workpiece within a batch. The operator is responsible for moving batches from the cell input queue to the first workstation input queue, for loading a workpiece of a batch from a workstation input queue into the equipment, for unloading the processed workpiece, for moving batches from the output queue of the first workstation to the input queue of the second workstation, and for moving batches from the second workstation output queue to the cell output queue.

Motivations for Multilevel Approach

The manufacturing control architecture in the application itself suggests a hierarchical modeling approach. The primary advantage is the consistency among the physical system, conceptual model, and software implementation. The multilevel framework also allows a straightforward substitution of abstract model components for detailed model components. For example, suppose that system designers are in the early stages of designing a new manufacturing cell that will be added to an existing set of manufacturing cells. The information to model the existing manufacturing cells in detail is available. However, the configuration of the new cell has not yet been determined. Using top-down design techniques, the designers could begin determining feasible design parameters with abstract or aggregate versions of the new cell model component, without needing to first specify each subcomponent in detail.

Classification Structure

The classification structure of the application is shown in Figure 5.10. The fundamental object class, CObject, provides certain Visual C++ [18] language-specific services such as diagnostic output and compatibility with libraries of "collection classes" such as doubly linked lists. The latter feature is the most important for our purposes as linked lists are used to model queues.

The next level in the classification structure consists of the object classes Batch and ModelObject. A batch is the level at which units of production are modeled. A ModelObject is an abstract simulation-object class that currently provides generic event timing attributes and behaviors. ModelObjects may be specialized into "Atoms" and "Coordinators." In the application, Atoms correspond to Equipment Level objects—operators, machines, and input/output queues. They have a direct correspondence to physical movement and manipulation (work) within the actual system. The work is managed and coordinated by specializations of the "Coordinator" object class. Coordinators may manage equipment level objects (as in the case of Workstation objects) or other Coordinators (as in the case of Cell ob-

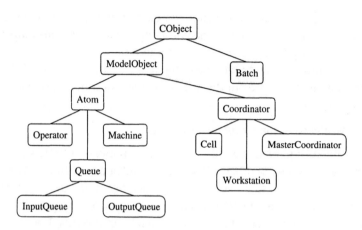

Figure 5.10 Classification structure of CMF application.

jects). Like ModelObject, Coordinator is also an abstract simulation-object class. It provides event timing mechanisms necessary to synchronize the behavior of lower level objects in the assembly structure. It currently also includes certain common batch management functions. All Coordinator classes also have their own input/output buffers (queues).

Assembly Structure

The assembly structure of the application is shown in Figure 5.11. The assembly structure shows the specific objects instantiated in the application and their part–whole relationships.

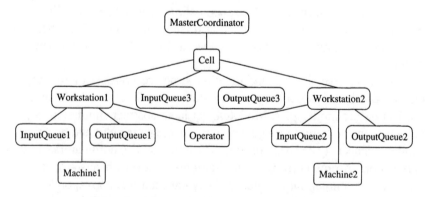

Figure 5.11 Assembly structure of CMF application.

Key Application Methods

The methods used to control the flow of batches are *acceptbatch, needbatch, nextbatch*, and *transfer_batch*. The message *acceptbatch* sends a batch to a

Cell, Workstation, or Queue from a parent Coordinator (Cell or Workstation). The message *needbatch* signals a Cell, Workstation, or Queue that a batch should be sent to its parent Coordinator. This is accomplished with *nextbatch* in most cases, and *transfer_batch* in the case of OutputQueues. These methods are illustrated in the case of a Workstation via pseudocode.

Workstation.

acceptbatch(batch,t)   (sent by Cell)
    if tL <= t <= tN
        send InputQueue *acceptbatch*(batch,t)
        if currentbatch = nil
            send InputQueue *needbatch*(t)
        tL = t
        tN = $mintN()$
    else synchronization error

needbatch(t)   (sent by Cell)
    if tL <= t <= tN
        send OutputQueue *needbatch*(t)
        send Cell *transfer_batch*(transferbatch,t)
        tL = t
        tN = $mintN()$
    else synchronization error

transfer_batch(batch,t)   (sent by OutputQueue)
    if tL <= t <= tN
        transferbatch = batch
    else synchronization error

nextbatch(batch,t)   (sent by InputQueue)
    if tL <= t <= tN
        piececount = 0
        currentbatch = batch
        send Machine *reportstatus*()
        if *reportstatus*() = NOT_SET
            send Cell *oper_request*(id,SETTING,t)
        else
            send Cell *oper_request*(id,LOADING,t)
    else synchronization error

The *nextbatch* method illustrates how requests for the use of a shared resource (the Operator) must be sent through the next level of control (the Cell). Rather than simply telling the Operator to perform an action, the Workstation must send an *oper_request* message to the Cell indicating the type of action desired. There are a number of ways that a Cell might deal with a resource request, including priorities, lookahead, or optimization strategies. In the application, we have implemented a simple FIFO "request queue." That is, if the Operator is currently idle and no other requests are pending, the request is granted immediately via the *use_oper* message. If not, the request is placed at the tail end of a queue of pending resource requests. Whenever the operator completes a task, a new task (if any exists) is selected from the head of the request queue. The Cell's *oper_request* method is illustrated below via pseudocode.

Cell.

oper_request(workstation, usage, t)   (sent by Workstation)
    if tL <= t <= tN
        if (operator-busy = FALSE)
            operator-busy = TRUE
            send workstation *use_oper*(usage, t)
        else add request to request queue
    else synchronization error

All of the methods described thus far fall into the "external event" category. In the prototype, internal events occur at the Operators and Machines. Machines have only one internal event type, workpiece completion. This event is activated as follows:

Machine.

internal_event_notice(t)   (sent by Workstation)
    if ((t = tN) AND (status = BUSY))
        status = IDLE
        tL = t
        tN = INFINITY
        send Workstation *workpiecedone*(t)
    else synchronization error

The Operator has three types of internal events:

Operator.

internal_event_notice(t)   (sent by Workstation)
    if ((t = tN) AND (status = IDLE))
        tL = t
        tN = INFINITY
        if status = SETTING
            status = IDLE
            send Workstation *setupdone*(t)

```
        else if status = LOADING
            status = IDLE
            send Workstation load_done(t)
        else if status = UNLOADING
            status = IDLE
            send Workstation unload_done(t)
    else synchronization error
```

Two methods are used by Coordinators to synchronize internal events, *internal_event_notice* and *mintN*. These operate as follows:

Coordinator (Cell or Workstation).

```
internal_event_notice(t)    (sent by parent Coordinator)
    if (t = tN)
        send minchild internal_event_notice(t)
        tL = t
        tN = mintN()
    else synchronization error

mintN( )        (sent by self)
    tN = INFINITY
    for each child
        send child report_tN()
        if (report_tN() <=tN)
            set tN = report_tN()
            set minchild = child
    return tN
```

5.6.   CONCLUSIONS AND FUTURE DIRECTIONS

This chapter describes multilevel simulation modeling from both a conceptual and a programming perspective. It combines object-oriented techniques with discrete-event simulation to provide multilevel simulations. Examples of simulation programs, written in Smalltalk and C++ style pseudocode for different applications, help to illustrate the important issues involved in developing multilevel simulation capabilities within object-oriented frameworks. These issues include language selection, abstraction mechanisms, control architectures, and object-oriented software design. The examples also provide materials for case studies in object-oriented analysis and design, illustrating the translation of physical objects to software objects. The principles developed in this work could be generalized across object-oriented languages, thereby providing researchers with a general foundation for future work in the area. The models illustrate prototype frameworks for a variety of potential applications.

A near-term goal is to compare the simulated performance of a system under different control architectures, for example, hierarchical versus heterarchical. Initial research could focus on the relative abilities of the two architectures, say, in a manufacturing control application, for handling resource contention under various scenarios. A heterarchical system could be built and its performance compared with that of the current hierarchical CMF prototype on measures such as fault tolerance and response time.

Because of the modularity of the CMF framework, it is feasible to use it in a distributed processing environment. There have been a number of recent advances in the development of interface standards and commercial software for general distributed object computing systems. *Distributed object-oriented simulation* has the potential to improve the design of large and complex systems such as distribution systems, aircraft, telecommunications systems, automobiles, and manufacturing control systems. Distributed processing enables the coordination of and collaboration between design team members, object-oriented modeling improves software engineering practices and network interoperability, and simulation provides risk-reducing predictive analysis. Further, distributed object-oriented simulation can enable realistic integrated training environments providing multiple user interfaces. CMF could be extended to operate in a distributed mode by using commercial distributed object computing software.

Multilevel modeling facilitates closer investigation of the behaviors of models at different levels. Future research will likely explore the comparative effectiveness of various abstraction techniques and mechanisms. Also, so far, creating an abstraction mechanism has been the burden of the user. That responsibility may be more appropriately apportioned by shifting some of it to the system. Part of this problem could be addressed by designing intelligent, friendly interfaces that effectively guide the user in abstracting model components.

References

[1] M. S. Ahn and T. G. Kim, "Simulation message-routing algorithms for hypercubes using DEVSIM++," in T. Beaumariage and C. Roberts, Eds., *Proc. Object-Oriented Simulation Conf.*, La Jolla, CA, Jan. 1993, pp. 137–142.

[2] R. G. Askin and C. R. Standridge, *Modeling and Analysis of Manufacturing Systems*. New York: Wiley, 1993.

[3] R. Belanger, "MODSIM II—A modular, object-oriented language," in *Proc. 1990 Winter Simulation Conf.*, New Orleans, LA, 1990, pp. 118–122.

[4] D. Bobrow, Ed., *Qualitative Reasoning about Physical Systems.* Cambridge, MA: MIT Press, 1986.

[5] G. Booch, *Object-Oriented Design with Applications.* New York: Benjamin Cummings, 1991.

[6] J. Boukachour, "Job shop simulation based on object-oriented programming," in *Proc. Object-Oriented Simulation Conf.*, Newport Beach, CA, Jan. 1992, pp. 8–12.

[7] P. Buchholz, "Definition of submodels and classification of aggregates," Integrated Modelling Support Environment (IMSE) Rep. R5.4-1, Version 2, Univ. Dortmund, Germany, 1989.

[8] P. Coad and E. Yourdon, *Object-Oriented Analysis.* Englewood Cliffs, NJ: Prentice-Hall, 1991.

[9] O. Dahl and K. Nygaard, "SIMULA—An ALGOL-based simulation language," *Commun. ACM*, vol. 9, Sept. 1966, pp. 349–395.

[10] D. Dilts, N. Boyd, and H. Whorms, "The evolution of control architectures for automated manufacturing systems," *J. Manufacturing Syst.*, vol. 10, no. 10, 1991, pp. 79–93.

[11] P. Fishwick, "The role of process abstraction in simulation," *IEEE Trans. Syst., Man, Cybern.*, vol. 18, Jan./Feb. 1988, pp. 18–39.

[12] P. Fishwick, "SimPack: Getting started with simulation programming in C and C++," Tech. Rep. TR92-022, Comput. and Inform. Sci., Univ. Florida, Gainesville, 1992.

[13] A. Goldberg and D. Robson, *Smalltalk-80: The Language.* Reading, MA: Addison-Wesley, 1989.

[14] N. Hilton, "An overview of the ERIC simulation language," in *Proc. Object-Oriented Simulation Conf.*, Newport Beach, CA, Jan. 1992, pp. 52–56.

[15] A. T. Jones and C. R. McLean, "A proposed hierarchical control model for automated manufacturing systems," *J. Manufacturing Syst.*, vol. 5, no. 1, 1986, pp. 15–25.

[16] G. Lomow and D. Baezner, "A tutorial introduction to object-oriented simulation and SIM++," in *Proc. 1990 Winter Simulation Conf.*, New Orleans, LA, 1990, pp. 149–153.

[17] S. Mathewson, "DRAFT," Dep. Management Sci., Imperial College of Sci. and Technol., London, England, 1977.

[18] Microsoft Corp., *Microsoft Visual C++ Development System for Windows: Programmer's Guides*, 1993.

[19] S. Y. Nof, "Is all manufacturing object-oriented?" in *Proc. Int. Conf. Object-Oriented Manufacturing Syst.*, Calgary, Alta., Canada, May 1992, pp. 37–54.

[20] C. Overstreet, "Using graphs to translate between world views," in *Proc. 1987 Winter Simulation Conf.*, 1987, pp. 582–589.

[21] T. Poggio and F. Girosi, "Networks for approximation and learning," *Proc. IEEE* (Special Issue on Neural Networks, I: Theory and Modeling), vol. 78, Sept. 1990, pp. 1481–1497.

[22] D. Popken, "Hierarchical modeling and process aggregation in object-oriented simulation," *Int. J. Comput. Simulation*, vol. 4, no. 1, 1994, pp. 1–19.

[23] D. Popken and A. P. Sinha, "An integrative framework for multi-level modeling of discrete systems," in C. Herring et al., Eds., *Proc. Object-Oriented Simulation Conf.*, Tempe, AZ, Jan. 1994, pp. 139–144.

[24] H. Schwetman, "Introduction to process-oriented simulation and CSIM," in *Proc. 1990 Winter Simulation Conf.*, New Orleans, LA, 1990, pp. 154–157.

[25] A. Srivastava and R. Ragade, "Object-oriented simulation of a SIMD computer using OMT and DEVS methodology," in C. Herring et al., Eds., *Proc. Object-Oriented Simulation Conf.*, Tempe, AZ, Jan. 1994, pp. 161–166.

[26] D. Taylor, "Using classes as high-level modules," *Object*, vol. 3, May/June 1993, pp. 14–16.

[27] P. Wegner, "Concepts and paradigms of object-oriented programming," *OOPS Messenger*, vol. 1, no. 1, 1990, pp. 7–87.

[28] B. P. Zeigler, *Multifacetted Modelling and Discrete Event Simulation*. New York: Academic, 1984.

[29] B. P. Zeigler, "DEVS-scheme: A Lisp-based environment for hierarchical, modular discrete event models," Tech. Rep. AIS-2, CERL Lab., Dep. ECE, Univ. Arizona, Tucson, 1986.

[30] B. P. Zeigler, *Object-Oriented Simulation with Hierarchical, Modular Models*. San Diego, CA: Academic, 1990.

Chapter 6

Design Strategies for Object-Oriented Simulation Testbeds that Support Software Integration

Michael L. Hilton

Department of Computer Science
University of South Carolina
Columbia, SC, USA

Craig S. Anken

U.S. Air Force Command
Rome Laboratory
Griffiss AFB, NY, USA

Editor's Introduction

We have investigated Object-Oriented Simulation techniques. But in the real world, systems must be designed, implemented, integrated, and tested. To ensure interoperability, it is often desirable to integrate automated decision tools into a simulation testbed to provide a realistic testing environment. There are two basic approaches to the design and implementation of simulation test beds: 1) an ad hoc approach to integrate existing systems that were not constructed with interoperability in mind, and 2) a deliberate approach in which systems are designed to communicate and cooperate via a common protocol.

In the ad hoc approach, each system must somehow be encapsulated and connected together. We will present a detailed account of a particular software integration environment, the Advanced AI Technology Testbed (AAITT). At the core of the AAITT is a generic object-oriented simulation capability.

The deliberate design approach is the most effective when the systems to be integrated all operate within the same restructed domain. A case study will be presented.

In addition to systems integration, there are some other concerns that must be addressed in the design of a simulation testbed. The testbed must be easily reconfigured to explore alternatives. Metrics and statistics on various aspects of the routine performance of each system must be collected and analyzed. The interactions between component systems must be observable and have the capability for debug.

6.1.   INTRODUCTION

For a variety of reasons, software components which are intended to operate together as parts of a larger system are often developed in isolation, far removed from their true operational environment. The testing of such components may be limited, and might not uncover significant errors or scalability problems. In addition, important interoperability issues may have been ignored. To address such concerns, it is often desirable to integrate such software components into a *simulation testbed* that will provide a more realistic testing environment.

Consider, for example, the case of military Command and Control (C^2) decision aids. Each decision aid is developed to solve a relatively narrow problem within the overall C^2 decision-making/management domain. To provide the user with guidance, an aid has sources of data and knowledge stored in some local format, a problem-solving methodology which uses the knowledge to reason over the data, and usually the ability to interact with a user. Testing is generally performed by presenting the aid with predefined scenarios and comparing the results to some standard. While this approach may be adequate in the laboratory setting, what happens when this aid is brought into the operational realm? That is, what happens when it is brought into an environment where information it needs may be stored in several databases at different geographic locations, and where multiple decision aids and/or conventional programs are working on various portions of the overall problem? Finally, how reliable will this system be, having been developed in isolation thousands of miles from the battlefield?

Aircraft mission planning is an example of a typical military problem domain which requires the use of multiple cooperating decision aids. To develop a viable plan which coordinates dozens or possibly hundreds of aircraft missions might require the use of one system which manages the availability of resources such as aircraft, personnel, and ordnance, a second system which performs route planning and airspace management, and a third system for monitoring enemy threats. These three systems need to share information and coordinate their activities. Some sort of simulation capability is also necessary to test how well these systems perform under a variety of conditions.

To thoroughly and realistically exercise C^2 decision aids, it is necessary to integrate them into a simulation testbed, such as that shown in Figure 6.1. The challenge is to integrate disparate systems, which have been developed in isolation and run on a variety of hardware and software platforms, so that they can cooperate together with a minimum of modification.

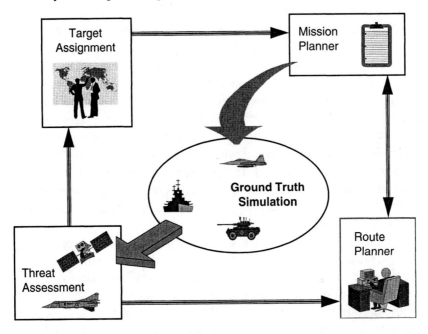

Figure 6.1 An example of a simulation testbed for military command and control experiments.

The development and testing of computer-integrated manufacturing systems is another area which can benefit from simulation testbeds [1], [2]. A computer-integrated manufacturing system is generally a collection of distributed computer systems and manufacturing devices, such as robots, numerically controlled machines, and materials-handling systems. A hierarchy of distributed, real-time control programs orchestrates the activities of the manufacturing devices. During the design, development, and testing of these control programs, it is not practical—and quite possibly hazardous—to use actual manufacturing devices. Instead, software simulations of these devices can be used. The individual device simulations may or may not be integrated together as part of a unified work cell or factory floor simulation.

This chapter identifies some of the issues involved in the construction of a simulation testbed for exercising and testing integrated software systems, and describes some ways of dealing with these issues. An in-depth case study of a testbed design environment is also presented.

6.2.   TESTBED INTEGRATION STRATEGIES

There are two basic approaches to the design of a testbed: an *ad hoc approach* that must be used when trying to integrate existing systems that were not constructed with interoperability in mind, and a *deliberate approach* in which systems are designed to communicate and cooperate via a common protocol. In the ad hoc approach, existing systems must somehow be encapsulated, connected together, and convinced to cooperate with each other. Economic factors and constraints imposed by the existing systems usually force a particular architecture on the testbed. In the deliberate approach, the component systems are designed with integration in mind, resulting in a more flexible and robust testbed. The deliberate design approach is most effective when the systems to be integrated all operate within some restricted domain; this facilitates the development of communications protocols and the sharing of resources.

In addition to the usual systems integration issues, there are other concerns that must be addressed in the design of a simulation testbed. How can the testbed be easily reconfigured to explore alternatives? How can metrics and statistics on various aspects of the run-time performance of each system be collected and analyzed? How do you observe (and possibly debug) the interactions between component systems? Which simulation architectures support the testbed concept best? Before turning our attention to these testbed-specific issues in Section 6.3, a case study of a testbed design environment, we first discuss some of the issues associated with any software integration effort.

6.2.1.   Integrating Software Systems

Building on the work of Nilsson *et al.* [3], we describe five dimensions of systems integration which are useful when comparing testbed designs:

1. *Integration Technology:* The "glue" that integrates the component systems by providing mechanisms for transporting data between systems and initiating actions in other systems.

2. *Component Architecture:* How the architecture of a component system influences the sharing of data and functionality with other systems.

3. *Semantic Integration:* Reconciling the semantic content of data in different systems.

4. *Control Strategy:* How the various systems in a testbed cooperate.

5. *User Interface Integration:* How the integrated system looks to the end user.

Different levels of integration may be achieved within each dimension; for example, a testbed may have a high level of semantic integration, but only a low level of integration technology. While these five dimensions are not orthogonal, they are independent enough to be discussed separately.

Integration Technology

The integration technology is the glue that is used to integrate the component systems together. The integration technology must provide the communications services which allow software systems to share data and control. Integration technologies range from the manual execution of testbed components and transfer of data by hand (a low level of integration technology) to distributed processing substrates that support the transparent exchange of data and control via message passing (a high level of integration technology), with a myriad of possibilities in between. Each of these levels of integration technology has advantages and disadvantages.

A low level of integration technology implies slow and possibly unreliable communication between systems, such as manual execution and data transfer. Manual integration has the advantages that it is extremely flexible, does not require that systems be able to directly communicate with each other, and has few or no development costs. The disadvantages are that it is time-consuming, error-prone, and may require highly skilled human operators. Although it may seem primitive, manual integration is probably the most widely used integration technology of all. Manual integration is quite appropriate for testbeds that are used infrequently, and in situations where the testbed components change very often.

A slightly higher level of integration technology is to use files for inter-systems communication and scripts or batch files to control the execution of the different systems components. A disadvantage of this approach is that the integrated systems are "passive" and cannot interact directly with each other [3]. A related technique for integrating passive systems is to use a common database through which the systems pass all information. One advantage of using a common database is that it encapsulates the communication between the component systems, thereby supporting flexible, modular design. Some disadvantages are that each component system must be designed to work with the database, and initiating and controlling actions in other systems can be difficult. Some experimental databases provide mechanisms for triggering actions in other systems as a result of changes to the database, but to our knowledge, none of the well-known commercially available database systems has such a triggering capability.

A medium level of integration technology is provided by byte-oriented communications facilities such as Unix sockets [4], [5] which allow interprocess communication, and network transport services such as those provided by TCP/IP [6]. These kinds of facilities are now widely available, and many have been standardized, allowing their use in heterogeneous systems.

The highest levels of integration technology allow the transparent (or nearly transparent) communication of both data and control between systems. One way to accomplish this is to implement all of the testbed components in a homogeneous, shared memory environment, such as Lisp [7] or Smalltalk [8]. We have developed several simulation testbeds in this manner. A great disadvantage of this strategy is the difficulty of integrating systems that were not developed in this special environment. Remote procedure calls [9] are another mechanism for a high level of integration technology. Emerging standards for high-level, platform-independent data transfer, such as those found in the upper layers of the ISO Open Systems Interconnection architecture [10], should make it much easier to integrate disparate systems in the future.

Recently, there have been a number of distributed computing environments developed that support the creation and execution of distributed applications on heterogeneous machines [11]–[13]. These environments support an object model of computation, and allow the communication of data and control information between systems via message passing. Cronus [14], [11], a distributed computing environment of this type, was chosen by Rome Laboratory as the substrate upon which to build the Advanced Artificial Intelligence Technology Testbed, which will be described in Section 6.3. As distributed computing environments like these become more readily available, they will have a significant impact on systems integration efforts.

Component Architecture

The architecture of each component system in a testbed influences how easy or difficult systems integration will be. The more open a component's architecture, the easier it is to integrate with other systems. By openness, we mean that a component has well-defined, explicit interfaces that make its functionality and data accessible to other systems. In contrast, a closed system acts like a "black box" whose functionality and data can only be accessed through its user interface. Closed systems can be extremely difficult to integrate with other systems. If the desired data and functionality cannot be accessed through the user interface, costly software modifications may be needed to provide the necessary access.

Providing access to a system's data is usually easier to accomplish than providing access to the system's functionality, especially if the system was not originally designed with integration in mind. If a system stores its data in an external database, then access can be provided using the database management system and query language. If the data are stored in some form internal to the system, it may not be too difficult to modify the system so that it can write (read) data to (from) a file, which can be used to communicate with other systems.

When multiple systems share data, care must be taken to avoid problems of semantic and temporal consistency. Semantic consistency will be dealt with shortly. Temporal consistency problems are usually caused by allowing different systems to each have a copy of the same shared data. If one system changes the data, the other systems will need to be notified so they can update their copy of the data. Implementing such a notification and update scheme can be expensive and is error-prone.

Rather than try to synchronize multiple local copies of data, it is often preferable to eliminate the duplication by keeping only one global copy of the data. One way to do this is to store the shared data in a single database that is accessed by all of the systems. While this may require substantial modification to some of the component systems, the technology required to manage communication with the database is well developed and readily available. A disadvantage of this approach is that accessing the common database may become a performance bottleneck. A different approach is to distribute the data among the systems, without duplication. If a system needs a piece of data that it does not "own," it must request the data from the system that owns the data. This approach may also require substantial modification to the component systems, and implies that at least a medium level of integration technology is available.

Providing access to a system's functionality is often impossible without making major software modifications, unless the system was designed with an open architecture. Open architectures promote the idea of systems as providers of services that may be accessed by clients, regardless of whether the clients are humans or other systems. The current trend in software engineering is toward open systems, and this trend is being supported by recent developments in object-oriented design and implementation techniques [15]. The effective use of object-oriented technology leads naturally to open systems, in which access to both data and functionality is provided through well-defined, explicit interfaces.

Having well-defined, explicit interfaces in an open system is not enough to ensure easy integration with other systems. What is also needed is some way to invoke the functionality from within another system. This implies that a medium to high level of integration technology should be used. At the medium level of integration technology, an open system must provide a front-end "command interpreter" of some sort to translate requests from a client into actions by the server, and to return usable information to the client. This is not difficult technically, but modifying the command interpreter each time a new service is desired is tiresome. A higher level of integration technology, such as remote procedure calls or object-based operating systems, allows direct invocation of functionality.

Semantic Integration

If multiple systems are going to share data, they must all agree on what those data mean, and perhaps how they are represented. Likewise, if multiple systems are going to communicate with each other, they must all agree on the communications protocol to be used. Both of these issues fall under the banner of semantic integration. Ensuring the semantic consistency of data across component systems can be a very difficult task. For one thing, it requires that the data semantics in the various systems be known; for many systems, documentation about such matters is poor or nonexistent. Semantic consistency of communication is often much easier to attain, and is usually a matter of obtaining agreement between those performing the integration task to adhere to some explicitly defined and documented protocol. Effective use of national and international computing standards can ease the task of semantic integration [16].

Semantic integration of data covers a broad range of concerns. At the relatively simple level are concerns about things like units of measure—for example, if velocity information is stored in meters per second or miles per hour. When common databases are used, the major concern is that the systems sharing the database properly understand the schema used to store the data. At a higher level, semantic integration must reconcile the basic concepts underlying different systems; for example, in a manufacturing testbed, the process models used by different component systems should be consistent. In general, the lower the level of a semantic disagreement, the easier it is to reconcile.

Two fortunate aspects of semantic integration are: 1) only the data which are shared by systems need to be reconciled, and 2) much of the reconciliation can be done by the communications interface which connects the applications. For example, the conversion of units or reformatting of data can be performed automatically when the data are transmitted between systems with different data semantics.

Control Strategy

The control strategy prescribes how the component systems in a testbed cooperate, and thus it has a major impact on testbed integration. There are basically two strategies for cooperation: centralized and decentralized control. Each strategy is characterized by the amount of knowledge each component system must have about the other components versus the degree of central control present in the testbed. Each strategy has its good and bad points.

Centralized testbeds are based on the concept of some type of controlling agent which coordinates the execution of individual component systems, and through which all information and data exchange takes place (see Figure 6.2). Individual components do not need to know information about the other components present in the testbed. Examples of centralized control include the blackboard [17], information broker, and metalevel controller architectures [18]. Centralized control facilitates the sharing of

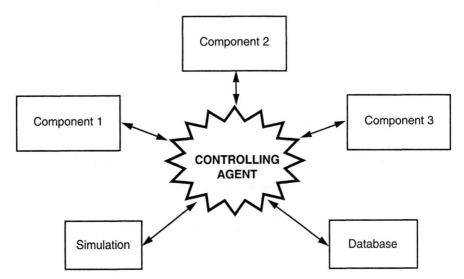

Figure 6.2 The centralized control strategy uses a controlling agent to coordinate execution and communication among the testbed components.

global data through a common database; while this aids in system recon-
figurability and extendibility, resulting bottlenecks can become a problem.

In a decentralized testbed, information flow and data exchange do not
travel through a common agent. The most popular examples of decentralized control are hardwired and broadcast architectures. In a hardwired
testbed, the component systems cooperate through direct calls to one another [19] (see Figure 6.3). Each component in the testbed is required to
know a lot about the other testbed components. In a broadcast system, each
component is connected to a common communication channel and uses
a common data representation (see Figure 6.4). Information requests are
broadcast over the channel, and any component that can service a particular type of request will do so. The decentralized approach can provide
more efficient distributed processing, but the sharing of global data and
reconfiguring the testbed are difficult.

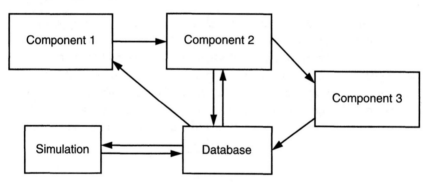

Figure 6.3 Testbed components communicate data and control directly in the hardwired
control strategy.

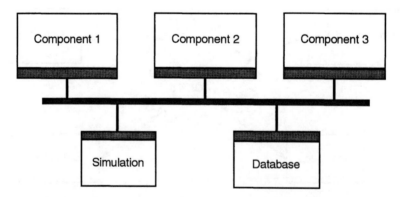

Figure 6.4 In a broadcast system, components are viewed as providers of
services. The shaded areas are component-to-network protocol interfaces.

Which control strategy to choose for a particular testbed situation depends on which one provides the most efficient and economical solution to the specific problems at hand. While all of the strategies mentioned have their advantages, they each have disadvantages as well. Problems such as extensibility, modularity, scalability, and performance bottlenecks are areas where each of these strategies, at some point, begin to fail.

User Interface Integration

When integrating a number of component systems into a testbed, one is confronted with the problem of managing the user interfaces provided by each of the components. This issue is particularly important in the case of distributed testbeds, where the component systems are run on different computers, and may even be separated geographically by large distances.

The lowest level of user interface integration is to simply leave the interfaces as is, and require a user to be present for each component system that needs user interaction. This solution is usually impractical, and it severely limits a testbed's utility.

A modest level of user interface integration is to redirect the component user interfaces to a limited number of workstations (perhaps just a single workstation), requiring fewer people to run the testbed. For example, interfaces built using the X Window System [20] can be operated transparently over a network.

Merely redirecting the component user interfaces is often not what is really desired. In many situations, it is desirable to *eliminate* a component's user interface entirely—that is, to separate the user interface from the component's functional interface—so that it is not necessary to know how to operate a particular component in order to run the testbed. This is particularly true for testbeds that are designed to support the exploratory development of new algorithms and technologies. For example, using a testbed designed to support experiments in the planning domain, a researcher who is developing a new temporal reasoning system might wish to incorporate this system into the testbed to observe how well it works with various plan generators under some standard scenario. It is unreasonable to require a researcher to learn how to operate all of the other components in the testbed; the researcher should only have to adhere to the functional interfaces of the particular systems with which the temporal reasoner communicates. The separation of a system's user interface from its functionality requires that a high level of integration technology be available to the testbed, and it is often impossible to accomplish economically with existing systems.

6.3.   THE AAITT: AN ENVIRONMENT
FOR BUILDING AD HOC TESTBEDS

To facilitate the development of ad hoc simulation testbeds, Rome Laboratory has sponsored the creation of the Advanced Artificial Intelligence Technology Testbed (AAITT). The AAITT provides a set of software integration tools that help encapsulate component systems and allow communication and coordination between components. Because no one control strategy is suitable for every testbed, the AAITT provides a "soft architecture" which allows a testbed to be configured and reconfigured until a desirable architecture is found. The AAITT allows a user to:

- Easily configure various application suites by providing tools to add or delete user-supplied software components and to modify the communication paths between various components.

- Control the execution of distributed testbeds from a single workstation.

- Observe and trace component actions and interactions.

- Select, gather, and view metrics and statistics on run-time performance.

- Rapidly change the flavor of the interactions among the components of the suite based upon the results of previous runs.

In addition, the AAITT provides generic database and simulation capabilities that can be tailored to the needs of a particular testbed application.

The components of the AAITT are shown in Figure 6.5. They are: the testbed manager, called the Modeling, Controlling, and Monitoring (MCM) Workstation; various user-supplied software components that are integrated into a testbed; an ORACLE database management system that can be used by the user-supplied software components; and a generic object-oriented simulation facility. These components are connected together via a distributed processing substrate.

6.3.1. Distributed Processing Substrate

The Distributed Processing Substrate (DPS) allows dissimilar software systems—databases, simulations, knowledge-based systems, and conventional software—running on heterogeneous hardware platforms to interact with one another via message passing. The substrate is provided by a combination of the Cronus distributed computing environment [14] and the ABE (A Better Environment) system [21]. Cronus provides heterogeneous

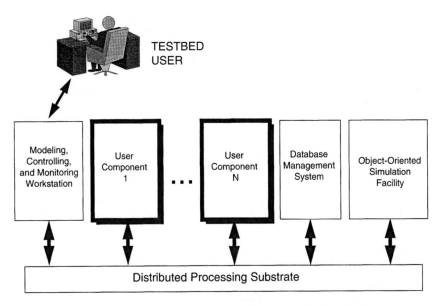

TESTBED
USER

Figure 6.5 The Advanced Artificial Intelligence Technology Testbed.

host support for distributed application development, and gives the user an object-oriented view of resources on a network. The ABE environment supports modules which are independent entities that communicate data and control among themselves through well-defined interfaces. The DPS allows the testbed builder to use the high-level computational and architectural model provided by ABE with the low-level distributed system environment support provided by Cronus.

The most basic responsibility of the DPS is to provide communications channels between testbed components. Each testbed component system must be provided with a Communications Interface Manager (CIM) which encapsulates the component system and serves as its interface with the rest of the testbed (see Figure 6.6). The combination of a software component and its CIM is called an AAITT *module*. The CIM receives and processes all of the DPS messages, which it then relates to its component by whatever means is appropriate. The various alternatives supported by the AAITT for implementing CIM-to-component communications cover the spectrum of integration technologies discussed within Section 6.2.1, including files, pipes, Unix sockets, direct subroutine calls, message passing, and shared memory. All outgoing communication is also funneled through the CIM, which then sends messages to other modules via the DPS. The AAITT provides facilities to aid in the construction of CIMs by guiding

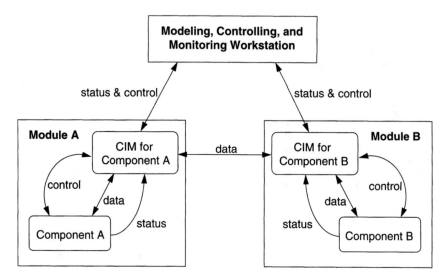

Figure 6.6 The Communications Interface Manager (CIM) interfaces each software component with the rest of the testbed.

the user through the CIM creation process and by providing a library of generic CIMs.

Certain types of outgoing messages may be used to implement concurrency and interprocess synchronization. The DPS is inherently concurrent; it supports multiple modules running concurrently on the same or different physical processor. Interprocess synchronization can be accomplished by using either: 1) remote procedure call messages, in which the calling CIM blocks its component until a reply is received; or 2) asynchronous rendezvous messages, in which the calling CIM allows its component to continue processing while the CIM waits for a reply from the message recipient. When the reply arrives, the CIM holds the reply until the component retrieves it.

The routing of intermodule messages is transparent to the modules, i.e., communication takes place without the modules needing to be aware of on which physical processor they reside. The DPS also provides the transparent translation of certain types of message data to ensure compatibility with the destination's hardware/language environment. For example, the byte ordering of a data item might be changed to accommodate communication between computers with a Big Endian–Little Endian data storage conflict.

Finally, the DPS also gathers data about intermodule message traffic, start and duration times of module execution, the hardware and software resources utilized by each module, and any user-defined monitored values. These data can be analyzed using utilities provided by the MCM Workstation.

The DPS currently runs on Sun workstations, Symbolics Lisp Machines, and VAXes running Unix. The DPS is capable of supporting up to 20 physical processors, each running up to 20 separate AAITT modules.

6.3.2. Modeling, Controlling, and Monitoring Workstation

The MCM Workstation provides a central user console for building and configuring testbeds, controlling testbed execution, and for the display and analysis of performance metrics gathered during application runs.

The modeling functions allow a user to graphically define the architecture of an application by specifying how data and control flow between modules during execution. Functions are also provided for specifying module-specific information, such as the physical location of the module's code and the processor on which the module will execute.

The control functions allow the user to load, initialize, execute, and reset components distributed across the testbed network. Breakpoint capabilities are available to aid in the debugging process.

The monitoring functions of the Workstation allow the user to specify measurements, monitors, and instrumentation. Measurements refer to quantifiable features that help the user understand system performance. Monitors are the procedures through which measurements are captured. Instrumentation allows the user to filter the resulting measurements and present them in an appropriate manner. The monitoring capabilities of the Workstation are very important in testing user-supplied software components and set the AAITT apart from testbeds that simply try to connect existing systems.

6.3.3. Generic Simulation Facilities

The AAITT provides a rich object-oriented environment for constructing simulations for use in exercising a testbed's software components. The ERIC simulation language and environment [22] are provided as the default simulation capability. ERIC is an object-oriented programming language designed to support the development of discrete, event-driven simulations. ERIC combines the pattern matching-based message handling originally found in the ROSS language [23], [24] with the more traditional object-oriented facilities of the Common Lisp Object System (CLOS) [25], [26]. ERIC is built on top of CLOS, extending CLOS in three ways:

- Classes in ERIC are first-class objects; they can have their own attributes and can be sent messages.
- A new type of message passing, based on pattern matching, is provided in addition to CLOS' generic functions.
- Facilities for supporting discrete-event simulations, such as an event-scheduling mechanism, are provided.

The full power of Common Lisp and CLOS can be utilized transparently within ERIC. A set of simulation development tools is provided, including a class browser, an object editor, a run-time instance viewer, and a graphical simulation clock manipulator.

Using these facilities as a substrate, a toolkit for constructing AirLand battle simulations has been constructed. This toolkit includes an object-oriented cartographic database, a map display system, basic air and ground force objects, and a scenario generator/editor. These tools have been used to create LACE (Land and Air Combat in Eric), the simulation which is currently being used to exercise C^2 decision aids at Rome Laboratory.

Classes and Instances

ERIC provides two kinds of software objects: *classes* and *instances*. Classes are used to describe the types of objects in a system and how they behave, while instances model the actual objects in a system. Classes can themselves be members (or *subclasses*) of more general classes (called *superclasses*). A subclass inherits the attributes and behaviors of its super-classes.

The most primitive class in ERIC is called something. Something provides the basic behaviors for all objects, such as how to print attributes, make instances, and define new behaviors. All other classes are built on top of something. New classes are defined with the DEFINE-CLASS special form. For example, a class called moving-object can be defined which has an x and y coordinate, a heading (whose default value is 0°), a current speed, and a maximum speed of 5 m/s:

```
(define-class moving-object
    (:parents something)
    (:documentation "Basic class for objects that move in two
                     dimensions.")
    (:class-attributes
        (maximum-speed 5))
    (:instance-attributes
        x y (heading 0) speed))
```

The :parents field specifies the new class' superclasses, which determine the attributes and behaviors that will be inherited. The optional

:documentation field can be used to supply a string which describes the new class. The :class-attributes field is used to declare attributes which belong only to the class object; they are not inherited by instances of the class. Class attributes can be used to store any type of information, but are generally used for storing information that is common to all members of the class. The :instance-attributes field declares the attributes which an instance of the defined class will have in addition to those it inherits.

An instance of the class moving-object can be created by sending the class a "make instance" message of the form

```
(ask moving-object make instance x)
```

where x is the name you wish to give the instance. A slightly different message allows you to specify initial values for the object's instance attributes:

```
(ask moving-object make instance x with {attribute value}+).
```

To create an object called George located at the origin and moving at a speed of 2 m/s with the default heading of $0°$, one could evaluate the form

```
(ask moving-object make instance George with x 0 y 0 speed 2).
```

Class objects keep track of all their created instances, and provide behaviors for iterating and filtering across the instances. For example, the following message causes a description of all the instances of moving-object to be printed:

```
(ask moving-object to ask your instances to print yourself).
```

Behaviors, Messages, and Methods

In addition to having attributes, objects are also capable of performing computations and communicating with one another. In ERIC, there are two mechanisms for doing this: *behaviors* and *methods*. Both of these mechanisms are a form of indirect function call, but one emphasizes expressiveness and the other emphasizes efficiency.

Behaviors.   A behavior is a class-specific procedure which is associated with a special sequence of symbols, called a *message*. Behaviors are invoked by sending messages to objects. Messages are sent to objects via the ASK special form, whose syntax is

```
(ask object message)
```

where *object* is either an ERIC class or instance object and *message* is the sequence of symbols denoting the message being sent to the object. For example, to find out George's current speed, we would send George the message

        (ask George recall your speed).

When an object receives a message, it executes the behavior that is associated with the most specific pattern that matches the message.

The expressive freedom provided by pattern matching allows programs to be written in a flexible, natural languagelike syntax. This makes ERIC easy to learn, and allows one to write code which can be easily understood by most nonprogrammers. Our experience has shown that these qualities help to gain end-user acceptance of simulations, and support the verification and validation of simulations by domain experts who may not be computer experts.

Behaviors are defined by sending a class object a message of the form

        (ask *class* when receiving *pattern actions*)

where *pattern* is a list specifying the message this behavior is to handle and *actions* is zero or more Lisp forms that are to be evaluated when the behavior is invoked. A message pattern is a sequence of symbols which may be either literals or variables. Variable symbols are prefixed by either a greater-than sign (>) or a plus sign (+). Variables prefixed by a ">" will match single forms such as an atom or a parenthesized list; variables prefixed by a "+" will match any number of consecutive atoms or lists. Pattern variables serve as a behavior's formal parameters; when a behavior is selected for execution, the pattern variables are bound by the matcher to the corresponding form in the message pattern. It is also permissible to use the ">" and "+" by themselves as wildcard variables which form no bindings.

For example, a behavior for increasing the speed of a moving-object instance could be written as follows:

```
(ask moving-object when receiving (increase your speed by >N meters
per second)
    (let ((new-speed (+ N (ask self recall your speed))
        (max-speed (ask self recall the maximum-speed for your
                    class))))
      (ask self set your speed to !(min max-speed new-speed)))).
```

The formal parameter for this behavior is N, which matches to a single item in the passed message because it is prefixed with a greater-than sign; within the body of the behavior, the N is used without this prefix. The exclamation mark (!) in the final line of the definition tells ERIC to evaluate the immediately following form before sending the message. (The exclamation mark is necessary because ASK is a Lisp macro which does not evaluate its arguments. If you wish to include in a message forms that do get evaluated, you must mark the forms with an evaluation prefix character.)

In addition to behaviors, ERIC provides before and after daemons, wrappers, a message trace facility, and a message recording facility, all of which support the pattern-matching paradigm. For example, you can trace invocations of all of moving-objects's messages that contain the symbol "right" with the message

```
(ask moving-object trace your messages matching (+ right +)).
```

These facilities are associated with message patterns, not with any particular behavior. Thus, they need not use the same exact pattern as any defined behavior. It is possible that one daemon may service many behaviors, and vice versa.

Methods.   Methods are class-specific procedures that are associated with a single symbol and are invoked just like a function call. The methods in ERIC are actually CLOS methods, both in their definition and implementation. Therefore, one could define a method for moving forward *n* meters as follows:

```
(defmethod move ((self moving-object) n)
    (with-slots (x y heading) self
        (setq x (* n (cosine heading)))
        (setq y (* n (sine heading)))))).
```

Why have both behaviors and methods?   Because each style has strengths and weaknesses. Behaviors provide a rich expressive capability that lets one encode procedural knowledge in an easily understood format, but the pattern matching involved in message passing is expensive. Methods are efficient and fast, but not very expressive. When should one use each? Methods should be used for mundane housekeeping chores (such as graphics) and in places where speed is important; behaviors should be used everywhere else.

Scheduling Events

Objects alone do not make a simulation; there must also be a temporal control mechanism which allows objects to interact over time. In ERIC, this mechanism is provided by the clock object. The clock controls the flow of time in a simulation, allowing actions to be scheduled for future execution. The clock is an instance of the class simulation-clock, which has three instance attributes: *simtime, event-list,* and *ticksize.*

Simtime is the current time in the simulation. Time is represented as a dimensionless integer. It is up to the programmer to decide what unit (if any) is to be associated with time, and to use this unit consistently throughout all object behaviors.

The *event-list* is a data structure which maintains the list of actions that have been scheduled to happen in the future. The clock moves forward in time by executing events in the event-list.

The clock allows a simulation to be stopped at regular intervals or run for a specific period of time. When the clock is sent a "tick" message, the simulation will run for a length of (simulated) time specified by the clock's *ticksize* attribute.

Two primitive messages are provided for scheduling actions to happen at some future time:

```
(ask clock to schedule object to action at time)
```

and

```
(ask clock to schedule object to action in x time units).
```

The first message schedules an action at some absolute time; the second schedules an action relative to the time when the message is sent. *Action* can be any message that *object* can handle. For example, we could ask the object George to increase its speed two time units from now:

```
(ask clock to schedule George
        to (increase your speed by 3 meters per second)
        in 2 time units)
```

The simulation programmer is free to define new scheduling behaviors which use the primitive scheduling behaviors. For example, one might wish to define a behavior with the message "schedule *object* to *action* in x hours and y minutes."

To support the use of artificial intelligence planning techniques, ERIC allows each object to efficiently manipulate its own scheduled events. Scheduled events are stored in the form of plans which contain three pieces of information: the action to be performed, the time when the action is to be performed, and who scheduled the action. Several behaviors are provided to manipulate an object's schedule. For instance:

- "recall your schedule" returns a list of the receiving object's plans;

- "forget your plans matching *pattern*" removes all of the plans whose action matches *pattern* from the receiving object's schedule;

- "forget your plans after time x," which removes all of the receiving object's plans that are scheduled to occur after time x.

These facilities can be used to implement "reactive" simulations capable
of sophisticated, contingency-based plan execution.

6.4.   RECOMMENDATIONS

Every simulation testbed is unique, with different goals, budgets, and component systems. Therefore, it is impossible to give specific recommendations on how to best structure a generic testbed. We have participated in
or observed the successful construction of simulation testbeds using all of
the integration technologies and strategies discussed in this chapter, and no
two of the resulting testbed architectures have been alike.

In ad hoc testbeds where few (if any) of the component systems were
built with integration in mind, often all one can do is cobble together a minimal testbed that is brittle and limited in capability. If the component systems were built using external data storage (such as a relational database),
the integration task becomes easier, and if the systems were designed to be
open or built using object-oriented techniques, the integration task becomes
easier still.

Based on our experiences using the ad hoc approach to testbed design,
we can make general recommendations to those embarking on the deliberate approach to testbed design for each of the five dimensions of systems
integration.

Integration Technology. Use as high a level of integration technology as possible. If your testbed is to be distributed across
multiple machines, build the testbed on top of a distributed processing substrate that will handle the intersystems communication in as
transparent a way as possible. Using a high level of integration technology does not ensure that integration will be easy or successful,
but it supports the development of open systems which will ease the
cost of integration. Whenever possible, use standardized services, languages, and tools; this helps ensure future compatibility with other
systems.

Component Architecture. Build open systems. Even if it initially
costs more to create an open system, there will be substantial savings
in long-term integration and maintenance costs. Design component
systems so their functionality is accessible separately from their user
interface. If the testbed is to serve a limited application domain, design
common protocols and data semantics before building the components.
Also, provide modules to perform common services rather than dupli-
cate such functionality within components.

Semantic Integration. Again, design a common data semantics before building component systems. If the integration technology can perform any required data translations easily, it is not necessary that every component have exactly the same data semantics. Utilize standard communications protocols such as those described in the ISO Open Systems Interconnection documents—avoid developing a unique local protocol if possible. Although the local protocol might appear more suitable, the use of standard protocols will provide better support for future growth and portability of the testbed and its component systems.

Control Strategy. Because one control strategy is not suitable for all testbeds, or even at all stages of a single testbed's life cycle, plan ahead for flexibility. Using a high level of integration technology and designing open systems support flexible control strategies.

User Interface Integration. Avoid directly tying the functionality of a component system directly to its interface. Use device-independent I/O protocols such as the X Window System, which supports remote execution of applications across networks, to implement user interfaces.

References

[1] N. B. Hadj-Alouane, J. K. Chaar, and A. W. Naylor, "The design and implementation of the control and integration software of a flexible manufacturing system," in *Systems Integration'90*, IEEE, Apr. 1990, pp. 494–502.

[2] A. W. Naylor and R. A. Volz, "Design of integrated manufacturing system control software," *IEEE Trans. Syst., Man, Cybern.*, vol. SMC-17, Nov./Dec. 1987, pp. 881–897.

[3] E. G. Nilsson, E. K. Nordhagen, and G. Oftedal, "Aspects of systems integration," in *Systems Integration'90*, IEEE, Apr. 1990, pp. 434–443.

[4] W. R. Stevens, *UNIX Network Programming*, Englewood Cliffs, NJ: Prentice-Hall, 1990.

[5] Y. Cao, J. H. Graham, and A. S. Elmaghraby, "Communications approaches for simulation–AI interactions," *Simulation Dig.*, vol. 23, Winter 1993, pp. 3–16.

[6] U. D. Black, *TCP/IP and Related Protocols*. New York: McGraw-Hill, 1992.

[7] G. L. Steele, Jr., *Common LISP: The Language*. Digital Press, 1984.

[8] A. Goldberg, *Smalltalk-80: The Language*. Reading, MA: Addison-Wesley, 1989.

[9] A. L. Ananda, B. H. Tay, and E. K. Koh, "A survey of asynchronous remote procedure calls," *Oper. Syst. Rev.*, vol. 26, Apr. 1992, pp. 92–109.

[10] M. T. Rose, *The Open Book: A Practical Perspective on OSI*. Englewood Cliffs, NJ: Prentice-Hall, 1990.

[11] J. R. Nichol, C. T. Wilkes, and F. A. Manola, "Object orientation in heterogeneous distributed computing systems," *IEEE Computer*, June 1993, pp. 57–67.

[12] J. D. Northcutt, *Mechanisms for Reliable Distributed Real-Time Operating Systems: The Alpha Kernel*. Boston, MA: Academic, 1987.

[13] R. Cooper and K. Birman, "Supporting large scale applications on networks of workstations," in *Proc. 2nd Workshop Workstation Oper. Syst.*, Pacific Grove, CA, Sept. 1989, pp. 25–28.

[14] J. C. Berets, N. Cherniak, and R. M. Sands, "An introduction to Cronus," Tech. Rep. 6986, BBN Syst. and Technol. Corp., Jan. 1993.

[15] G. Booch, *Object-Oriented Analysis and Design with Applications*, 2nd ed. Redwood City, CA: Benjamin Cummings, 1994.

[16] D. R. Kuhn, "On the effective use of software standards in systems integration," in *Systems Integration'90*, IEEE, Apr. 1990, pp. 455–461.

[17] P. H. Nii, "Blackboard sytems: The blackboard model of problem solving and the evolution of blackboard architectures," *AI Mag.*, Summer 1986.

[18] M. Grover et al., "Cooperating expert systems (COPES)," Tech. Rep. RADC-TR-90-104, Rome Air Develop. Cen., 1990.

[19] J. Benoit et al., "Airland loosely integrated expert systems: The ALLIES project," Technical Rep. MTR-86W00041, The MITRE Corp., 1986.

[20] R. W. Scheifler and J. Gettys, "The X Window System," *ACM Trans. Graphics*, vol. 5, Apr. 1986, pp. 79–109.

[21] F. Hayes-Roth et al., "Frameworks for developing intelligent systems: The ABE systems engineering environment," *IEEE Expert*, vol. 6, June 1991, pp. 30–40.

[22] M. Hilton and J. Grimshaw, "ERIC manual," Tech. Rep. RADC-TR-90-84, Rome Air Develop. Cen., 1990.

[23] D. McArthur and P. Klahr, "The ROSS language manual," Tech. Rep. RAND Note N-1854-AF, The RAND Corp., 1982.

[24] P. Klahr, "Expressibility in ROSS: An object-oriented simulation system," in *AI Applied to Simulation, Proc. European Conf. at Univ. Ghent*, Soc. for Comput. Simulation, 1986, pp. 136–139.

[25] D. Bobrow et al., "Common Lisp object specification," X3J13 Document 88-002R, 1988.

[26] R. P. Gabriel, J. L. White, and D. G. Bobrow, "CLOS: Integrating object-oriented and functional programming," *Commun. ACM*, vol. 34, Sept. 1991, pp. 28–38.

Chapter 7

Automation of Transformation Schemas for Object-Oriented Simulations[1]

Christopher J. Coomber   *School of Computing and Mathematics*
                         Deakin University, Geelong, Australia

Editor's Introduction ───────────────────────────────

In this chapter, we will examine the automation of transformation schema for object-oriented simulations.

The transformation schema is a modeling notation which extends the common data-flow diagram to include control and timing features. A system modeled as a transformation schema can be executed visually by moving tokens around the schema according to certain rules. As a result, the transformation schema is a powerful tool for modeling and demonstrating the functional and temporal requirements of real-time systems.

The problem of automating transformation schema execution has been tackled in two ways: 1) Petri nets, and 2) time-ordered execution plans.

In this chapter, we report further research on automating transformation schema execution. A novel execution approach based on mapping a transformation schema to a system of interacting objects is presented. The approach addresses quantitative and hierarchical execution and implementation efficiency. The object model derived from a transformation schema serves as a substrate for driving an interactive simulation. We will discuss how such an object model is executed using a unique object-oriented simulation strategy.

7.1.   INTRODUCTION

The design of systems that must adhere to stringent functional and temporal requirements is a difficult exercise. These "real-time" systems are typically

───────────────────

1. Figures 7.3a, 7.4a, 7.4b, 7.4c, and 7.10–.14 are reprinted from "An object-oriented simulation procedure for automating transformation," by C. Coomber, in *International Journal in Computer Simulation* with permission from the author and Ablex Publishing Corporation.

221

very complex, and have very tight operational tolerances and performance constraints [15]. The failure to meet a required constraint, even marginally, can cause a disaster. Furthermore, these systems must always behave in a predictable manner, even in abnormal situations. There are many examples of real-time systems which have gone out of control, for one reason or another, and in the process have killed people and damaged equipment [9].

Simulation has an obvious benefit in the design of real-time systems [4]. It allows the modeling and examination of both normal and abnormal conditions before system implementation to see whether operational constraints are always going to be met. In particular, simulation allows the designer to prototype critical aspects of the system and to test them thoroughly.

In this chapter, we will examine transformation schemas as a means of modeling real-time systems for object-oriented simulations. Transformation schemas are interesting because they can be simulated (or executed) interactively, and they help to validate critical requirements rapidly. We will see how transformation schemas can be mapped to an underlying, automatable simulation model.

7.2.   THE TRANSFORMATION SCHEMA

A transformation schema [17] is an extended data-flow diagram which incorporates control and temporal information. The notation defines graphical constructs for modeling data and control flow, shown in Figure 7.1, syntactic constraints, and execution rules to predict the behavior of a sys-

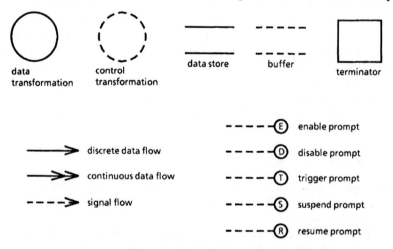

Figure 7.1 Graphical constructs.

tem through interactive simulation. A transformation schema is well suited to modeling stimulus–response systems, and has been used to model, among other things, a bottling factory [16], a car cruise controller [6], and a nuclear reactor control system [7].

7.2.1. Data Flows, Signal Flows, and Prompts

As in data-flow diagrams, flows are directed arcs which carry some form of data from one component to another. However, a transformation schema may contain several types of flows, which are distinguished by the type of data they can carry. A flow may be discrete in nature (its data defined at discrete points in time), or continuous (its data defined continuously over an interval). A flow may be one of the following types: a continuous data flow, a discrete data flow, a signal flow, a trigger, an enable prompt, a disable prompt, a suspend prompt, or a resume prompt. A flow may also split or merge to indicate multiple sources and destinations.

A continuous data flow is drawn as a solid line with a double arrowhead, and is an abstraction of a real-world quantity such as temperature or flow rate. A discrete data flow is drawn as a solid line with a single arrowhead, and is an abstraction of a transient real-world quantity. Both continuous and discrete data flows carry variable data.

In circumstances where it is important to indicate the occurrence of some event, such as "temperature too hot" or "danger," a signal flow is used. This type of flow is drawn as a dashed line with a single arrowhead. The data it carries are discrete, but not variable.

Prompts are special signal flows which represent control imposed by one component on another. There are five types, distinguished by a letter placed in a small circle at the head of the flow. A trigger forces a component to perform a time-discrete action. The enable and disable prompts initiate and terminate the activity of a component. A suspend places the activity of a component in abeyance, and a resume causes a suspended component to continue from where it left off.

7.2.2. Transformations, Stores, and Terminators

The transformation schema notation provides fives types of components for modeling the intended behavior of a system. These components are the data transformation, control transformation, data store, buffer, and terminator.

A data transformation is shown as a circle drawn with a solid line, and represents a basic functional component of a system. A data transformation receives data from its environment, transforms the data according to an internal algorithm (its specification), and then produces outputs. The production of outputs may also be associated with a delay.

A component which directs the operation of other components by sending signals is termed a control transformation, and is shown as a circle drawn with a dashed line. The logic underlying a control transformation may be shown as a state transition diagram, typically a Mealy machine, represented as rectangles (states) connected by directed arcs (transitions). A transition can have conditions (input signal flows disjunctively related) and actions (output signal flows or prompts).

As an example, Figure 7.2 shows part of a transformation schema and the state transition diagram for the control transformation called "control." The state transition diagram is entered through the "off" state and moves to the "on" state when a "start" signal is received, and sends an enable prompt to "process$_1$" and a "go" signal to "process$_2$." From the "on" state, when a "stop" or a "done" signal is received, a disable prompt is sent to "process$_1$."

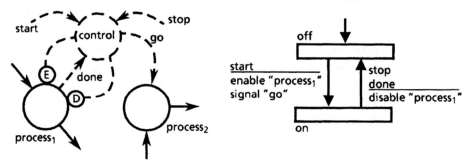

Figure 7.2 A simple transformation schema and the state transition diagram for "control."

Apart from providing constructs for modeling functional behavior, the transformation schema notation also provides storage constructs for modeling information repositories. The first type, the data store, is drawn with a solid pair of horizontal lines and acts as a general file object. The next type, the buffer, is drawn with a dashed pair of horizontal lines and acts as a first-in first-out queue.

Special components called terminators serve to model the environment of a system. They represent real-world devices such as buttons, gauges, and various machines. A terminator may represent anything that is external to the system, but is nevertheless needed for its operation and completeness. Terminators are typically shown as rectangles, but may be depicted as icons or symbols in order to convey their meaning more aptly.

7.2.3. Interactive Execution of Transformation Schemas

Besides being able to construct a static representation of a system, the transformation schema notation provides a method for engaging interactively in the dynamic operation (or execution) of the system. The execution method is based loosely on the execution of a Petri net, and is visualized in terms of token movement (small black squares) around the schema. A token placed on a component indicates some or potential activity, and a token placed on a flow indicates that the flow is carrying data. The interaction between components and flows and the interpretation of token placements are dictated by a number of prescribed rules, which are summarized as follows.

Prior to the first execution step, all data and control transformations that are the destination of an enable prompt are assumed to be disabled; all others are enabled by default. If a data transformation is currently disabled and a token is placed on one of its incoming enable prompts, the token is removed from the prompt, and is placed on the transformation to indicate that it is now enabled. The token indicates that the transformation may produce outputs from available inputs. Furthermore, while a transformation is enabled, each continuous data flow it produces must carry a token. If tokens are now placed on one or more of the incoming flows (except prompts), the transformation may signify the production of an output by placing a token on one or more of its output flows. As long as the input is not a continuous data flow, its token is then removed.

If a token is now put on an incoming disable prompt, the data transformation will be disabled (the token on it is removed), and also, schemas it comprises (its schema hierarchy) will also be disabled (tokens are removed from all flows and components on these schemas).

In the case of a control transformation, a token is associated with the current state of its state transition diagram. Placing a token on an incoming signal flow may cause the transformation to change state. For this to happen, a condition associated with an arc that leaves the current state must be satisfied. If such an arc exists, the token on the current state is moved to the destination state of the arc, thus becoming the new current state. As a result, tokens may be placed on appropriate signal flows and prompts that leave the control transformation to show outputs caused by the state change. Finally, the token is removed from the input flow. If more than one arc could be involved in a state change, the inability of the state diagram to decide which arc to take causes an undesirable deadlock situation.

A token is placed on a buffer for every item of data it contains. Tokens are not placed on data stores because they do not enter directly into the execution of a schema.

7.2.4. Symbolic and Functional Execution

The above execution rules may be carried out in either a symbolic or functional manner. In symbolic execution, tokens have no data values, and activity is based on the structure and interaction among the various components in the schema. Symbolic execution typically employs an execution plan: a table in which a row represents an execution step of token-based interactions at a single point in time. The columns of the table show the parts of each step, including preconditions (token placements caused by preceding steps), output selections to resolve indeterminacies, and resulting token placements.

On the other hand, in functional execution, tokens can carry values, and the specifications of data transformations are actually executed. Therefore, functional execution simulates the qualitative as well as the quantitative elements of execution.

Ideally, the execution of a transformation schema should be entirely automated by computer; otherwise, it becomes very tedious and time consuming. To date, [3] has automated a simple execution plan scheme, [11] a symbolic approach involving Petri nets for single-level transformation schemas, and [8] a functional execution procedure using object-oriented modeling. This last automation procedure, which was developed by the author, is implemented as the simulation kernel of the Schema Execution Environment (SEE) [7].

7.3. THE SEE OBJECT-ORIENTED MODELING SCHEME

The simulation kernel of SEE was developed as part of an ongoing project concerned with mission-critical systems. The object-oriented nature of the kernel facilitates efficient simulation in terms of model design, performance, and future extensibility. The intention of the following discussion is to examine in detail the object-oriented modeling procedure we have used in SEE for expressing a transformation schema in an automatable form. Unlike previous approaches, we have considered as a unified whole hierarchical (multilevel) schemas, functional execution, and computational efficiency.

7.3.1. Objects, Messages, and Inheritance

The design of the simulation kernel was approached from an object-oriented perspective because it seems to be a more natural way of designing a system than the traditional function-oriented approaches. Object-oriented design resembles the way people perceive and interact with the world, which is seen as containing objects that communicate by sending messages.

In contrast to function-oriented design, which is primarily a top-down process involving partitioning, object-oriented design is more of a bottom-up process concentrating on assembling reusable components. However, in practice, a hybrid middle-out approach is normally adopted. Moreover, with libraries of reusable components at hand, significant productivity gains are expected.

Although some authors see object-oriented design as being superior to and superseding other approaches, this view is not shared by the author. Rather, object-oriented design offers a complementary viewpoint [1], [5], [18]. For example, Ward has suggested that object-oriented and functional design could be mixed. Some stages in the design process may be better managed using a functional approach, and other stages with an object-oriented approach.

In order to appreciate how object-oriented design may facilitate modeling, it is important to understand some basic concepts. First, at the center of object-oriented design is the concept of an object. An object provides a mechanism for representing things in the problem domain, while messages invoke operations in the problem domain. An object has its own private data (attributes) and a set of operations for manipulating its data.

An object is requested to perform one of its operations by sending it a message (which may carry parameters). The receiver of the message responds by choosing the operation that implements the message name, executing this operation, and then returning control to the sender. Message sending is represented (in Smalltalk) by placing the message to the right of the object. For example, the expression *circle radius* represents the message *radius* being sent to the object *circle*. C++ and Eiffel show message sending with a dot notation (*circle.radius*).

An object has a number of important properties. First, it is a self-contained entity which has its own private data and its own set of operations. No object can change the private data of some other object, except by sending an appropriate message. Second, an object cleanly encapsulates the operations associated with its private data, and therefore every object has a well-defined communication interface. Third, an object can be modified without propagating changes to other objects. This property is valuable during testing. And fourth, an object is an abstraction mechanism that provides a way to manage complexity.

In relation to this last point, object-oriented design affords a powerful structuring and grouping mechanism—the hierarchical tree structure. Objects can be classified using this concept into what is called an inheritance tree (or class hierarchy). In an inheritance tree, a class of object inherits operations and attributes from the class above it (or superclass). This inheritance extends through increasingly general classes, ultimately ending with the most general class (which is called Object in Smalltalk).

7.3.2. Object Representation

Various notations exist for representing objects (see, for example, [12]). All have their strengths and weaknesses. In the logical design of the SEE simulation kernel, the author has used the notation illustrated in Figure 7.3. The box represents an object (an instance of a particular class) whose attributes refer to other objects by arrows or identifiers. An instance of a class C is termed "a C." When an object is created, all of its attributes initially refer to nothing (or the object nil).

As a concrete example, in Figure 7.3(b), "a MotorBike" denoted as john's_bike refers to two different instances of Wheel via its wheels attribute, and to "an Engine" via its engine attribute. Each Wheel has a diameter of 50 (cm), and the engine has two pistons and a capacity of 500 cm^3. Also, the bike's attribute of "a CollectionOfBikes" refers to john's_bike.

By representing objects and assigning attributes in the above fashion, a system of communicating objects is created. A particular object may then send messages to objects it references.

7.3.3. Classes of Objects in a Hierarchical Transformation Schema

The first step in the logical design of the SEE simulation kernel was to identify objects in a hierarchical transformation schema. Once known, the various classes of objects can be represented in the chosen notation and hierarchically related to one another. Objects identified include the entire transformation schema hierarchy, the individual transformation schemas that make up the hierarchy, and the various kinds of components, such as data and control transformations, stores, terminators, and flows. Each of these objects can be thought of as being members of some class of object.

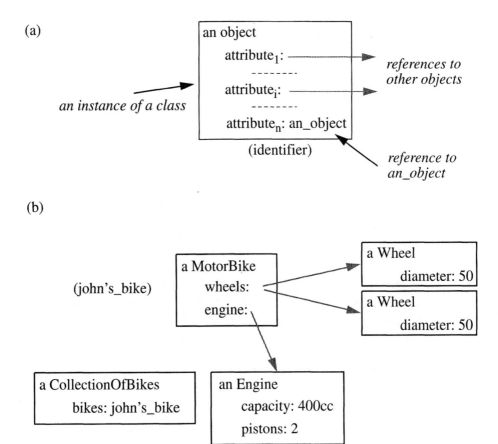

Figure 7.3 (a) General object format. (b) Objects associated with a motorbike.

For example, transformation schema would belong to the class Schema, and discrete data flow to DiscreteDataFlow. The full list is shown in Table 7.1.

The classes in Table 7.1 can be defined in terms of their attributes and messages, and can also be organized into a hierarchy by subsuming classes with like attributes and operations under a common class. For example, DataTransformation and ControlTransformation both represent kinds of transformations, and therefore can be placed under the class Transformation. Store and Buffer represent kinds of storage devices, and can be placed under StorageDevice. Transformation and StorageDevice can be placed under the class Component, which represents a general constructive element.

The different classes of flow can also be organized into a hierarchy. DiscreteDataFlow and ContinuousDataFlow can be subsumed under the class DataFlow (since they both carry data). The different classes of prompts

Table 7.1   Objects to Class

OBJECT	CLASS
Transformation schema hierarchy	TSHierarchy
Transformation schema	Schema
Data transformation	DataTransformation
Control transformation	ControlTransformation
Data store	DataStore
Buffer	Buffer
Terminator	Terminator
Signal flow	SignalFlow
Discrete data flow	DiscreteDataFlow
Continuous data flow	ContinuousDataFlow
Enable prompt	EnablePrompt
Disable prompt	DisablePrompt
Suspend prompt	SuspendPrompt
Resume prompt	ResumePrompt

can be generalized by the class Prompt. DataFlow, SignalFlow, and Prompt can be placed under Flow. Flow and Component can then be placed under the general class SchemaObject whose superclass is Object.

Terminator can also go under SchemaObject, and may be given subclasses to represent external entities, such as bar gauges, lights, buttons, etc. These devices are represented in Table 7.2.

Table 7.2   Subclasses of Terminator

DEVICE	CLASS
A bar gauge	BarGauge
A digital display unit	DigitalDisplay
A light	Light
A button (for sending signals)	SignalButton
A button (for sending values)	DataButton
A keyboard	Keyboard
An external machine (e.g., power station)	ExternalFunction
A continuous data source (e.g., voltage, pressure)	ContinuousSource
An external data repository (e.g., water tank)	ExternalStore

Figure 7.4 illustrates the branches of the class hierarchy discussed thus far. Figure 7.4(a) shows the relationship between the various transformations and stores. Notice that DataTransformation has the subclasses PrimitiveDataTransformation and AbstractDataTransformation. The former represents a data transformation that has a specification (pre- and postcondition rules), and the latter represents a data transformation comprising another

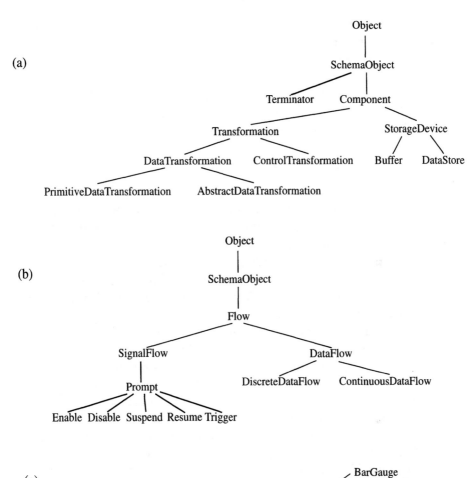

(a)

(b)

(c)

(d)

Figure 7.4 The class hierarchy derived for the transformation schema.

schema. Figure 7.4(b) shows the relationship between the various flows that connect transformations and stores, and Figure 7.4(c) shows the class hierarchy of terminators for modeling external entities. Finally, Figure 7.4(d) shows where TSHierarchy and Schema are in the hierarchy. Observe that each class has a particular line of inheritance. For example, Primitive-DataTransformation inherits attributes and messages from DataTransformation, Transformation, Component, SchemaObject, and Object.

7.3.4. Attributes and Object Mappings

The next step in the logical design is to define attributes for each class, and subsequently model transformation schemas as systems of objects. The attributes of the more general classes shown in Figure 7.4 will be defined first, working down to specific classes.

The first class to consider is Object—the progenitor of all other classes. It has neither superclass nor attributes. The class immediately below Object is SchemaObject, which embodies the common characteristics of transformations, stores, terminators, and flows. Since all of these belong on transformation schemas, the attribute context is defined for SchemaObject. When a SchemaObject is instantiated, its context will refer to a Schema.

Next in line is the general notational component on a transformation schema which is represented by the subclass Component. This class embodies the common characteristics of data transformations, control transformation, data stores, and buffers, all of which may be the source or destination of various flows. Consequently, the attributes enteringFlows and leavingFlows are defined for Component to capture this connective information. The immediate subclasses of Component are Transformation and StorageDevice. Transformation embodies the common characteristics of data and control transformations, and StorageDevice embodies the common characteristics of data stores and buffers. In addition, because a transformation may be either enabled, disabled, or suspended, it is necessary to define the attribute status for Transformation.

The subclass ControlTransformation has the attribute stateMachine, which refers to an instance of the class STDiagram (a state diagram). The adjacent subclass, DataTransformation, has no attributes itself (except those inherited from superclasses), but its refinements PrimitiveDataTransformation and AbstractDataTransformation do. PrimitiveDataTransformation represents a simple function, and has the attribute specification which refers to the procedure for transforming inputs into outputs. A more abstract data transformation (one which can be decomposed into several functions)

is represented by the class AbstractDataTransformation. The attribute abstractedSchema is defined which references a subordinate Schema.

The other immediate subclass of Component is StorageDevice, which
has the subclasses DataStore and Buffer. A data store and a buffer both retain
information; therefore, the attribute contents are defined for StorageDevice.
A buffer may also have a limited capacity. This entails the attribute capacity
for Buffer. The class hierarchy represented in a textual fashion and showing
attributes is as follows.

```
Object
    SchemaObject(context)
        Component(enteringFlows, leavingFlows)
            Transformation(status)
                DataTransformation
                    PrimitiveDataTransformation(specification)
                    AbstractDataTransformation(abstractedSchema)
                ControlTransformation(stateMachine)
            StorageDevice(contents)
                DataStore
                Buffer(capacity)
```

Attributes for the classes of Flow may be defined in like fashion. As
before, we do this by finding common characteristics. Three areas of com-
monality may be found. First, a flow carries information from one component (source) to another component (sink). Second, it is found on a
transformation schema. Third, it may branch out to other schemas in the
hierarchy.

These common characteristics are embodied in the class Flow by defining the attributes source, sink, flowChain, and context. The attribute context
points to the schema on which the Flow is found. The source and sink of
a Flow will be instances of Component or Terminator, or a special object
called BoundaryLink which forms connections with other schemas. The
subclasses, SignalFlow and DataFlow, have their own special properties.
SignalFlow has the attribute signal (0 or 1) and DataFlow has the attribute
data (information). Further subclasses have no additional attributes. In the
situation where information must flow in and out of the boundary, the attribute flowChain will refer to forward branches on other Schemas.

For example, Figure 7.5 shows a transformation schema hierarchy and
a partial mapping of several flows and components to objects. The top
schema, labeled "1," is the context schema. The other schemas are subordinate members of the hierarchy. Data transformation 1.1 abstracts transformation schema 1.1, and data transformation 1.2 abstracts transformation

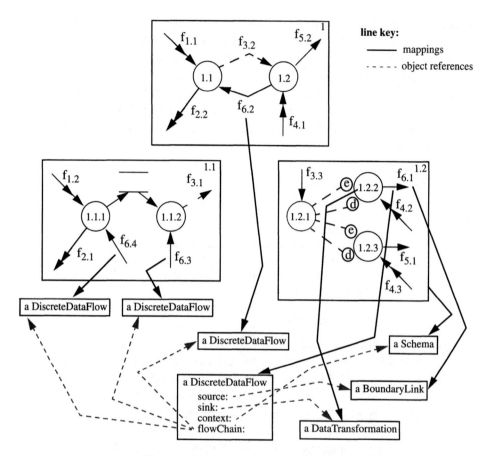

Figure 7.5 Branches of flows on different schemas.

schema 1.2. Each flow is also subscripted to indicate name and related branches. The first number names the flow, and the second number identifies the branch. For instance, $f_{5.1}$ and $f_{5.2}$ have the same name and $f_{5.2}$ is the next branch of $f_{5.1}$.

The discrete data flow $f_{6.1}$ leaves the boundary of schema 1.2, emerges as $f_{6.2}$ leaving data transformation 1.2 in schema 1, and then heads down into schema 1.1, branching into $f_{6.4}$ and $f_{6.3}$. Therefore, $f_{6.1}$, when mapped to an instance of DiscreteDataFlow, will have a PrimitiveDataTransformation as a source (the mapping of data transformation 1.2.2), a BoundaryLink as a sink, a Schema (the mapping of schema 1.2) as a context, and the objects mapped from $f_{6.2}$, $f_{6.3}$, and $f_{6.4}$ as members of its flowChain. A message sent to the DiscreteDataFlow will propagate across the objects in its flowChain.

This establishes communication among Schemas. In summary, the textual format of the Flow hierarchy after attributes have been defined is as follows.

```
Object

    SchemaObject(context)
        Flow(source, sink, flowChain)
            SignalFlow(signal)
                Prompt
                    Enable
                    Disable
                    Suspend
                    Resume
                    Trigger
            DataFlow(data)
                DiscreteDataFlow
                ContinuousDataFlow
```

The next portion of the class hierarchy to consider is that which describes external components (or terminators). Some of these classes represent devices that only produce data (e.g., Keyboard), and some represent devices that only receive data (e.g., Light). Therefore, many of the classes will not define both enteringFlow and leavingFlow attributes. This is indicated by the fact that Terminator is not placed under Component, but instead under SchemaObject. Rather than categorizing terminators under three separate headings (input, output, or both), the necessary enteringFlow and leavingFlow attributes are defined in each class.

BarGauge has the attributes value (current reading), min (minimum level), max (maximum level), and enteringFlows. DigitalDisplay has the attributes value (current reading) and enteringFlows. Light has status, which indicates whether an instance of Light is either on or off, and the attribute enteringFlows. SignalButton has the attribute leavingFlows. DataButton has specification (the value to be sent) and leavingFlows. Keyboard has the attributes keyBuffer for retaining key strokes, and also leavingFlows. ExternalFunction has the attributes status (either on or off), specification (the values to be repeatedly sent), and leavingFlows. ContinuousSource has the attributes value (a discrete sample of a continuous quantity that is sent to other objects), min (minimum level), max (maximum level), and leavingFlows. Finally, ExternalStore has contents (retained data), and both enteringFlows and leavingFlows. The above classes also inherit context from SchemaObject. In summary, the textual format of the Terminator hierarchy with the above attributes defined is as follows.

```
Object

    SchemaObject(context)
        Terminator
            BarGauge(value, min, max, enteringFlows)
            DigitalDisplay(value, enteringFlows)
            Light(status, enteringFlows)
            SignalButton(leavingFlows)
            Keyboard(keyBuffer, leavingFlows)
            DataButton(specification, leavingFlows)
            ExternalFunction(specification, status, leavingFlows)
            ContinuousSource(value, min, max, leavingFlows)
            ExternalStore(contents, enteringFlows, leavingFlows)
```

The only attributes to define now are those for TSHierarchy and Schema. However, at this point, only a partial definition is possible. TSHierarchy represents a hierarchy of transformation schemas. Thus, TSHierarchy must have an attribute schema for referring to constituent Schemas. Furthermore, as we shall see later, a hierarchy of transformation schemas can be executed in simulated real time using a token-passing strategy. This suggests a clock attribute and an object-oriented execution strategy. The clock points to an instance of Counter which models a real-time clock. The execution strategy increments the clock each time an execution step is performed.

Finally, Schema represents a single-level transformation schema, and as such, must have attributes, components, and flows for referring to the Components, Terminators, and Flows. Schema has other attributes that are used during execution, but these are defined later when execution is discussed.

7.4.   OBJECT MAPPING EXAMPLE—A DOOR
SECURITY SYSTEM

We are now in a position to use the knowledge we have about mapping transformation schemas to objects to attempt a working example. We will consider the specification of a door security system, and later return to the same to illustrate the execution procedure. The discussion in this section begins by describing how the security system can be modeled as a transformation schema. We then apply our knowledge of mapping schemas to objects.

7.4.1. Problem Description: Security System
Requirements

The security system can be in one of three states: disarmed, armed, or alarm. In the first state, the security system is inactive: the door being monitored can be opened and closed without an alarm sounding. In the second state, the security system is operational, so that a person opening the door has 20 s to key in a correct entry password to disarm the system before an alarm is sounded. If the system is in the third state, a person has previously opened the door without disarming the system within 20 s, thereby triggering an alarm bell. Once the alarm bell starts to ring, it can only be turned off by entering the correct entry password into the security system.

To arm the security system, a person must enter the correct entry password into the system, and then leave the room and close the door within 20 s before the system becomes operational. Anyone who now opens the door, or even closes it immediately after entering the room, will cause an alarm bell to sound unless the system is disarmed within 20 s.

7.4.2. The Transformation Schema Model

To model the door security system as a transformation schema, it is necessary to identify the different activities the system can perform, the states it can assume, and the data it requires in order to operate. Modeling begins by looking at the context (top schema) of the system, and then other more detailed parts. Once data and control flow has been modeled, the specification of each primitive data transformation and the state machine of each control transformation can be constructed.

The context schema of the door security system is very simple. A sensor on the door tells the system whether the door is open or closed, and a numeric keypad is used to supply the system with an entry password for arming and disarming. There is also an alarm which can be switched on and off by receiving an appropriate signal from the security system. These external devices can be modeled by terminators named "sensor," "keypad," and "alarm," respectively.

The security system needs to be able to interpret the code entered at the keypad by comparing it with a stored password, and only if the two are the same can entry be granted. A data transformation, "check_password," can be used to interpret the code, and a data store, "entry_code," to retain the password. The system must also know whether the door is open or closed. This can be achieved by having a data store, named "door_status," which retains either an "open" or "closed" value, depending on input from "sensor." Data from "sensor" are directed to the system via a data transformation "monitor_door." The actual operation of the security system, apart from its peripheral behavior of password entry and door status detection, can be represented by a data transformation "operate_security_system." The context schema is illustrated in Figure 7.6(a).

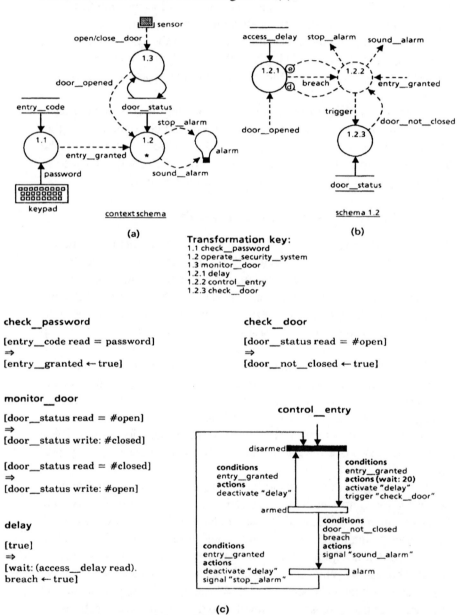

Figure 7.6 Transformation schema for a door security system and associated specifications.

On the schema composed by "operate_security_system," a control transformation "control_entry" can be used to describe the three different states of the system. Its internal state transition diagram will need to respond to a correct password being entered by either arming or disarming the system, and to activate an alarm if a break-in occurs. Also, a data transformation is needed to cause a 20 s delay as soon as the door is opened so that a person has enough time to disarm the system before security is breached, and it is appropriately named "delay." Another data transformation for giving someone time to arm the system, leave the room, and close the door is also required. This transformation, denoted as "check_door," will need to know whether the door is open or not, and therefore must have access to the data store called "door_status" on the context schema. Figure 7.6(b) illustrates the completed transformation schema.

The specification of each primitive data transformation and the state machine of the control transformation "control_entry" are shown in Figure 7.6(c). Simple pre-/postcondition rules are used to specify the operation of the data transformations. "check_password" has one rule. The precondition is met when the access code in "entry_status" is the same as a "password" sent from "keypad." The postcondition sends an "entry_granted" signal to "operate_security_system." The specification of "monitor_door" has alternative rules. The precondition of the first is met when the contents of "door_status" equal #open. The postcondition changes the contents of "door_status" to #closed. The precondition of the second rule is met when the contents of "door_status" is #closed, and the postcondition changes the contents of "door_status" to #open. "monitor_door" is triggered into performing one of these rules by receiving an "open/close_door" signal from "sensor."

"delay" has one pre-/postcondition rule in its specification. The precondition is always true, so whenever the transformation is triggered by a "door_opened" signal, and provided the transformation has already been enabled by "control_entry," the postcondition is performed. In such an event, "delay" is made to wait for the number of clock ticks in "access_delay" before sending a "breach" signal to "control_entry." However, it is possible for "delay" to be disabled by "control_entry" while it is still waiting, thereby stopping the "breach" signal from being sent. This occurs when the correct entry code is received to disarm the system. "check_door" has one pre-/postcondition rule. When "check_door" receives a "trigger" signal from "control_entry," it checks the contents of "door_status" to see whether it equals #open, and if so, sends a signal across "door_not_closed." Someone failing to close the door in time after arming the security system will cause a "door_not_closed" signal to be sent from "check_door" to "control_entry."

"control_entry" has a state transition diagram as its specification. It is initially in the "disarmed" state, and will change to "armed" when an "entry_granted" signal arrives. However, prior to making the state change, a 20 s delay must expire, which gives someone arming the system reasonable time to leave the room and close the door. Only then is "delay" enabled and a "trigger" signal sent to "check_door." From the "armed" state, either the "disarmed" or "alarm" state can be adopted. If an "entry_granted" signal is received, "delay" will be disabled and the "disarmed" state adopted, but if a "breach" or "door_not_closed" signal is received, a "sound_alarm" signal will be sent and "alarm" adopted as the current state. The "alarm" state indicates that someone has failed to disarm the system after opening the door. From this state, an "entry_granted" signal must be received in order to adopt the "disarmed" state, send a "stop_alarm" signal, and to disable "delay."

7.4.3. Mapping the Transformation Schemas to a System of Objects

Each transformation schema in Figure 7.6 is represented as a system of objects by mapping its constituent parts to objects, and then adding suitable references from one object to another. The name of each transformation, terminator, store, and flow is also carried over to its corresponding object. The resulting systems of objects are illustrated in Figures 7.7 and 7.8. Figure 7.7 shows the objects mapped from the context schema, and Figure 7.8 shows the objects from schema 1.2.

The transformation, store, and flow mappings are straightforward, but the terminator mappings need some explanation. Of the terminator classes, a Keyboard is best suited for representing "keypad," a Light for representing "alarm," and a SignalButton for representing "sensor." A press of the SignalButton indicates that the door has closed if it was previously open, or opened if it was previously closed.

Notice that each figure has an instance of Schema (labeled with a "1" in Figure 7.7 and a "16" in Figure 7.8) which references other objects in the figure. Furthermore, the context of each of these objects also refers to the Schema. In other words, a Schema may send messages to the objects it references, which may also send messages to the Schema. The types of messages that can be passed between the different objects are discussed in subsequent sections.

Some references in Figure 7.7 come from or go to certain objects in Figure 7.8. For example, the flowChain of "entry_granted" refers to an

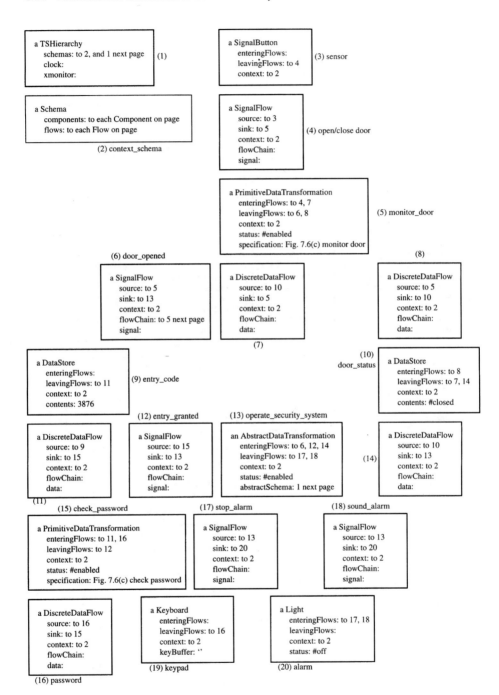

Figure 7.7 Objects mapped from the context schema in Figure 7.6(a).

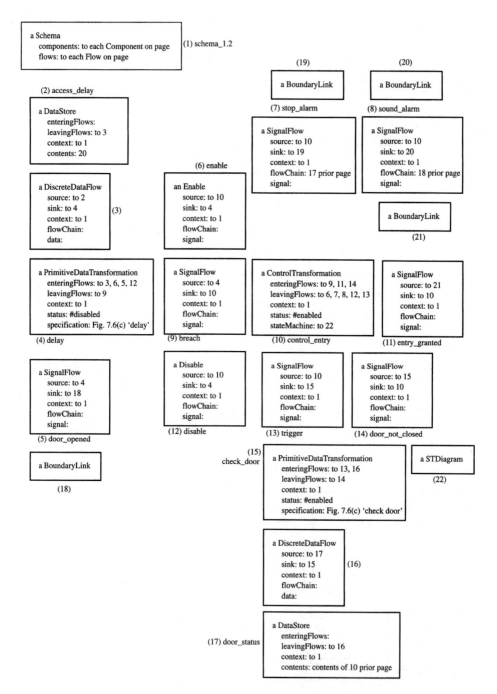

Figure 7.8 Objects mapped from schema 1.2 in Figure 7.6(b).

object by the same name in Figure 7.8. Also, the abstractedSchema of "operate_security_system" refers to the instance of Schema in Figure 7.8.

The attributes of some objects are assigned special values. For example, the status attributes of the DataTransformations "operate_security_system" and "monitor_door" are assigned #enabled, but the same attribute of "delay" in Figure 7.8 is initially assigned #disabled because it is referenced by instances of Enable and Disable. In addition, the contents of "entry_code" are 3876, the contents of "access_delay" are 20, and the contents of "door_status" in Figure 7.7 are initially #closed. "door_status" has a counterpart in Figure 7.8 by the same name that shares its contents. Also, the keyBuffer of "keypad" refers to an empty string, and the status of "alarm" is initially #off.

Finally, each PrimitiveDataTransformation refers to a set of pre-/postcondition rules from Figure 7.6, and the ControlTransformation in Figure 7.8 refers to an instance of STDiagram. These behavioral specifications are used when the objects are sent messages.

7.5.   EXECUTING A SYSTEM OF OBJECTS

We now have an object-based model of a door security system. But what does it tell us about the behavior of the system? We can find this out from the original transformation schema by applying the execution rules. But at present, these rules have not been translated to the object model. In the following section, we will discuss how the system of objects mapped from a single-level transformation schema is executed. An execution procedure is devised which controls message passing among objects on the single-level schema. We will then generalize the procedure to multilevel schemas, and return to the security door example to demonstrate object-based execution.

7.5.1. The Execution Approach

As a transformation schema is being executed, several activities will usually be happening concurrently. For example, many transformations may be receiving inputs and generating outputs at the same time. In a system of objects, these activities are represented as message passing between objects. That is, interaction among components in a transformation schema is mapped to messages in a system of objects. One way to coordinate message passing is to use a clock. Therefore, execution must be divided into discrete time intervals (execution steps) in which objects may send and respond to messages.

This approach to executing a system of objects resembles the way discrete-event simulations are often performed. At regular time intervals, entities in the system respond to queued events (an occurrence in time which may alter the system's state), causing more events to be queued, and so on. Messages can be viewed as events because they cause objects (entities in the system) to perform actions and to send messages to other objects. The operation of the procedure for coordinating message passing is illustrated in Figure 7.9.

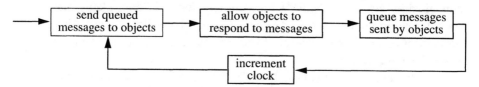

Figure 7.9 Operation of the execution procedure.

A consequence of adopting an execution procedure of this sort is that continuous quantities will be treated as discrete samples. The TEAM-WORK system [3] and the Petri net approach [11] mentioned previously also assume that continuous quantities are sampled at discrete points in time. This does not limit the effectiveness of the simulation, since the aim of executing a transformation schema is to validate critical requirements rapidly. Therefore, a simple discrete simulation strategy will generally do. Most continuous simulation procedures involve complicated differential equations, and for this reason, they are difficult to automate and are computationally inefficient.

7.5.2. Data Flow and Message Sending

The first step in describing the execution procedure is to establish a relationship between data flow and message sending. Consider Figure 7.10, which illustrates a simple transformation schema (left) and the relevant parts of its object mapping (right). A token carrying $data_1$ is on flow D, and a token representing a signal is on flow F. These tokens indicate that data transformation E has just transformed data on flow C.

The same situation can be represented in the system of objects by interpreting tokens as messages. Placing a token carrying $data_1$ on flow D can be represented by sending the message data[$data_1$] (the message data with parameter data1) to DiscreteDataFlow D. Similarly, placing a token on signal flow F can be represented by sending the message signal to SignalFlow F.

The sender of these messages is PrimitiveDataTransformation E, whose leavingFlows refer to the DiscreteDataFlow and the SignalFlow. Therefore, an object X that references an object Y indicates that object X can send messages to object Y. Hence, placing data-bearing tokens on discrete and continuous data flows is represented in a system of objects by sending data[value] messages to ContinuousDataFlows and DiscreteDataFlows. And placing tokens on prompts and signal flows is represented by sending signal messages to SignalFlows and Prompts.

The sending of data[value] and signal messages is coordinated from one execution step to the next by using the following queues.

Queues for current execution step
active_dts
active_cts
active_flows
active_input_terminators
active_output_terminators

Queues for the next execution step
next_active_dts
next_active_cts
next_active_flows
next_active_input_terminators
next_active_output_terminators

Queues for delayed and prompted Transformations
delayed_transformations
prompted_transformations

The "active_" queues contain objects that are involved in the current execution step, and the "next_" queues collect objects for the next execution step. The other two queues, delayed_transformations and prompted_transformations, are for Transformations in special conditions.

An execution step involves allowing the objects in the "active_" queues to respond to messages sent to them in the previous execution step. As this happens, data[value] and signal messages may be sent to other objects, which are consequently placed in appropriate "next_" queues. At the end of the execution step, the "next_" queues are transferred to the "active_" queues.

The execution step illustrated in Figure 7.10 will now be considered to illustrate how the above queues function. Observe that PrimitiveDataTransformation E has just sent a data[data$_1$] message to DiscreteDataFlow D and a signal message to SignalFlow F. Therefore, it must be in active_dts.

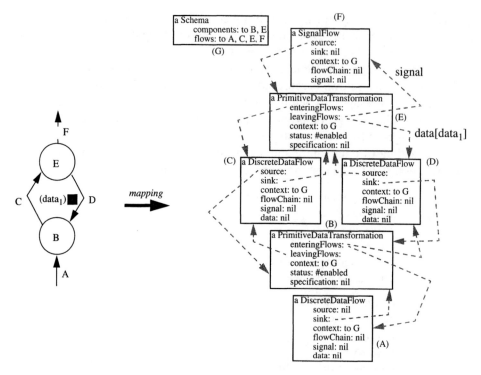

Figure 7.10 Example showing the correspondence between data flow and message passing.

This queue is for PrimitiveDataTransformations involved in the current execution step. Similarly, the queues active_cts, active_source_terminators, and active_output_terminators are for ControlTransformations, source Terminators, and output Terminators, respectively.

When DiscreteDataFlow D receives the message data[data$_1$], two things occur. First, the DiscreteDataFlow and data$_1$ are put in next_active_flows. This queue is for Flows that will carry data or signals in the next execution step. Second, the DiscreteDataFlow will send a schedule message to its sink, PrimitiveDataTransformation B, causing it to be placed in next_active_dts, which contains PrimitiveDataTransformations to be invoked in the next execution step. SignalFlow F is also placed in next_active_flows. Figure 7.11(a) shows the relevant queues after these messages have been sent.

In general, a DataFlow responds to a data[value] message, and a SignalFlow (not subclass instances) responds to a signal message by placing itself in next_active_flows and sending a schedule message to its sink. The object referenced by the sink is then placed in an appropriate "next_" queue. For example, PrimitiveDataTransformations are placed in next_active_dts,

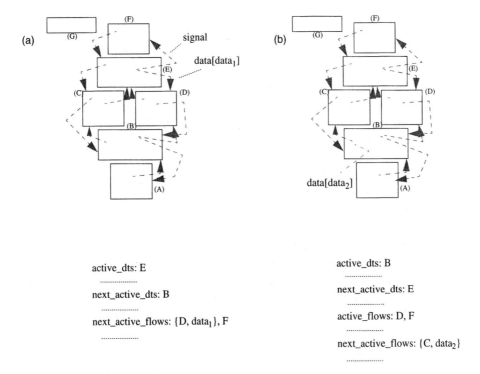

active_dts: E
....
next_active_dts: B
....
next_active_flows: {D, data$_1$}, F
....

active_dts: B
....
next_active_dts: E
....
active_flows: D, F
....
next_active_flows: {C, data$_2$}
....

Figure 7.11 Contents of queues for Figure 7.6 during an execution step.

ControlTransformations are placed in next_active_cts, and output Terminators are placed in next_active_output_terminators.

Note that a Prompt responds in a different way to a signal message. It is still placed in next_active_flows, but instead of sending a schedule message to its sink, it sends a prompt message. This causes the object referenced by the sink to be placed in prompted_transformations, which contains Transformations whose status attributes are to be updated at the beginning of the next execution step.

Placing objects in queues by sending them schedule or prompt messages is denoted as self-scheduling. The "self" prefix indicates that an object, upon receiving one of these messages, will place itself in an appropriate queue. This is an important consideration for computational efficiency because objects can exchange messages with a minimal amount of interference from the execution monitor. A large part of the overhead associated with discrete-event simulations comes from the processing an execution monitor must do to coordinate the set of interacting entities [14]. Self-scheduling helps to minimize this overhead by imparting more responsibility to the objects.

Furthermore, only those objects queued (a subset of all objects) will participate in execution. Therefore, before performing an execution step, it is not necessary to examine every object in the system to find those wanting to be invoked. Instead, during an execution step, those objects receiving schedule or prompt messages will automatically queue themselves for the next execution step.

At the end of an execution step, the objects self-scheduled in the "next_" queues are moved to the "active_" queues. In addition, for each DataFlow in next_active_flows, the associated value is assigned to its data attribute, and the signal attribute of each SignalFlow is set to 1. As shown in Figure 7.11(b), PrimitiveDataTransformation B is moved to active_dts, and DiscreteDataFlow D and SignalFlow F are moved to active_flows. Also, $data_1$ is assigned to the data attribute of the DiscreteDataFlow, and 1 is assigned to the signal attribute of the SignalFlow.

When a new execution step begins, the objects in all "active_" queues, except those in active_flows, are sent step messages. A step message causes an object to perform its action.

In Figure 7.11(b), a step message is sent to PrimitiveDataTransformation B, invoking its specification. The DiscreteDataFlows referenced by the enteringFlows attribute of the PrimitiveDataTransformation are then sent data messages. This causes them to return their respective data attributes, which are then transformed by the specification before sending data[value] messages. If we assume data[$data_2$] is sent to DiscreteDataFlow C, which is referenced by the leavingFlows attribute of the PrimitiveData-Transformation, the DiscreteDataFlow will respond by placing itself in next_active_flows with $data_2$, and by sending a schedule message to its sink, PrimitiveDataTransformation E, which then places itself in next_active_dts, as shown in Figure 7.11(b). ControlTransformations and Terminators respond to step messages in a similar manner.

Sometimes, the specification of a PrimitiveDataTransformation or the stateMachine of a ControlTransformation will require a delay to expire (a certain number of execution steps) before messages are sent out. For this, the Transformation is removed from the "active_" queue to the delayed_transformations queue until the delay expires. It is then moved back to the "active_" queue, and the postponed messages are sent to their destinations.

7.5.3. Single-Level Schema Execution

The above approach to executing a system of objects is described in the following steps, which constitute the single-level execution algorithm.

1. Initialize queues.

2. Send step messages to Terminators in active_source_terminators.

3. Update the status of Transformations in prompted_transformations.

4. Decrement the delays of Transformations in delayed_transformations.

5. Send step messages to DataTransformations in active_dts.

6. Send step messages to ControlTransformations in active_cts.

7. Send step messages to Terminators in active_sink_terminators.

8. Transfer "next_" queues to "active_" queues.

9. Increment clock.

Steps 2–9 form a single execution step. Step 1 is performed once to set up the queues with objects that are to participate in the first execution step.

An execution step is begun by sending step messages to the Terminators in active_source_terminators (2). Then, each Terminator is allowed to perform its appropriate action. For example, a SignalButton will send signal messages to its leavingFlows. The queue is then cleared and Terminators for the following execution step are placed in it (2).

Next, the status of each Transformation in prompted_transformations is updated (3). This involves examining the enteringFlows attribute of each Transformation for Prompts with assigned signal attributes. If there are many Prompts with assigned signal attributes, we have to determine which one will take priority. For our purpose, the priority order from greatest to least is: Disable, Suspend, Resume, and Enable.

If the status of a Transformation is changed to disabled or suspended, then the Transformation is taken out of all "active_" and "delayed_" queues. If suspended, the Transformation will ignore step messages until it receives a signal message from a Resume, which reinstates the status as enabled. When all Transformations in prompted_transformations have been serviced, the queue is then emptied. The delays associated with Transformations in delayed_transformations are then decremented (4). If a delay reaches zero, the Transformation is moved to one of active_dts or active_cts.

Steps 5–7 involve sending step messages to the PrimitiveDataTransformations in active_dts, the ControlTransformations in active_cts, and the Terminators in active_sink_terminators. A PrimitiveDataTransformation responds by performing its specification, a ControlTransformation its stateMachine, and a Terminator its activity (e.g., a Light would change its status from off to on).

As a PrimitiveDataTransformation performs its specification, it may send read and write[value] messages to StorageDevices it references (via its enteringFlows and leavingFlows attributes). For example, if a Discrete-DataFlow referenced by the leavingFlows of a PrimitiveDataTransformation has a DataStore as a sink, then the PrimitiveDataTransformation can place a value in the DataStore by sending the message write[value] to the DiscreteDataFlow, which in turn delivers a write[value] message to the DataStore. Reading is performed similarly, except that read messages are used.

If a PrimitiveDataTransformation or a ControlTransformation encounters a delay statement (wait: delay) in the course of performing its specification, it is moved to the delayed_transformations queue. If not, it sends data[value] and signal messages to Flows referenced by its leavingFlows attribute. Subsequent schedule and prompt messages cause objects referenced by the sinks of these Flows to be put in "next_" queues and/or prompted_transformations queue.

When instructed to be placed in a queue, a PrimitiveDataTransformation first determines whether it is there already. If it is, the queue is not updated. However, a PrimitiveDataTransformation may be in prompted_transformations as well as next_active_dts. To cause this to happen, the PrimitiveDataTransformation must receive a message from a Prompt and some other Flow simultaneously. The message from the Prompt takes priority.

After sending the step messages, the "next_" queues are transferred to the "active_" queues (8). The "active_" queues are first cleared, then each "next_" queue is moved to a corresponding "active_" queue. Then, the active_flows queue is traversed in order to assign data and signal attributes. Finally, the number of execution steps is incremented (9). We then return to step 2 to begin another execution step.

7.5.4. Multilevel Schema Execution

It is now a relatively straightforward matter to generalize the above to multilevel schemas. In essence, an execution procedure is needed to coordinate message sending among a collection of Schemas using the single-level algorithm.

First, we must define the message "step" for Schema, which implements the single-level execution algorithm. This necessitates that the queues manipulated by the execution algorithm be made attributes of Schema. Moreover, objects referenced by the Schema must have access to these queues to perform self-scheduling. An object can then send the message getQueue to its context to retrieve the required queue. The object can then place itself in that queue.

A Schema now has the necessary attributes and messages for coordinating the execution of its constituent objects. What we can do next is work out a way of coordinating the execution of a hierarchy of Schemas. Interaction among Schemas can be coordinated in the same manner as other objects by using queues and self-scheduling. To do this, we need to define the queues active_schemas and next_active_schemas for TSHierarchy, and also a context attribute for Schema. The context attribute will be used by a Schema to place itself in the next_active_schemas queue.

As it stands, Schema possesses some queues that go unused in all but the topmost Schema. In a hierarchy of Schemas, only the topmost Schema, which represents the system context, can refer to Terminators. Hence, queues associated with Terminators in lower level Schemas will never be used. This problem is solved by making these queues attributes of ContextSchema, a subclass of Schema. The extended class hierarchy is summarized as

> Object
>> Schema(components, flows, context, active_dts, active_cts, active_flows,
>>> next_active_dts, next_active_cts, next_active_flows,
>>> delayed_transformations, prompted_transformations)
>> ContextSchema(active_input_terminators,
>>> active_output_terminators,
>>> next_active_input_terminators,
>>> next_active_output_terminators).

Therefore, the context schema of a transformation schema hierarchy is mapped to an instance of ContextSchema. Other schemas are mapped to instances of Schema. ContextSchema inherits the attributes of Schema. ContextSchema and Schema also have their own step messages, defined as follows.

Step message for Schema
> 1. Update the status of Transformations in prompted_transformations.
> 2. Decrement the delays of Transformations in delayed_transformations.
> 3. Send step messages to DataTransformations in active_dts.
> 4. Send step messages to ControlTransformations in active_cts.

Step message for ContextSchema
> 1. Send step messages to Terminators in active_source_terminators.
> 2. Send step messages to Terminators in active_sink_terminators.
> 3. Perform the step message from Schema.

transferQueues message for Schema
> 4. Transfer "next_" queues to "active_" queues.

The step messages are essentially the same, except that the one for ContextSchema considers Terminators. ContextSchema also performs the step message of Schema. The transferring of "next_" queues to "active_" queues is done by the message transferQueues. This message is sent to each Schema in the TSHierarchy only when all Schemas have completed an execution step. This is necessary because, even though a Schema may have finished executing, other Schemas still going might send messages to that Schema, causing objects to be self-scheduled. Therefore, each Schema must first be allowed to complete a step, and then each can be sent a transferQueues message.

The next thing we must consider is how step messages affect an AbstractDataTransformation. We know that a PrimitiveDataTransformation is made to execute its code specification. In a similar manner, an AbstractDataTransformation must be made to execute its enclosed schema (pointed to by abstractedSchema). To work out how to coordinate the execution of such a layered structure, consider the relationship between the TSHierarchy and the hierarchical transformation schema shown in Figure 7.12. The tree structure on the left represents a hierarchy of transformation schemas (horizontal lines). s_1 has two abstract data transformations which decompose into s_2 and s_3, respectively, and similarly for the other schemas. On the right of the figure, the transformation schema hierarchy is depicted as a system of objects. The top box represents a ContextSchema, and the other boxes represent Schemas. ContextSchema s_1 will have two AbstractDataTransformations, one referring to Schema s_2, and the other referring to Schema s_3. The other Schemas have similar references.

Ward [17] suggests that the execution of a transformation schema hierarchy, such as this, may be simplified by first flattening the hierarchy. In

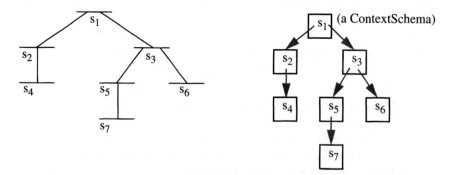

Figure 7.12 A schema hierarchy and object representation.

other words, each abstract data transformation is replaced by the transformation schema it composes. For example, in Figure 7.12, the abstract data transformations in schema s_1 are replaced by schema s_2 and s_3. Then, the abstract data transformation on schema s_2 is replaced by schema s_4, and so on. A single-level transformation schema results which can be executed by applying the rules found in [17].

However, it is also possible to execute the transformation schema hierarchy without flattening it. This is done by first executing each transformation schema in the hierarchy as a single-level schema. If an abstract data transformation is encountered, it is skipped. Then, for each transformation schema, the data on outgoing flows are delivered to another schema. A flow is outgoing if it leaves a schema from the boundary or enters an abstract data transformation.

However, this execution approach can be computationally inefficient because some of the transformation schemas may not have any components that need to be executed. This problem is easily solved. The Schemas are simply divided into those with empty and nonempty queues. Only those Schemas with nonempty queues will participate in the current execution step. All others remain untouched.

The active_schemas and next_active_schemas queues of TSHierarchy are used to hold these active Schemas. Schemas participating in the current execution step are held in active_schemas, and those to participate in the next execution step are collected in next_active_schemas.

To place a Schema in next_active_schemas, it must receive a schedule message from an AbstractDataTransformation. This happens when a Flow referenced by the enteringFlows attribute of an AbstractDataTransformation receives a data[value] or signal message. Consequently, the Flow sends a schedule message to the AbstractDataTransformation. The AbstractDataTransformation then places itself in the next_active_dts queue of its context, and sends a schedule message to the Schema referenced by its abstractedSchema. The Schema then retrieves next_active_schemas from its context (the TSHierarchy) and places itself in that queue.

For example, if in Figure 7.12 the AbstractDataTransformation referencing Schema s_3 were to receive a schedule message from a DataFlow (which means that the DataFlow was previously sent a data[value] message), then Schema s_3 would be placed in next_active_schemas. Schema s_3 would now have at least one nonempty queue because the data[value] message would also have been sent to an ingoing DataFlow on the boundary of Schema s_3.

The next matter to consider is how individual Schemas communicate with each other in a coordinated manner when data enter or leave the boundary. Consider Figure 7.13, which shows the correspondence between token and message passing, and also how messages are sent from Schema to Schema by propagated signal and data[value] messages.

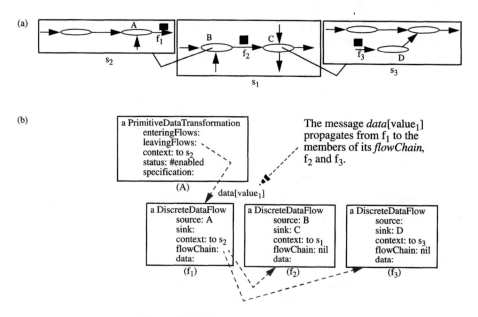

Figure 7.13 Message passing to other Schemas.

In Figure 7.13(a), if data transformation A sends data on flow f_1, then a token is placed on this flow and on flows f_2 and f_3. If the data transformation and flows are mapped to objects [Figure 7.13(b)], then we can see how messages can be sent from Schema to Schema. When the PrimitiveDataTransformation sends a data[value$_1$] message to DiscreteDataFlow f_1, the message is propagated to DiscreteDataFlows f_2 and f_3, which are referenced by the flowChain attribute of DiscreteDataFlow f_1.

Upon receiving the data[value$_1$] message, DiscreteDataFlow f_1 places itself in the next_active_flows queue of Schema s_2. Similarly, DiscreteDataFlow f_2 places itself in the next_active_flows queue of Schema s_1. Moreover, its sink, AbstractDataTransformation C, is placed in next_active_dts. Schema s_3, which is referenced by the abstractedSchema of the AbstractDataTransformation, is placed in next_active_schemas. When DiscreteDataFlow f_3 receives the data[value$_1$] message, it is placed in the next_active_flows queue of Schema s_3, and its sink, PrimitiveDataTransformation D, is queued in next_active_dts.

Observe that only DiscreteDataFlow f_1 has flowChain references. The other forward branches of DiscreteDataFlow f_1, that is, DiscreteDataFlows f_2 and f_3, remain unassigned because we must ensure that no more than one data[value$_1$] message is ever sent to DiscreteDataFlow f_3. Otherwise, if this were not done, a data[value$_1$] message would be sent from the flowChains of both DiscreteDataFlows f_1 and f_2, and PrimitiveDataTransformation D would receive multiple copies of value$_1$.

Therefore, as a rule, only the flowChain attributes of Flows having a "primitive" source attribute, either a PrimitiveDataTransformation, a ControlTransformation, or an input Terminator, will be assigned.

To summarize the use of flowChain attributes, when a Flow receives either a data[value] or signal message, it places itself in the next_active_flows queue of its context, queues its sink, and also sends the same message to each Flow referenced by its flowChain. Each of these Flows places itself in the next_active_flows queue of its context, and also causes its sink to be queued. If the sink references an AbstractDataTransformation, the Schema referenced by the abstractedSchema attribute is placed in next_active_schemas.

We can construct an algorithm based on queuing Schemas and propagating messages, as described in the above discussion, to coordinate multilevel Schema execution. The steps in the algorithm are as follows:

1. Initialize the queues of each Schema.
2. Queue required input Terminators.
3. Send a step message to each Schema in active_schemas.
4. Remove the Schemas in active_schemas with empty queues.
5. Move the Schemas in next_active_schemas to active_schemas.
6. Send transferQueues messages to each Schema in active_schemas.
7. Increment the clock.

Step 1 initializes the queues of each Schema with objects for the first execution step. Steps 2–7 entail the main body of a single execution step.

Step 2 involves queueing and manipulating input Terminators. For example, we may want to queue a DataButton or change the status attribute of an ExternalFunction from #on to #off.

Step 3 involves sending step messages to the Schemas in ac-
tive_schemas so they can run for a single execution step. During this activity, some Schemas may be placed in next_active_schemas, and data[value]
and signal messages may propagate across Schemas, causing objects to be
scheduled in "next_" queues.

Note that as Schemas are being executed, AbstractDataTransformations that receive data[value], signal, and prompt messages are queued
in exactly the same manner as PrimitiveDataTransformations. However,
if an AbstractDataTransformation is instructed to update its status, this
must also be reflected in Schemas subordinate to the AbstractDataTransformation. For example, if in Figure 7.13 the AbstractDataTransformation
referencing Schema s_3 were #disabled, the status attributes of Transformations in Schemas s_3, s_5, s_6, and s_7 would also be #disabled. Therefore,
when the status of an AbstractDataTransformation is updated at the beginning of its execution step, an appropriate message must also be sent to the
abstractedSchema of the AbstractDataTransformation. This message, denoted as status[aSymbol] where aSymbol is #enable, #disable, #suspend,
or #resume, will update Transformations in and subordinate to the Schema.

In step 4, the Schemas in active_schemas that have empty queues are removed. The remaining Schemas will participate in the next execution step.

In step 5, the Schemas in next_active_schemas are moved to ac-
tive_schemas. If a Schema in next_active_schemas is already present in
active_schemas, it is passed over.

In step 6, each Schema in active_schemas is sent a transferQueues
message. This causes the "next_" queues in the Schema to be transferred
to the "active_" queues.

Finally, in step 7, the clock keeping the number of elapsed execution steps is incremented. At this point, the algorithm returns to step 2 to
begin again.

7.6.   EXECUTION EXAMPLE—DOOR SECURITY
SYSTEM REVISITED

We will now return to the door security system discussed previously to show
how the associated systems of objects (Figures 7.7 and 7.8) are executed
with the multilevel schema execution algorithm. The exercise will involve
arming the security system. We will show what happens as someone opens
the door when the security system is disarmed, then enters the correct arming code, and finally leaves the room and closes the door before 20 s elapse.
The contents of queues and the responses made to messages are explained.

Initially, it is assumed that "context schema" is queued in active_schemas, and that "sensor" is queued in active_source_terminators of "context schema." The arming sequence is then begun by opening the door. To show this, a step message is sent to the TSHierarchy, and consequently, a step message is sent to "sensor" which then sends a signal message to "open/close_door." This causes "open/close_door" to place itself in next_active_flows, and "monitor_door" (the sink of "open/close_door") to put itself in next_active_dts. At the end of the execution step, these queues are transferred to corresponding "active_" queues of "context schema," and "context schema" remains queued in active_schemas [see Figure 7.14(a)].

By again sending a step message to the TSHierarchy, "monitor_door" will be made to execute its specification, causing the contents of "door_status" to become #open, and a signal message to be sent to "door_opened." As a result, "door_opened" is placed in next_active_flows, and its sink, "operate_security_system," is put in next_active_dts. Moreover, "operate_security_system" places its abstractedSchema, "schema 1.2," in next_active_schemas. Also, the flowChain of "door_opened" refers to a SignalFlow by the same name in "schema_1.2." This SignalFlow also receives a signal message and is placed in the next_active_flows queue of "schema_1.2," and its sink, "delay," is placed in the next_active_dts queue. Finally, queues of each Schema are transferred, and both Schemas are placed in active_schemas [see Figure 7.14(b)].

Before another step message is sent to the TSHierarchy, "keypad" is sent the message add[3876] and also placed in active_source_terminators. This indicates that a person is now entering the correct password to arm the system. When a step message is now sent to the TSHierarchy, "context schema" will execute and send a step message to "keypad," which will send a data[3876] message to "password." Consequently, "password" and "check_password" are appropriately queued. Next, "schema_1.2" is executed. However, even though "delay" is sent a step message, it does not perform its specification because its status is #disabled. The relevant queues at the end of this execution step are shown in Figure 7.14(c).

If another step message is now sent to the TSHierarchy, then "context schema" will execute and cause "check_password" to compare the contents of "entry_code" with the data carried by "password." Since the contents and data are the same, a signal message will be sent to "entry_granted." This causes "entry_granted" to queue itself, to send a signal message to the SignalFlow that its flowChain references on "schema_1.2," and to send a schedule message to its sink, "operate_security_system." Consequently,

(a) execution step 1

context schema
queues during step
active_source_terminators: sensor
next_active_flows: open/close_door
next_active_dts: monitor_door
queues after step
active_flows: open/close_door
active_dts: monitor_door

(b) execution step 2

context schema
queues during step
next_active_flows: door_opened
next_active_dts: operate_security_system
queues after step
active_flows: door_opened
active_dts: operate_security_system

schema 1.2
queues during step
next_active_flows: door_opened
next_active_dts: delay
queues after step
active_flows: door_opened
active_dts: delay

(c) execution step 3

context schema
queues during step
active_source_terminators: keypad
next_active_flows: {password, 3876}
next_active_dts: check_password
queues after step
active_flows: password
active_dts: check_password

(d) execution step 4

context schema
queues during step
next_active_flows: entry_granted
next_active_dts: operate_security_system
queues after step
active_flows: entry_granted
active_dts: operate_security_system

schema 1.2
queues during step
next_active_flows: entry_granted
next_active_cts: control_entry
queues after step
active_flows: entry_granted
active_cts: control_entry

(e) execution step 5

schema 1.2
queues after step
delayed_transformations: {control_entry, 20}

(f) after another 10 execution steps

context schema
queues during step
active_source_terminators: sensor
next_active_flows: open/close_door
next_active_dts: monitor_door
queues after step
active_flows: open/close_door
active_dts: monitor_door

schema 1.2
queues after step
delayed_transformations: {control_entry, 10}

(g) after another 10 execution steps

schema 1.2
queues during step
active_cts: control_entry
next_active_flows: trigger, enable
next_active_dts: check_door
prompted_transformations: delay
queues after step
active_flows: trigger, enable
active_dts: check_door

(h) execution step 24

all queues empty
(security system armed)

Figure 7.14 Contents of queues for an arming sequence of a door security system.

"operate_security_system" is queued, and so is "schema 1.2" and "control_entry" [see Figure 7.14(d)].

When "schema 1.2" is next executed by the TSHierarchy, "control_entry" will receive a step message, and then postpones itself in the queue "delayedTransformations" for 20 execution steps. This allows the person entering the password to leave the room and close the door before the system becomes operational (see Figure 7.14(e)). And, because "schema 1.2" has a nonempty queue, it is also queued again.

After ten execution steps, "sensor" is again placed in the active_source_terminators queue and sent a step message. Consequently, "open/close_door" receives a signal message, is placed in next_active_flows, and its sink, "monitor_door," is placed in next_active_dts of "context schema." At the end of this execution step, "open/close_door" will be moved to active_flows, and "monitor_door" will be moved to active_dts of "context schema" [see Figure 7.14(f)]. Note that "schema 1.2" is queued in active_schemas because "control_entry" is still counting down a delay in delayed_transformations.

In the next execution step, "monitor_door" will perform its specification and change the contents of "door_status" to #closed. Also, the delay associated with "control_entry" will be decremented. After a further nine execution steps have occurred, the delay associated with "control_entry" will have expired. Therefore, "control_entry" will be moved to "active_cts" and sent a step message. Consequently, a signal is sent to "trigger" and to "enable." This causes "check_door" to be queued in next_active_dts, and "delay" to be queued in prompted_transformations. At the end of the execution step, queues are again appropriately transferred [see Figure 7.14(g)].

During the next execution step, the status of "delay" is changed to #enabled, and the specification of "check_door" is performed. Because the contents of "door_status" is #closed, a signal message is not sent to "door_not_closed."

The arming sequence is now complete, and as the execution sequence seems to suggest, the transformation schemas in Figures 7.7 and 7.8 correctly model the arming operation of the system.

7.7.   CONCLUSION

In this chapter, we have seen how single- and multilevel transformation schemas can be mapped to systems of objects for interactive simulation. This underlying object model can be executed by the Schema Execution

Environment (SEE) [7] and the results of simulation displayed graphically. The modeling scheme is highly extensible, and can be adapted to suit a wide range of scenarios by the addition of new functional components and external entities. Presently, SEE has been used to simulate things ranging from the complex control dynamics of a nuclear reactor to the operation of a water catchment system.

The "simulation engine" driving transformation schema execution in SEE has been purposely designed to be highly extensible and to make the most of object reuse. New modeling components (terminators, for example) can easily be dovetailed to the class hierarchy by borrowing relevant functionality from existing classes. Other systems for designing real-time systems, such as CAPS [13], TEAMWORK [3], PAISLEY [19] and REVS [10], do not appear to offer the same sort of flexibility as SEE.

7.8.   APPENDIX

7.8.1. Message Definitions

Of the messages already described, the step and schedule messages form the basis of the procedure for executing a system of objects. However, there are other messages, not as yet mentioned, which are indirectly invoked by step and schedule. There are also certain standard messages which serve to complete object class definitions (e.g., messages for accessing attributes). In this section, relevant messages for each class are defined.

7.8.2. Component Messages

Messages for SchemaObject

context
  Return the object referenced by the context attribute.
context[aSchema]
  Assign aSchema to the context attribute.
schedule
  Retrieve the right queue from the context attribute (using getQueue) and join the queue.
  This message is used when a data[value] or signal message is received by a Flow.

Messages for Component (Superclass Is SchemaObject)

enteringFlows/leavingFlows
  Return the objects referenced by the enteringFlows/leavingFlows attribute.

enteringFlows/leavingFlows[aNumberOfFlows]
Assign aNumberOfFlows to the enteringFlows/leavingFlows attribute.

Messages for Transformation (Superclass Is Component)

status
Return the symbol referenced by the status attribute (#enabled, #disabled, or #suspended).

status[aSymbol]
Assign aSymbol to the status attribute.

initializeStatus
Assign the status attribute an initial symbol (#enabled or #disabled). The initializeStatus message is sent to a Transformation by its context. The message causes a Transformation to assign an appropriate symbol to its status attribute, in accordance with [17].

updateStatus
Examine the Prompts in the enteringFlows attribute and update status accordingly. The updateStatus message is used to change the status attribute of a Transformation found in the prompted_transformations queue of its context. This message also makes use of the status[a_symbol] message.

prompt
This message causes a Transformation to be placed in the prompted_transformations queue of its context. This happens when a Prompt referenced by the enteringFlows of the Transformation receives a signal message. Later, the Transformation will receive an updateStatus message.

Messages for DataTransformation (Superclass Is Transformation)

getQueue
Return next_active_dts from the context attribute. The getQueue message is used by subclass instances to access the next_active_dts queue of its context.

Messages for PrimitiveDataTransformation (Superclass Is DataTransformation)

specification[code]
Assign code to the specification attribute (pre- and postcondition rules).

step
Perform the specification, providing status is #enabled (uses the data attributes of Flows referenced by enteringFlows, and sends data[value] and signal messages to certain Flows in leavingFlows).

Messages for AbstractDataTransformation (Superclass Is DataTransformation)

abstractedSchema

Return the Schema referenced by the abstractedSchema attribute.

abstractedSchema[aSchema]

Assign aSchema to the abstractedSchema attribute.

status[aSymbol]

Redefine the status[a_symbol] message from Transformation. This is done because, when an AbstractDataTransformation receives an updateStatus message (also inherited), it must not only update its own status, but also that of Transformations on other Schemas reachable from the abstractedSchema. Therefore, the inherited status[aSymbol] message is performed, as well as sending status[aSymbol] to the abstractedSchema.

step

Do nothing.

schedule

Perform this message from SchemaObject, and then send schedule to abstractedSchema.

Messages for ControlTransformation (Superclass Is Transformation)

stateMachine

Return the STDiagram referenced by the stateMachine attribute.

stateMachine[aSTDiagram]

Assign aSTDiagram to the stateMachine attribute.

step

Perform the stateMachine (similar to PrimitiveDataTransformation's step message, except that enteringFlows and leavingFlows will only refer to SignalFlows).

getQueue

Return next_active_cts from the context attribute.

Messages for StorageDevice (Superclass Is Component)

contents

Return the object referenced by the contents attribute.

Messages for DataStore (Superclass Is StorageDevice)

read

Return the objects referenced by the contents attribute.

write[aValue]

Add aValue to the objects referenced by the contents attribute.

Messages for Buffer (Superclass Is StorageDevice)

read
Return the first object referenced by the contents attribute (break reference link).
write[aValue]
Add aValue after the last object referenced by the contents attribute.

7.8.3. Flow Messages

Messages for Flow (Superclass Is SchemaObject)

source
Return the object referenced by the source attribute.
source[anObject]
Assign anObject to the source attribute.
sink
Return the object referenced by the sink attribute.
sink[anObject]
Assign anObject to the sink attribute.
flowChain
Return the Flows referenced by the flowChain attribute.
flowChain[someFlows]
Assign someFlows to the flowChain attribute.
getQueue
Return next_active_flows from the context attribute.
makeFlowChain
Determine the Flows to be referenced by the flowChain attribute, and then assign them.

Messages for SignalFlow (Superclass Is Flow)

signal
Join the queue returned by getQueue, and send a signal message to each SignalFlow referenced by the flowChain attribute. Finally, send a schedule message to the sink attribute.
hasSignal
Return true if the signal attribute contains 1; else return false.
setSignal
Assign 1 to the signal attribute.
clearSignal
Assign 0 to the signal attribute.

Messages for Prompt (Superclass Is SignalFlow)

signal

Join the queue returned by getQueue, and send a prompt message to the sink attribute (Prompts do not have flowChains).

Messages for DataFlow (Superclass Is Flow)

data

Return the object referenced by the data attribute.

data[value]

Join the queue returned by getQueue along with value, and send a data[value] message to each DataFlow referenced by the flowChain attribute. Finally, send a schedule message to the sink attribute.

clearData

Assign nil to the data attribute.

7.8.4. Schema and TSHierarchy Messages

Messages for Schema (Superclass Is Object)

context

Return the context attribute.

context[aTSHierarchy]

Assign aTSHierarchy to the context attribute.

components

Return the objects referenced by the components attribute.

components[someComponents]

Assign someComponents to the components attribute.

flows

Return the objects referenced by the flows attribute.

flows[someFlows]

Assign someFlows to the flows attribute.

activeDts

Return the active_dts queue.

activeCts

Return the active_cts queue.

activeFlows

Return the active_flows queue.

nextActiveDts

Return the next_active_dts queue.

nextActiveCts

Return the next_active_cts queue.

nextActiveFlows

Return the next_active_flows queue.

delayedTransformations

Return the delayed_transformations queue.

promptedTransformations

Return the prompted_transformations queue.

status[aSymbol]

Send this message to each Transformation referenced by components.

step

Perform the single-level execution algorithm.

transferQueues

Transfer the "next" queues to the "active" queues.

schedule

Join the next_active_schemas queue of the context.

Messages for ContextSchema (Superclass Is Schema)

activeInputTerminators

Return the active_input_terminators queue.

activeOutputTerminators

Return the active_output_terminators queue.

nextActiveInputTerminators

Return the next_active_output_terminators queue.

nextActiveOutputTerminators

Return the next_active_output_terminators queue.

step

Perform the single-level execution algorithm.

transferQueues

Transfer the "next" queues to the "active" queues (also performs the transferQueues messages in Schema).

Messages for TSHierarchy (Superclass Is Object)

schemas

Return the Schemas referenced by the schemas attribute.

schemas[someSchemas]

Assign someSchemas to the schemas attribute.

activeSchemas

Return the active_schemas queue.

nextActiveSchemas

Return the next_active_schemas queue.

incrementClock

Increment the execution step counter, the clock attribute.

step

Perform the hierarchical execution algorithm.

References

[1] B. Alabiso, "Transformation of data flow analysis models to object oriented design," in *OOPSLA Proc.*, Sept. 1988, pp. 335–353.

[2] O. Balci, "The implementation of four conceptual frameworks for simulation modeling in high-level languages," *Proc. 1988 Winter Simulation Conf.*, San Diego, CA, IEEE, Dec. 1988, pp. 287–295.

[3] R. Blumofe and A. Hecht, "Executing real-time structured analysis specifications," *ACM Software Eng. Notes*, vol. 13, pp. 32–40, July 1988.

[4] B. Boehm, "Verifying and validating software requirements and design specifications," *IEEE Software*, pp. 75–88, Jan. 1984.

[5] G. Booch, "Object-oriented development," *IEEE Trans. Software Eng.*, vol. SE-12, pp. 211–221, Feb. 1986.

[6] W. Bruyn et al., "ESML: An extended systems modelling language based on the data flow diagram," *ACM Software Eng. Notes*, vol. 12, pp. 58–67, Nov. 1987.

[7] C. J. Coomber and R. E. Childs, "A graphical tool for the prototyping of real-time systems," *ACM Software Eng. Notes*, vol. 15, pp. 70–82, Apr. 1990.

[8] C. J. Coomber, "An object-oriented simulation procedure for automating transformation schema execution," *Int. J. Comput. Simulation* (Special Issue on Object-Oriented Simulation), vol. 5, no. 4, 1995.

[9] D. Craigen, Ed., "Formal methods for trustworthy computer systems (FM89): Report from FM89—A workshop on the assessment of formal methods for trustworthy computer systems," Halifax, Canada, July 1989.

[10] A. M. Davis, "Rapid prototyping using executable requirements specifications," *ACM Software Eng. Notes*, vol. 7, pp. 39–43, Dec. 1982.

[11] R. Dew, "Schematic execution using Petri nets, and prototypical execution using software generation of real-time system specifications," M.Sc. thesis, Deakin Univ., Australia, 1992.

[12] B. Henderson-Sellers and J. M. Edwards, "The object-oriented systems life cycle," *Commun. ACM* (Special Issue on Object-Oriented Design), vol. 33, pp. 142–159, Sept. 1990.

[13] Luqi, "Software evolution through rapid prototyping," *IEEE Computer*, pp. 13–25, May 1989.

[14] L. F. Pollacia, "A survey of discrete event simulation and state-of-the-art discrete event languages," *Simulation Dig.*, pp. 8–25, Mar. 1990.

[15] R. Pressman, *Software Engineering: A Practitioner's Approach*. New York: McGraw-Hill, 1992.

[16] P. Ward and S. Mellor, *Structured Development for Real-Time Systems*. New York: Yourdon, 1985.

[17] P. Ward, "The transformation schema: An extension of the data flow diagram to represent control and timing," *IEEE Trans. Software Eng.*, vol. SE-12, pp. 198–210, Feb. 1986.

[18] P. Ward, "How to integrate object orientation with structured analysis and design," *IEEE Software*, pp. 74–82, Mar. 1989.

[19] P. Zave, "Salient features of an executable specification language and its environment," *IEEE Trans. Software Eng.*, vol. SE-12, pp. 312–325, Feb. 1986.

Chapter 8

Steps to an Ecology of Actor Simulation

Alain Senteni   *DIRO, Université de Montréal,*
Montréal, Canada

Editor's Introduction

Now, with the background gained from the previous chapters, we are able to attack this final chapter, which presents a progression of steps for the application of object-oriented techniques to discrete-event or behavioral simulation problems, starting from simple objects (or actors), up to whole ecologies of reflective agents. This chapter introduces aspects of ecologies of Object-Oriented Concurrent Programming (OOCP). The first step is concerned with the minimal extensions needed in an actor language to make it suitable for Discrete-Event Simulation. The second step introduces concurrency issues as an improvement. The third step shows how the rollback problem can be solved by the introduction of reflection. The next step introduces agents as a step ahead in actor programming. We introduce the concept of ecosystems where agents become a community of concurrent processes which, in their interactions, strategies, and competition for resources, behave like ecologies. Finally, the last step adds a reflective dimension to the agents, thus making them able to reason about the ecosystem where they belong, and eventually, to change it or to change themselves: that is, to adapt. From this set of experiments, we conclude that object-oriented concurrent programming can be refined in a significant way, in order to provide a very flexible and a powerful toolkit for different kinds of discrete-event or behavioral simulation problems.

Abstract

From an early definition of the actor concept to whole communities of concurrent processes behaving in their interactions, strategies, and competition for resources like whole ecologies of reflective agents, object-oriented concurrent programming has gone through several conceptual steps, giving rise to a structured methodology. To apply concurrent object-oriented techniques to discrete-event and behavioral simulation problems, the same kind of incremental methodology has to be defined. The first step provides minimal extensions of an actor language for discrete-event simulation. For an improvement of efficiency, the second step introduces concurrency issues in the form of a message-driven time-warp system. The third step introduces reflection as a solution to the rollback problem. It is shown how reflective techniques can be used to dynamically restore an actor's state. The fourth step defines agents as reflective actors aware of their environment, described as an ecosystem. This awareness makes agents able to make local decisions based on imperfect knowledge about the whole system or inconsistent and delayed information. In this case, reflection gives an agent a proper view of the ecosystem where it belongs. The agent becomes more adaptable to evolving circumstances: it can reason about its environment, change it, or modify itself. This constructivist approach of actor simulation techniques makes modeling easier, while it provides a flexible and powerful toolkit to solve several kinds of discrete-event or behavioral simulation problems.

Key Words

Agent systems, Behavioral simulation, Computational reflection, Concurrent object-oriented simulation, Conditional message passing, Discrete-event simulation, Sharing mechanisms, Time-referenced message passing.

8.1.   INTRODUCTION

From the early definition of actor concepts given by Hewitt in 1976 [12] to the ecology of computation introduced by Huberman [13] to describe communities of concurrent processes behaving in their interactions, strategies, and competition for resources like whole ecologies of reflective agents, Object-Oriented Concurrent Programming (OOCP) [30] has gone through several conceptual steps. The increasing complexity of systems appeals to new techniques either to refine knowledge representation aspects or to solve problems related to computational aspects. Both dimensions are usually intertwined, bringing forward a need for tools that would help distinguish different layers. This chapter proposes a constructivist approach of actor simulation that follows the evolution of object-oriented concurrent programming from actors to agent ecologies. Sketching different steps in the evolution of object-oriented concurrent programming techniques, it introduces each step as a specific solution of a given problem in simulation:

- knowledge   representation   (*model,   expressive   power   of   the formalism*)

- concurrency (*time warp*)

- reflection (*rollback, dynamic modifications at run time*)
- social dimensions (*relations among different subsystems, open systems*).

From a historical point of view, simple object or actor concepts have been refined with a focus on given dimensions of object-oriented concurrent programming, up to the definition of reflective agents systems with an ecological metaphor:

- **Actors** are self-contained, concurrently interacting entities of a computer system. They communicate via message passing, which is asynchronous and fair. Actors can be created dynamically, and the topology of an actor system can change dynamically. The model supports encapsulation and sharing, and provides a natural extension of both functional programming and object-style data abstraction to concurrent open systems [1], [12]. The actor model belongs to the general object-oriented concurrent programming paradigm.

- **A reflective actor** is an actor provided with a causally connected representation of itself. Causally connected means that when the actor changes, the representation does as well (and vice versa) [26], [20]. *In an approach of reflection with meta-actor*, the reflective representation of an actor is a metacircular description of some given aspect of the actor (either behavioral or computational) as an actor program. *In a modular approach of reflection*, low-level register of the actor's interpreter [14] such as namespaces or continuations are made available as data, so that the actor's interpretation can be modified.

- **An agent** is an actor system in relation with others. Actors and agents belong to the same paradigm, but differ in granularity. Actors represent the implementation level of agents. To quote Huberman who introduced the expression *ecology of computation* [13]: "A new form of computation is emerging. Propelled by advances in software design and increasing connectivity, distributed computational systems are acquiring characteristics reminiscent of social and biological organizations. These open systems, self-regulating entities which in their overall behavior are quite different from conventional computers, engage in asynchronous computation of very complex tasks, while their **agents** spawn processes in other machines whose total specification is unknown to them. These **agents** also make local decisions based both on imperfect knowledge about the system and on information which at times is inconsistent and delayed. They thus become a community of concurrent processes which, in their interactions, strategies, and competition for resources, behave like whole **ecologies**." Actor model, reflection, and agent system [6] are integrated into the unifying concepts of ecosystem in [5] and [9].

At the base level, actors provide a framework for object orientation and concurrency. Reflection introduces metacognition in the actor universe, and adds a wide range of possibilities for both knowledge representation and computational aspects by providing an actor with a handy representation of itself. A reflective actor can reason and can act upon its own state and behavior, while a plain actor cannot. One step further, the agent concept brings in the agent's environment as a new dimension. An agent must be able to reason and act not only on itself, but upon its environment as well. It has to be provided with a partial representation of its surroundings.

To show how these paradigms can be applied to discrete-event or behavioral simulation, the chapter follows a progression similar to the historical evolution of object-oriented concurrent programming. The approach is problem-driven rather than technology-driven since a new step is presented as an improvement of the solution of a problem that could not be tackled before:

- **The first step** is concerned with the minimal extensions needed in an actor language for discrete-event simulation. Starting with knowledge representation, it presents the basic sharing mechanisms—inheritance and delegation—used by both object and actor systems for sharing knowledge and behavior. The impact of one or the other sharing mechanisms on discrete-event simulation programs is shown in some examples. A beehive model is taken as a first example of standard actor programming. This model introduces some extensions of the actor message-passing paradigm (*time-referenced* and *conditional messages*). These techniques are then applied to a steam machine model as a sample of a process control problem where delays are crucial for decision making.

- **The second step** introduces concurrency issues as an improvement of the efficiency of such frameworks. It shows how a classical time-warp system and a rollback mechanism based on the history of the actor is implemented in a message-driven system. However, the cost becomes too high memorywise. New techniques must be introduced in the architecture.

- **The third step** introduces reflection to solve the rollback problem, and to dynamically restore the state of an actor. In this paradigm, reflection provides the actor with a local, private, and somehow *reversible* interpreter [19] in which the effect of a given message can be cancelled by the antimessage of the message. Reflection helps clean up the implementation of rollback and reversible actors.

- **The fourth step** introduces agents as actors aware of their environment, described as an ecosystem. This framework for ecosimulation relies on the concept of ecosystem as *"a system involving the interactions between a community and its nonliving environment."* Agents make local decisions based on imperfect knowledge about the whole system or on inconsistent and delayed information. Agent programming improves the example of the beehive revisited by making bees aware of their environment. To be aware of its ecosystem, an agent is provided with a reflective dimension from which it can reason not only about itself, but about the ecosystem where it belongs as well. Then, it can eventually bring some changes into the system or into itself. Somehow, it adapts (optimize, trace, accept new coming entities, etc.) according to evolving circumstances.

8.2.   KNOWLEDGE REPRESENTATION WITH ACTORS

8.2.1. Bits of History

The original actor interpreter that first served as a basis for this work is called Plasma, standing for Planner-like System Modeled on Actors. Initially designed by Carl Hewitt at M.I.T., the language has been revisited at the Langages et Systèmes Informatiques (LSI) Laboratory of the Institut de Recherches en Informatique de Toulouse (IRIT) in Toulouse, France [24], while a portable Plasma interpreter was developed on an LILA virtual machine. Plasma is a lambda-language derived from Lisp, and is based on the concept of actors exchanging messages. To the application of a Lisp function to its arguments, Plasma substitutes that of the transmission of a message to an actor which will take care of it.[1]

---

1. The examples or algorithms found in the chapter refer to implementations with different actor languages, mainly Plasma and Actalk (standing for actors in Smalltalk-80). In order to make their descriptions more general and accessible, independently of any specific implementation, we have chosen to provide either figures or pseudo code descriptions, in a style inspired by Lieberman [19], instead of pure code.

8.2.2. Basic Principles of Actor Programming

Some previous experiments have shown that the actor methodology is quite powerful and flexible for the design of user-friendly interfaces, and enables the incremental and modular building of a system. Extended to discrete-event simulation, the approach shows that the dynamic nature of actors greatly improves the isomorphism between the conceptual model and the code itself, making design, maintenance, and debugging much easier.

The actor methodology leads to the development of abstractions from a set of concrete experiments, making the building of a system comparable to the molding from a sketch, in much the same way as a sculptor works. This approach contrasts with a centralized one where everything has to be fixed at the beginning. Thus, a physical system is modeled through the definition and specialization of autonomous processes, entities, or events, able to exchange information and cooperate. All styles of simulation modeling take advantage of the highly expressive character of actor systems, which also relieves the simulationist from the constraints of a predefined class hierarchy. The actor approach has already proved itself to be quite interesting for the design of user-friendly graphical interfaces, where actors are physically represented by graphical objects with a specific *behavior* and *knowledge*. An actor interface for education was built on a Xerox 1109 at Université de Montréal [12], showing how the actor methodology enables an incremental and modular building of a system.

The main feature of this method of system building is the absence of class hierarchies that allows the work to be done using only instances which can be cloned and specialized to better suit the special needs of a new instance. The actor approach differs from a "class"ical one, such as that of Smalltalk, because it does not imply the *a priori* definition for a group of abstract concepts. Sharing knowledge between actors is done by *delegation*, a mechanism that allows a scarcity of concepts, in the early stage of system design and implementation. Actors can refer knowledge or behavior to one another, and therefore can be specified only by their differences with other actors. An actor is not the end of a long conceptual chain in a hierarchy. Therefore, it becomes unnecessary to have a global idea of all the elements in a system before starting its implementation. It is very interesting to compare this approach with the one using classes in which abstractions have to be defined at first (defining class comes under bottom-up reasoning), and then applied to the particular and concrete cases (defining instances comes under top-down reasoning). Actor systems offer the alternative of a more "horizontal" path, as well as a "differential" approach: an actor can be used to define another one by analogy. It is often difficult to determine *a priori* the characteristics necessary for the definition of a concept. Actor languages appear as a very efficient tool to empirically develop complex systems. The actor model gives access to the main features of the object-oriented paradigm without imposing a predefined formalism. Instead, actors enable to define in a natural manner one's own formalism adapted to a given application. In a bottom-up style, the actor model builds abstraction out of concrete prototypes, to finally come up with a general model. Thus, the building of an actor system starts from a series of practical experiments, in contrast with the approach usually used in systems with class hierarchies. In the same way that [16] points out the advantages of using object-oriented languages to model physical systems, [25] shows that actors constitute a step further toward a more flexible and evolutionary environment.

8.2.3. Limitations

We mentioned how the absence of class hierarchies in actor systems allows one to start from instances which can be cloned and specialized to suit special needs. One should be aware that this brings flexibility, but at the cost of much of the support usually found in larger industrial systems. Often, creative programming and new powerful paradigms show what industry considers a weakness: a lack of software reliability and a lack of uniformity. Thus, a dark side of the distributed non"class"ical approach is that it may leave programmers on their own, when most of us have strong sequential thinking habits and little experience about parallel process coordination.

From another point of view, pure actor systems like Plasma-II [17] usually provide a poor programming environment, while new parallel algorithms that work are scarce. The event order in an actor program changes from one run to another, not making programs easy to put together and debug, especially when they are large. This weakness has been overcome by systems such as Actalk [3] built on top of Smalltalk-80, whose strong programming environment remains available. However, Actalk is more of a toy system for testing actor architecture than a robust actor system able to face industrial applications.

Most of the research in the area of parallel language has been practical, but with a limited formal basis. When it is formal and theoretical, it is too often at the expense of realism. In spite of this, large-scale systems such as air traffic control are developed from an actor substrate supporting agent programming [6]. We think that the field is very promising, and we know that there exists a real effort to bridge the gap between theory and practice, such as the research work done at the Open System Laboratory (University of Illinois) [1].

8.2.4. Actor-Sharing Mechanisms

Object-oriented systems, since SIMULA-67, traditionally propose the mechanisms of class, subclass, and inheritance to share knowledge between objects. A class is an explicitly identified abstraction, holding the common description of a set of related objects whose common behavior comes from inherited chunks. Class instances are *detached* objects which, once generated, behave on their own. Classes introduce a sort of typing that makes it difficult to deal with idiosyncratic objects or small deviations in form. Such objects are often called *independent* or *detached* in reference to SIMULA.

On the other hand, prototype-based languages, such as actor systems, instead use delegation as an alternative to inheritance. Delegation realizes sharing by the forwarding of messages to a prototype, combining the behaviors of both a template and an instance. Clone generation is part of the competence of this prototype actor, belonging to the same logical type as its clones. Then, clones are actors whose competence needs to extend only to the idiosyncratic treatment of requests since any message that they cannot handle is delegated to the prototype proxy. In that sense, clones are not detached actors. This mechanism removes the class/instance distinction, and allows an actor to change its behavior and that of its descendants on the fly. Lieberman first raised the question of the implementation of one sharing mechanism in terms of the other, concluding that delegation could implement inheritance, but that the reverse mapping was not possible. The debate is open between holders of traditional inheritance systems and those of systems using prototypical objects and delegation, although everyone agrees to recognize the flexibility of prototypes and their superiority for rapid and exploratory programming. So far, the temporary conclusion is that class and prototype facilities refer to two essential patterns of the world of cognition:

1. *templates* correspond to predefined structures for forming new objects

2. *empathy* is a quality for sharing knowledge and behavior in response to a message.

EXAMPLE—A Model of a Beehive. ────────────────────────────────
Worker bees are waiting in a FIFO queue, and arrive every *ta*—random uniform—to
feed their queen, taking *lunch time*—random uniform—simulated time units—so-called
similisecs—to eat a piece of food brought by one of the workers.

───

Belonging to the same family, worker bee instances can be created by a
bee generator from which they will inherit a generic behavior. They can,
as well, be clones of a prototype bee to whom they will refer every time
they must apply their generic behavior.

Sharing Behavior by Inheritance

Although an actor language usually has no predefined classes, it provides
the basics for the definition of generators, a dynamic equivalent of classes.
In Smalltalk or SIMULA, an instance has access to some piece of knowledge stored in its class through a *hard-wired lookup loop*. Instead, in an
actor system, everything has to be defined by the user. A *closure* and its
hidden *binding environment* (the set of local variables and their values)
inherited from the generator play the same role as instance objects in an
object-oriented system. A *receiver* is an actor usually built incrementally by
embedding blocks, each block defining a new binding. The name receiver
denotes the idea that one such actor expects messages. A binding may define an atom or a *cell* (assignable local variable) representing a piece of
knowledge, or it may encapsulate other receivers providing some specific
local behaviors as well. The hierarchy of embedded closures is similar to a
class hierarchy. In this discipline, an actor, once generated, is completely
detached from the matrix that served to cast it. When it is created, an actor
inherits every piece of knowledge it will need afterwards, so that it can behave on its own and perform the calculation for which it has been defined.
This means precisely that a copy of all the bindings is kept in the hidden
closure of every actor generated, making them grow larger and larger as
one goes down the hierarchy. This implies as well that the behavior of a
group of detached actors cannot be changed at run time, unless this change
was expected at the time of their creation. Even in this case, they each must
be notified of the change individually.[2]

A process generator for bees is a "class-like" entity that generates an
instance of bee every time it receives a *New* message. It knows about the
bee processes it creates and gives them names: *Bee1, Bee2, Bee3*, etc. Its
closure contains a random generator, *ta*, to issue the successive arriving

─────────────────────

2. In this case, the behavior of an actor can be modified dynamically at run time by a
reflective operation.

times of *Bees* with a uniform distribution. A generated bee has the form
of a *closure* whose behavior is a copy of the generator's *self*, closed in a
binding including the bee's name—*Bee5*—and a date—*TA*—that will be
used by *Bee5* as the date of arrival of its successor. Each bee process is
able to answer a specific request for its name or to apply its behavior. The
behavior of bees refers to the management of a simulated time dimension,
which will be discussed in a later section, after the introduction of time-
referenced messages. A pseudocode description of a generator would look
like the following:

```
Bee Process-Generator Definition:
if I am a Bee-Process-Generator actor then

    I know about the number Num of bees I have generated;
    I know about a random number generator ta;
    I expect a New message to activate my behavior, i.e.,
      build up the Name of a bee Bee_i to be created;
      cook up its arrival time TA;
      produce a new bee actor:

    Bee Self Definition:
    if I am a new bee actor then
      I know about my own name Bee_i;
      I know about the next arrival time TA;
      I expect two possible messages:
        either Name to identify myself;
        or Behav to act as a generic bee.
        (Here would come the definition of the behavior.)
```

Sharing Behavior by Delegation

Delegation removes the class/instance distinction. In the closure of an actor
prototype, one finds its own behavior and a receiver Defclone, whose behavior consists of creating clones. One such clone, specified by a difference
with its prototype Bee0, is therefore minimal. Whatever is not idiosyncratic
belongs to the prototype, and need not be held in the clone's closure. When
any piece of behavior is needed, it is asked of the prototype. A question
rapidly arises: As all the pieces of common behavior are now performed
by the prototype, what guarantees that they are performed as if the clone
did it?

   One no longer disposes of a *self* variable as in traditional object-
oriented systems. Delegation solves the problem by delegating a compound
message that contains the message itself and the address of the actor that
first received it, called the Client of the message. One of the significant

advantages of this style of code is certainly its reusability. Extension and modification of the prototype behavior have an immediate impact on any clone either already created or to be created, since everything is done by reference to the initial prototype. A pseudocode description of a prototype would look like the following:

```
Bee Proto Definition:
if I am a Bee-Proto actor then
I know about a DefClone actor

 DefClone Definition:
 if I am a DefClone actor then
 I expect a New message to produce a Clone actor:

    Clone Definition:
    if I am a clone of Bee-Proto then
      I know about my one name Bee_i;
      I expect two possible messages:
        either Name to identify myself;
        or Behav that I will delegate to Bee-Proto
        (along with my name, so that Bee-Proto will know
         who is asking).

  I know about the number Num of my clones
  I know about a random number generator ta;
  I expect several possible messages:

     Name to identify myself Bee0;
     New transmitted to DefClone
     to produce a new clone;
     NextArrival to produce a random arrival time TA;
     Num to generate the number of the next clone
     {Behav,Client} to make me perform
     the behavior of a prototypical bee
     as if Client were performing it.
     (Here would come the definition of the behavior.)
```

8.3. THE FIRST STEP: DISCRETE-EVENT SIMULATION WITH ACTORS

The contribution of artificial intelligence languages to discrete-event simulation is already largely acknowledged among the simulation community [16], [21], [30]. In the same vein, our extended actor environment offers tools to specialize the actor paradigm to the domain of discrete-event simulation.

This paper discusses some extensions of an actor language to discrete-event simulation and the application of this simulation package to some discrete-event simulation problems. After some bits of history about actor languages, we present several mechanisms available in actor languages for sharing knowledge and behavior: *generators*, using inheritance, and *prototypes*, using delegation. The use of generators leads to a classification comparable to the traditional object-oriented class-instance description, while the prototype approach is original to actor languages. The impact of each choice on discrete-event simulation is studied later in the example of *"the dance of bees."* A queueing network example is provided as a sample of the main dimensions of standard actor programming, as well as an introduction to some extensions of the actor message-passing paradigm, especially built for discrete-event simulation.

Actors use *envelopes* to pack messages and to express some specifications about how they should be processed: for example, the name of the actor expecting the reply to the message can be written on the envelope enclosing the message itself. The actor simulation toolkit presented here is based on two new types of envelopes:

1. *Time-stamped envelopes* contain both the message and the date (simulated time) at which it must be sent;

2. A *waituntil envelope* encloses a message and a condition (predicate actor), thus allowing for conditional sequencing among event or process actors in discrete-event simulation. For every simulated time step (*similisec*), the condition is reevaluated, and the message in the form is sent only if the result of that evaluation is *true*.

These new types of envelopes alter the flow of message transmissions, and introduce simulated time or conditions related to simulation as virtual dimensions of the usual sequence of interpretation. The flow of simulated time or the state of the model entities are now processed by the actor interpreter at the same level as the usual sequence of messages, with the effect of efficiently lightening the style of simulation programs. This combination of actor paradigm expressiveness and specific simulation programming tools results in an interesting environment for the development of experimental simulation software.

The first example, the dance of bees, demonstrates the efficiency of a style of actor programming based on delegation for discrete-event simulation programming, especially when it comes to behavioral simulation.

The simulation of a cybernetic self-regulated system is a second example that could easily be modeled in a standard actor context. However, the introduction of time-referenced message transmission adds the possibility of studying the effect of delays in the internal communication among the various parts of a whole system. This example could be easily generalized to a large class of process control problems, where the effect of delays in decision making is crucial.

8.3.1. Time-Referenced Messages

Time-referenced messages introduce a new paradigm for time sequencing, called *time-referenced message passing*, associating to a message a simulated date until which its transmission will be held. The actor message-passing model uses envelopes which may contain, aside from the message, the actor to which the reply must be sent. An envelope is a form whose head is an envelope identifier.

Time sequencing can be simplified a great deal by the use of a new type of dedicated time-referenced *at envelopes*, from the name of their identifier:

```
(at date message)
```

An *at envelope* allows a transmission to make a direct reference to a simulated time dimension. It evaluates as one of its kind, enclosing the evaluated values of the enclosed actors: if the value of *date* is *10* and that of *message* is *Hello*, then this *at envelope* above evaluates to (*at 10 Hello*).

When an *at envelope* is read by the extended actor interpreter, the corresponding transmission is inserted into a time-ordered event list. When this task is achieved, the value *unbound* is returned, and the interpreter carries on with the normal continuation of the current computation. In actor languages, the normal continuation of a message transmission may be seen as what normally follows this transmission when nothing unexpected occurs. It is usually determined by the syntactic context of the current instruction. Continuations are more precisely studied in [17].

```
((at date2 "message2) => act)
((at date1 "message1) => act)
```

In the above sequence, for example, the two transmissions are evaluated in increasing order of dates, and not in the order in which the sequence is written.

```
((at 12 "message) => act)
```

results in embedding an event notice such as

```
Event: send message to the actor act Time: 12
```

in a "sequencing list," and carrying on the usual continuation, that can be simply understood as the remaining computation. As soon as there is no continuation left, the interpreter starts evaluating the stack of held transmissions.

8.3.2. Conditional Transmissions

The previous section shows how a time-referenced message tells an actor to activate its behavior at a given simulated time. However, in simulation programs, we may want to express that some model entity has to be in a given state, before it is asked to perform a specific action. In the actor context, this means specifying that an actor must wait until an external condition becomes true before it activates its behavior. Such conditional sequencing is implemented in SIMULA by the *waituntil* primitive discussed in [27].

The communication system is completed by the introduction of the following new paradigm for conditional sequencing. For this purpose, the same operation that was used for time sequencing may be generalized to a new kind of form, whose head is the standard atom **when**:

```
(when true "message) is equivalent to "message,
(when false "message) is never forwarded
                          since its condition is always false.
```

This type of envelope includes a predicate actor whose state can change along with its interaction with other actors of the model:

```
((when <predicate> "message3) => act)
((at date2 "message2) => act)
((at date1 "message1) => act).
```

Until *<predicate>* becomes true, the transmission is held, and the following *at* transmissions are evaluated in the order of increasing times. However, after each of these transmissions, the held *when* transmission is tried again, in case *predicate* has become true. Then, *message3* is transmitted to the receiver *act*. *When* forms provide a general conditional sequencing statement that can be used to specify that an actor is waiting for an external condition to become true before it performs some action.

8.3.3. The Behavior of Bees in Terms
of Time-Referenced and Conditional Messages

In the previous illustration of a bee generator or a prototype bee, the definition of the behavior, involving time-referenced message passing and conditional transmissions, was left blank. Applied to the definition of behavior, the pseudocode description of the generic bee would look like the following:

Generic Bee Behavior Definition:
if I am a *Generic Bee Behavior* actor then

I expect a *Behav* message to
  <u>at time TA</u>, send the *Generator* (or *Proto*)
  a message *New* to create a new bee;
  place myself in the Queue;
  <u>when the Queen is available</u>, then activate the queen.

This behavior can be described as follows:

- Create one's successor. Schedule successor's execution at time: <current simulated time> + <time interval to next arrival>. One creates its successor just by scheduling the transmission of a time-stamped message (*at TA "New"*) to the generator that activates a new bee at the instant TA.

- Take one's turn in queue. Remove oneself from sequencing set. Queue is a specialized actor that places the current process into a waiting line. Queue actors' competence also includes statistics collection.

- If the queen is available, activate it. To activate the queen, one sends it a conditional message (*when("AvailableP => Queen*).

- If the queen is not available, nothing specific happens, and the control passes as well. Since there is no continuation to this transmission, the next step consists of passing the control any way to the scheduling monitor integrated into the interpreter.

8.3.4. Toward an Actor Approach of Discrete-Event Simulation

The Queen Process

Actor systems present most of the ingredients needed for a simple process model, holding a state. As actor languages use static binding, once an identifier is bound to a value, it cannot be reassigned during the same computation. Assignment in an actor language is done:

- either through *become*, which changes an actor's behavior or an actor's state by a replacement of its whole behavior

- or, in a less pure actor style, through cells, the only entities to which values can be assigned in the usual sense.

In this example, local variables—*cells*—represent the actor's state and provide the actor with a private memory. During the computation of the example, the queen process changes and recalls its own state, modeled by a cell local to this actor.

Besides recalling its state, the queen process may generate service duration with a random generator *lunch time* as well, and answer a few specific requests (messages):

- *Name* to identify

- *EatingFor* to produce a lunch duration

- *AvailableP* to produce queen's state (true or false)

- *Available* to change queen's state to true

- *Busy* to change it to false.

The behavior of the queen process is quite simple:

- If queue is empty, change one's state to true (when its state is true, queen is available) and deactivate. Deactivation is performed by the continuation's interplay.

- If queue is not empty, change one's state to false; then remove the first bee in line. Hold for a random *lunch time*. Holding is simply done by a transmission whose date is computed by the queen itself when it is sent the message *ServingFor*.

- The queen's behavior is cyclic: any time it is activated, its sequence of behavioral actions is resumed from the beginning. For a more complex behavior that has to be interrupted between two actions, a coroutine actor would be recommended.

Model Consistency Maintenance: The Dance of Bees

EXAMPLE—The Dance of Bees. ————————————————————————
The second example offered by the behavior of bees is based on the special flight called by entomologists the "dance of bees." The problem consists of modeling a swarm of bees in their search for pollen. When a bee finds a spot of flowers that is a potential source of pollen, it flies back to the hive and delivers this information to its sister bees. The knowledge to be shared includes the kind of flowers involved and the direction, distance, and capacity of the spot. The language used to communicate this information consists of given sequences of flight comparable to a choreography, so beekeepers call it a dance. Once a source is exhausted, bees learn about another one, if any, from a lucky one that found it. One wants

to do a simulation for two spots of flowers, namely, clover, direction NW[3], distance 300 m, amount 25,000, and alfalfa, direction SW, distance 250 m, amount 35,000. The unit for amount is such that when a bee gets to the spot, it decreases by one. The capacity of the beehive is 65,000 bees. One wants to know how long it will take the swarm to exhaust the two sources of flowers.

The beehive *BeeH* is represented by a list of bees, implemented by a list (Plasma would rather talk of a sequence, denoted by square brackets):

`[Bee1 Bee2 ... Bee7].`

The first bee to be activated performs its actions, and then goes at the end of this list so that a rotation takes place. At reception of some message, a bee first checks if any of its friends, ignorant about the flowers, is left in the hive. In this case, the activated bee teaches the left-out worker, i.e., creates a new one with the same behavior, and then flies to the flowers. Its behavior is held for the duration of the trip which depends on the distance and the direction (as far as the wind is concerned) of the flowers. When it arrives on the spot, the activated bee checks the number of flowers left. If this amount is not null, it decreases it by one, and then sends some message to the next one in the sequence. But if the spot is exhausted, our bee has to select another source and let it be known by the others. One must take into account that this can happen at any moment, whether all the bees have been generated or not. In the latter case, the behavior of newly generated bees has to be changed, as well as that of all existing bees. This is done very easily using prototypes and delegation.

Figures 8.1(a) and (b) gives a schema of the behavior of bees for both kinds of implementation of the creation of the swarm. In this example, the population of bees is very large; then it becomes important to be able to change their behavior on the fly without having to address each of them. With the use of generators or classes, the change would be done by changing the behavior of the generator, or in a traditional object-oriented system, by creating a subclass and new instances of this subclass. In traditional object-oriented languages such as Smalltalk, SIMULA, or C++, instance objects, once created, carry on during all their lifetime with the behavior and knowledge provided at their creation, unless this behavior and knowledge are changed explicitly on an individual basis, by recompiling methods, for example. The prototype and delegation model, whose details are given

---

3. So far, real life bees do not use a compass, but rather locate a direction relative to the sun. For the purpose of the paper, one must consider that cardinal orientation is much easier to understand.

in the form of pseudocode descriptions, makes it easier to dynamically change the behavior of existing objects just by changing the behavior of a prototype. The change then has an immediate effect on all clones attached to this prototype.

The inheritance style produces larger actors, while delegation imposes a longer search for knowledge and behavior, but this issue addresses more implementors than simulationists. Beyond the question of the so-called "speed-for-space tradeoff," the major issue for the simulation community lies in the facility of expression and flexibility. The next example shows that a differential approach like delegation is more natural and concrete than one using the abstract concept of class, especially for interactive simulation. Furthermore, this approach proves to be more efficient when the behavior of the actors in the model is subject to dynamic changes.

The Steam Machine: An Example of Process Control

EXAMPLE—The Steam Machine. ─────────────────────────

The third example, the steam machine of Figure 8.2, can be modeled as a cyclic self-regulated system composed of three parts interacting with one another: a water tank, a burner and its oil alimentation, and a regulator. The water tank contains water and steam

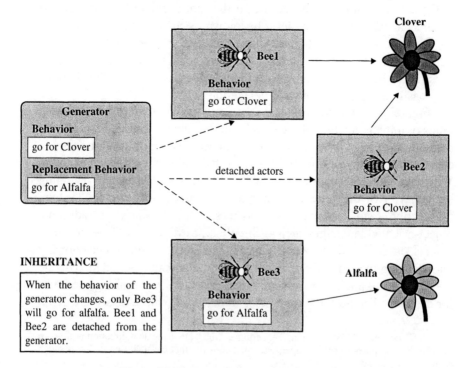

Figure 8.1(a) Creating the swarm with a generator.

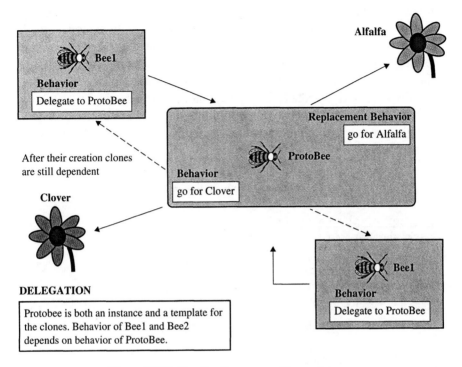

Figure 8.1(b) Creating the swarm with a prototype.

whose pressure serves as a power supply for a given mechanism. It is heated by the oil burner. The pressure in the tank is roughly proportional to the amount of oil supplied. Then, it is obvious that, after a while, the water tank would explode without a regulation system, the regulator, which lowers the oil alimentation when the pressure gets too high.

Figure 8.2 shows the steam machine whose pseudocode description is given above. There is no problem modeling such a system with standard actors.

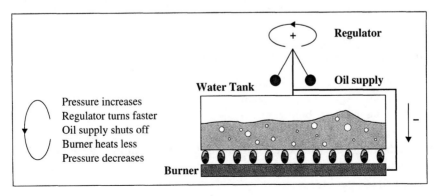

Figure 8.2 The steam machine.

In such a case, one would see which pressure is needed to activate the regulator, knowing that beyond this limit, the tank would explode. However, in the real world, when the regulator is activated, it takes some time before its action becomes effective enough to make the pressure decrease. The use of at envelopes allows one to study the effect of a *delay* in the negative feedback introduced by the regulator on the behavior of the whole system. A delay of 10 between the moment the pressure in the tank gets to a given value and the moment the regulator reacts is modeled with an at envelope:

```
(at (+ 10 (simtime))("Pressure => WaterTank))
```

Behavior of the Water Tank
Check whether burner is heating or not.

  If burner is heating, then check steam pressure.

  If pressure is lower than last-security-level,
  then augment it by 1; else BOOM!!!

  If burner is not heating, then decrease pressure by 1.

Behavior of the Burner
Check whether regulator is active or not.

  If regulator is active, then set HeatingP to false.

  If regulator is not active, then set HeatingP to true.

Behavior of the Regulator
At <current time> + <delay>, get water tank pressure.

If pressure is greater than first-security-level, then set my activity indicator, ActiveP, to true; else set it to false.

Behavior of the Steam Machine
Until simtime is expired, run a cycle consisting of

  Activate water tank behavior
  Activate regulator behavior
  Activate burner behavior.

When the delay does not exceed four simulated time units—*4 similisecs*—the regulator still has enough time to play its role and avoid something really bad happening:

```
("On => Burner) --->          WaterTank_1
                    Burner_true
                    WaterTank_2

            <a few similisecs later...>
                    WaterTank_13
                    Burner_false
                    RegActive
                    WaterTank_12
                    Burner_false
                    RegActive
                    WaterTank_11
                    Burner_false

            <a few similisecs later...>
                    Stop
```

The pressure can reach the value 14, quite close to the limit, but then the action of the regulator becomes effective, and the pressure starts going down.

What happens if, for any reason, the delay reaches *5 similisecs*?

```
((at (+ 5 (simtime))("Pressure => WaterTank))) ?

("On => Burner) ---> WaterTank_1
                Burner_true
                WaterTank_2

        <some similisecs later...>

                WaterTank_14
                Burner_true
                RegNeutral
                WaterTank_15
                Burner_true
                RegActive
                WaterTank_BOOM
```

This approach can easily be applied to the study of process control where the activity of a production division depends on decisions taken at a control level, while the control level uses the feedback it gets from the production to make those decisions. The good functioning of such a cyclic system depends heavily on the rhythm of information exchanges and on the delays in decision making. The extended actor context provides a good environment for modeling this class of problem. Just like a flowchart can give a *static* viewpoint on the critical steps of a set of tasks, such as an assembly line, the kind of actor simulation proposed here would give a *dynamic* one, and would allow one to play *interactively* with delays at some point of the line and see the effects on the whole line.

Summary of the First Step

The first step has shown that actor languages offer an interesting framework for the exploration of various styles of discrete-event simulation. However, the introduction of simulated time as an extra sequencing dimension brings to the fore a need for a specialized time control. Hewitt explains that one of the major benefits of the actor approach consists of replacing "hairy control structures" by patterns of passing messages. The introduction of a virtual time dimension in the context of standard actors appears as a drawback, for it puts the monitor at the same level as the actors representing the entities of the model, not bothering with the conceptual difference between them. This forces a programming style in which time control becomes too explicit, and where the transmissions of messages related only to the management of simulated time are mixed with the ones related to process events or entity interactions. The lack of transparency of these control structures stands up against the expressivity which is supposed to be a strength of the actor approach. It is possible to offset this drawback by creating new patterns of actor transmissions, using time-referenced envelopes, that make simulated time a new dimension in the evaluation of a transmission. The use of these new patterns of passing messages improves the isomorphism between the model description and the code itself. This approach can be extended to the definition of special forms for conditional transmissions, enlarging the scope of the actor interpreter to the modeling of systems in which the sequence of events depends not only on the simulated time, but also on the state of other components of the model, like an activity scanning world view. Time-referenced and conditional transmissions appear as an abstraction barrier that leads to a style of actor simulation programming where the programmer can ignore (until a certain point) the underlying control algorithm.

To share knowledge and behavior, actors use delegation as an alternative to inheritance. The inheritance style produces larger actors, while delegation imposes a longer search for knowledge and behavior, but this issue addresses more implementors than simulationists. Beyond the question of the "speed-for-space tradeoff," the simulation community should feel more concerned with the facility of expression and flexibility. A differential approach like delegation seems more natural, especially for interactive simulation, than the usual one, based on the abstract concept of class. It is also more efficient when the behavior of some model components is subject to dynamic changes.

It appears that these specialized dimensions, added to an actor language, provide a good environment to define and test nonclassical models of simulation. This specialization of actors helps in enhancing the structural correspondence between the real world and the models, already largely improved by the use of the object-oriented or the actor paradigms.

But so far, no room is made for the essence of actor systems: fine-grained concurrency. Up to this point, actors are just dealt with as flexible, class-independent objects, endowed with sophisticated knowledge-sharing mechanisms and customizable communication structures. Concurrency would bring parallelism into simulation, improving its efficiency, but bringing in, as a side effect, synchronization problems. Finding solutions to such problems is the purpose of our second step, especially concerned with actor Time Warp, synchronization, and concurrency issues. Actor synchronization relies on the use of *serializers*, providing the actor with a mailbox where pending messages are waiting in the order of arrival. Actor time warp uses a similar mechanism, except that time-referenced messages wait to be processed in the order of simulated time arrival. A message whose simulated time stamp is smaller than the first stamp in the line causes a local rollback. Local rollbacks cascade among the actors of the model since later messages sent by an actor that rolled back will eventually force other actors of the model to roll back themselves.

8.4.   CONCURRENCY ISSUES AND THE ACTOR MODEL OF COMPUTATION

The major principles of the actor model of computation are:

- maximal concurrency
- bounded nondeterminism
- asynchrony
- locality
- no assignment.

For maximal concurrency, the actor model assumes that concurrency is the default [1].

The concept of serializer. Since sequential execution must be obtained by construction, two kinds of actors must be considered: on the one hand, history-insensitive actors, comparable to mathematical functions, are called *pure actors*. The order of message arrival has no influence on the result of their internal computation; their behavior looks constant. On the other hand, history-sensitive actors are called *serialized actors*. Because of asynchrony, the message flow has to be buffered. Since an actor computes messages one at a time. i.e., *serially*, mutual exclusion is automatically achieved. An *event* is the reception of a message by its actor target. Therefore, events with the same target are ordered according to the order of message arrival at the target. The buffer in which messages wait to be processed is a FIFO queue called the *mailbox* of the actor. This explains the schematic representation of an actor found in Figures 8.3–8.5.

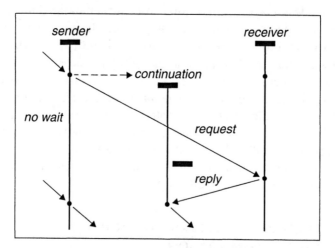

Figure 8.3 The concept of continuation.

The concept of continuation (Figure 8.3). The basic idea behind the model is to keep computation fluid, i.e., to perform little computation for each request. Communication is one-sided, i.e., the sender must specify the actor to whom the answer of a message must be transmitted. Rather than performing by itself the whole computation, an actor initiates it and delegates the remainder—*the continuation of the computation*—to some other actor that it creates for that purpose. (Such a continuation is called a *customer*. It is usually transmitted on the envelope that contains the message.)

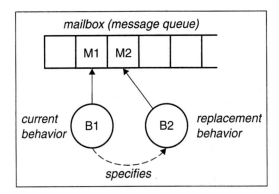

Figure 8.4 The concept of replacement behavior.

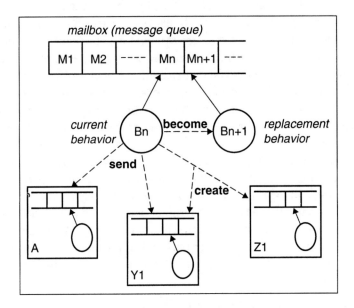

Figure 8.5 The three actions of a behavior.

The concept of replacement behavior (Figure 8.4). In the same spirit, an actor's behavior—the autonomous process associated to the actor—computes only one message. When computing a message, the current behavior specifies its *replacement behavior*, the one that will compute the next message. This means that the way the next message will be computed is concurrently specified by the current behavior while it takes care of the current message. As soon as this replacement behavior is specified, computation of next message may take place.

The three actions of a behavior (Figure 8.5). A behavior can perform concurrently three specific kind of actions:

- *specify* its replacement behavior (become <next behavior>)
- *create* new actors
- *send* messages to other actors.

8.5.   THE SECOND STEP: ACTOR TIME WARP

8.5.1. Parallel Discrete-Event Simulation

Jefferson's Time Warp (TW) is known to be one of the most popular distributed simulation algorithms [15]. The algorithm[4] can easily be implemented in an actor context in which actors represent logical entities that simulate the physical processes of the system to be modeled, while process actor communication uses time-referenced messages, as explained in the first section of the chapter. So far, with a concern for clarity, no mention was made of communication aspects related to asynchronous message passing. In order to maximize concurrency, thus avoiding the need for the sender of a message to wait for a possible answer, most Object-Oriented Concurrent Programming (OOCP) models, especially Agha's actor model of computation, considers asynchronous message passing as the fundamental mode.

This section focuses on such concurrency issues; more precisely, on the definition and the implementation of TW under Agha's model of computation, it studies the details of the implementation of TW in that context, demonstrating, in particular, the need for antimessages. We assume, in the rest of this section, that the autonomous logical processes that simulate the physical processes of the system to be modeled are identified to Process Actors (PAs).

- A PA maintains an implicit local clock (stamp of the last message processed).
- A PA receives messages.
- A PA performs its behavior (internal computation).[5]
- A PA sends messages.

---

4. This section sketches the implementation of TW, rollback, and antimessages in the actor context. For a more general description of TW, one should refer to Jefferson's original paper on virtual time.

5. The kind of actions that can be performed by an actor's behavior is explained later, with the details of the gear work of actor computation.

Each PA may or may not be placed on its own processor since this is managed at the actor level in order to maximize parallelism and to balance the workload of each component of the system. Therefore, it is transparent to the programmer. Generally speaking, the PDES algorithms themselves may tend to limit parallelism in order to prevent the simulation from deadlocking and to ensure correctness. In an actor system, such control belongs to the interpreter or to the virtual machine, and therefore is beyond the reach of the PDES algorithm.

Among the techniques developed to address deadlocking and correctness, we focus on TW and the rollback mechanism it uses for synchronization. Because of the lack of determinism in the succession of events during actor computation, causality between events may be impossible to maintain without a specific algorithm to take care of it. Otherwise, there is no guarantee that the real-time chronology of events in the actor system is coherent with the simulated time chronology of the corresponding events in the physical system. In order to maintain causality between events, TW makes the entire system roll back and cancel any operations that violated causality.

In order to get into more detail about the actor implementation of the algorithm, we must take into consideration the concurrency mechanisms underlying the actor model of computation that were presented in the previous section.

8.5.2. History-Sensitive Actors

To restore a previous state of the system before reexecuting the operations that violated causality, actor TW keeps a local perspective: when a PA detects an incoherence, i.e., receives a message whose time stamp is less than its Local Virtual Time (LVT), it is forced to *roll back* to a time before the time stamp of the arriving message. Rollback propagates, by way of antimessages, among the acquaintance[6] PAs of the PA that started it.

Each PA keeps track of its own history, a list of pair message-behaviors. Here appears the power of the actor model of computation as defined in [1], [12]:

> Intuitively, an ACTOR is an active agent which plays a role on cue according to a script. Our formalism shows how all of the modes of behavior can be defined in terms of *one* kind of behavior: *sending messages to actors.*

---

6. The acquaintances of an actor A are other actors whose "mail address" is known by A.

The uniformity of the model, as emphasized by Hewitt, allows one to keep an actor history in terms of time-stamped messages and corresponding behaviors, as shown in Figure 8.6.

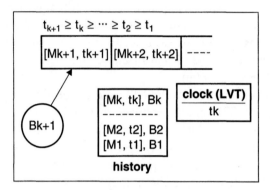

Figure 8.6 The history of an actor.

8.5.3. Actor Rollback: What Happens at Run Time?

To roll an actor back according to a virtual time dimension is conceptually tantamount to resetting its state at any point of its history, which is easy from a local point of view:[7] it is like "erasing" a slice of virtual time in the actor's life. However, to locally reset an actor's state is not sufficient, since during this slice of time, the actor may have been the cause of several events, as shown in Figure 8.7(a). Since a behavior performs three classes of actions, a rollback mechanism has to undo any action, belonging to one or another of these three classes, in the lapse of virtual time to be erased:

- Since *become events* are internal to the actor, they are undone locally.
- *Create events* cannot be undone, but no call to actors created during an erased lapse of virtual time will occur in the future. Therefore, they will be garbage collected.
- Every *send event* has to be undone explicitly by the antimessage corresponding to the message sent. An antimessage either erases its corresponding time-stamped message if this message is still in the mailbox, or it erases the pair message-behavior if the message is already part of the history.

Figure 8.7 shows details of the effect of a virtually backdated message on actors that were created or that exchanged messages before the time

---

7. Later, we will show how reflection helps to make it technically easy.

stamp of the new coming message. In Figure 8.7(c), the antimessage *[N2, t2]* erases only [N2, t2]. Message [M'2, t'2] that was sent by A2 remains in the mailbox, or would have remained in the history together

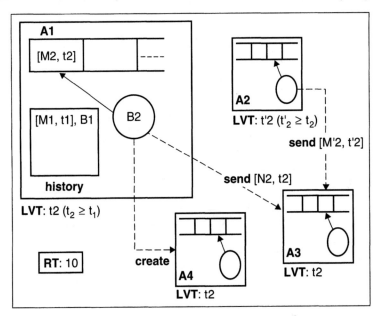

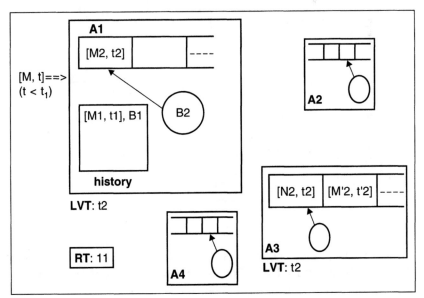

Figure 8.7 Different phases of actor Time Warp at run time.

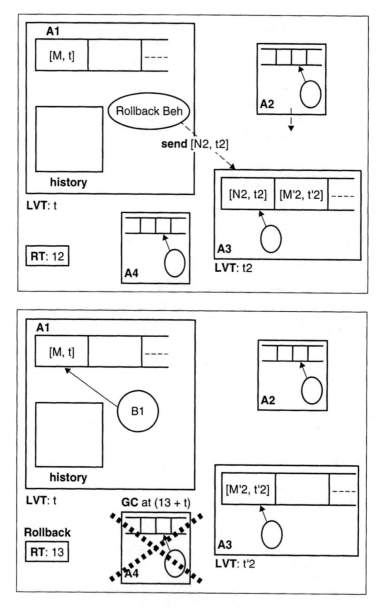

Figure 8.7 *Continued*

with the behavior that took care of it. It will be processed later. A4 that was created by A1 at LVT t2 becomes a ghost actor. Becoming unknown, it does not receive messages any longer, and is then garbage collected after a while.

8.5.4. Summary of the Second Step

The second step shows that concurrency, and thus efficiency issues, can be introduced through a classical TW algorithm. In order to describe an actor approach of TW, we had to get a little deeper into the gear work of Agha's actor model of computation. Since our major concern was to describe and to understand *what happens at run time* in an actor TW system, we did not look too closely at the implementation, instead emphasizing the different phases witnessed in an actor TW system.

The third step takes into account the implementation aspects that were so far neglected. Previously, it introduced reflection as a new dimension to be added to the system in order to make its customization much easier: rollback will be implemented at the *metalevel* without any major modification of the actor system in a reflective architecture. For this reason, we can say that reflection provides an economic solution to the rollback problem linked to any TW system. The section begins with a short introduction of the major ideas behind reflection based on an example of a reflective system which is used, further on, to give an outline of an implementation of a rollback mechanism.

8.6.   COMPUTATIONAL REFLECTION

Lisp programmers have always been familiar with the concept of metacircularity. In a metacircular interpreter, "program is data" becomes "*language is data*." These data are a description of the programming language in its own syntax. These are close family links between reflection and metacircularity, the former appearing as a structured and dynamic systemization of the latter. Smith initiated this work thread with 3-Lisp in the early 1980s [26]. Since then, the concept has been thoroughly explored:

- Reflection implements dynamically monitoring aspects [20].

- Reflective systems have shown their practical interest for implementing systems because of their ability to represent the functionality and the implementation of a system within the system itself.

- Reflective systems provide programmers with hooks on a programming language to customize it: Clos uses reflection as a metacircular description of classes and objects (*the metaobject protocol*) that helps customize the core of the object system.

- MUSE applies reflection to the design of an operating system.

- Reflective systems provide a general framework to support and structure mechanisms somehow adaptive.[8] It can be used as the essential dimension of "adaptive" processes evolving in a dynamic environment in [7]–[10].

Computational reflection is the activity performed by a computational system when doing *meta*computation about its own *base*computation which affects this *base*computation [20]. According to Maes' early work, a reflective system is:

> . . . a computational system which is about itself *in a causally connected way*: Any program is *about a domain*, which means that its internal structure incorporates some aspects of this domain. A program and its domain are said to be causally connected if changes in one lead to a corresponding effect on the other, just like the image seen in the viewfinder of a camera is causally connected to the piece of reality aimed at by the camera. A reflective system is to a system which incorporates structures representing some aspects of itself.

Therefore, reflection is the ability for a system to reason about itself and its own behavior (computation and actions).

8.6.1. "What Do You Mean, *Meta?*"[9]

We rely on Smith's essential work on reflection to introduce the basic ideas underlying the concept: "*The metalevel is probably the most identifiable feature of a reflective system.*" For a language to be reflective, there has to be a (potential) *metalevel* that describes some of its elements in terms belonging to the language itself.

- The metalevel description of a reflective system may be potential (also called *delayed*) in order to keep the system from being too heavy. Since metacomputation is a kind of computation performed by the system about its own structure or its own behavior, it consumes resources that are not available in the meantime for any computation related to the domain.

- The metalevel description of a reflective system *reifies* some aspects of the system it *denotes*, known as the *base level* (*denotation*).

---

8. The last part of the paper presents some applications of this dimension of reflective architectures to ecosystem modeling and behavioral simulation.

9. The striking title of Brian Cantwell Smith's position paper, "What do you mean meta?" *ECOOP/OOPSLA'90 Workshop on Reflection and Metalevel Architectures in Object-Oriented Programming Proceedings*, Ottawa, Canada, 1990.

Reification (also called "thingification" by Seymour Papert) is the process of changing some hidden part of a system into data. *Reify* is tantamount to "*uncompile*".

- Any change at one level reflects immediately at the other: a reflective system is said to be "in a causally connected way about itself" [20]. This means that a reflective actor is provided with a "causally connected representation" of itself. "Causally connected" simply means that when one changes, the other one does as well.

Reflection may be applied either:

- *introspectively*—about one's self and one's internal thought process, or
- *externally*—about one's behavior and situation in the world.

Further on in this section, a reflective implementation of rollback makes heavy use of introspective reflection. First, it is necessary to take a closer look at actor's reflection.

8.6.2. Actor and Meta-Actor

A reflective actor system can use a metaobject approach. This is the case of Reactalk [9], a reflective version of the Actalk actor kernel developed on top of Smalltalk-80 [3]. However, the structure of a meta-actor is implementation-free, as proves another one realized in Plasma-II.

In a meta-actor structure,

- *What is reified?* Every step of message circulation, from message arrival to next message arrival.
- *How is the link between actor level and meta-actor level implemented?* A Meta instance variable is given to any actor (eventually) provided with a meta-actor.
- A <u>Denotation</u> variable denotes (point on) the actor. Its value is often the actor's address itself.
- *When should one go from the actor level to the metalevel?*

Some kinds of messages provoke:

- the creation of the meta-actor if it does not exist already
- a shift to the metalevel.

In an actor language, actor interaction and evolution are message-driven. Thus, it is not surprising that messages provide a privileged lever to reflection.

In Reactalk, the gear work of message processing is "taylorized" [8]; messages are pieces progressing on an assembly line. At any moment, either workers (actors) or pieces (messages) can be removed from the line, replaced, or modified, and then put back on the line once fixed. Workstations along the "message-processing line" are associated to agents working concurrently. This "organizational" view of actor computation helps to improve the grain of parallelism.

8.6.3. Actor Reflection without Meta-Actor

A reflective actor system can also follow an approach without meta-actor [27]. Reflection appears as an attempt to give programs some knowledge about their own text and about the context in which they are executed. In early work on reflection such as 3-Lisp, a program had access to the data structures of its own interpreter:

- an expression e to be evaluated
- a binding environment r
- a continuation k to which the value of e on r is to be sent.

In an actor language like Plasma-II, these data structures are:

- a binding environment vars, defined through message passing by pattern matching
- a script body
- a local binding environment state-vars (that many contain cells)
- a FIFO queue storing messages waiting to be processed by the actor.

Reflection without meta-actor in an actor language uses *reifying* messages and *reflecting* ones to manipulate these data structures.

Reflective Counter Definition:
```
if I am a Reflective Counter actor then
I know about the number Num of messages I have processed;
I expect

    either a Reify message to output
    the binding environment [Num value]
    in which my script is evaluated;
```

```
or a Reflect message [Num new_value]
to install a new binding environment
in which my script is evaluated.
```

Reifying messages can be:

- either nonfreezing, when one wants a snapshot of the internal register of an actor,
- or freezing when one wants to stop the computation, and get the internal register of an actor.
- In this case, the actor will wake up when it receives a *reflect* message that will reinstall the registers with new "reflected" values.

8.7.   THE THIRD STEP: ROLLBACK IN A REFLEXIVE ARCHITECTURE

8.7.1. The Life and Time of a Message

During the lifetime of a message, many events may occur either at message reception or during message processing:

At message reception

- Transmission of the message.
- Arrival of the message at the actor's address.
- Reception of the message by the actor.
- Storage of a message in the mailbox.

During message processing

- Request for the next message to be performed.
- Selection of the next message meeting a given criterion.
- Retrieval of a selected message from the mailbox.
- Performance of an action *before* the execution of the script.
- Processing of the message by the script.
- Performance of an action *after* the execution of the script.

These events underline the overall architecture of the message factory since they determine the interactions between agents. The metalevel is defined so as to reify and isolate any event that can be manipulated and modified. Each actor in the metalevel description of the computational behavior is dedicated to a single given task.

8.7.2. Rollback from a Metalevel Viewpoint

In the actor model of computation, any behavior can be expressed in terms of *one* kind of behavior: *sending messages to actors*. Since the metalevel describes most events occurring either at message reception or during message processing, rollback can be expressed in the same way: specific components of the meta-actor can be notified to take care of given tasks whose conjunction will result in a rollback. The whole rollback mechanism can thus be set up dynamically by message transmission to these components of the meta-actor.

Ordering the Mailbox

In the first part of the chapter, time-stamped messages were put in a queue in increasing order at the interpreter level. Therefore, the simulation interpreter was slightly different from the regular one: changes had to be hardwired in the interpreter; stack processing was specific to discrete-event simulation.

In the metalevel architecture, the Mailbox Manager is in change of anything regarding the organization of the Mailbox. The Mailbox Manager is a complex actor whose behavior can be changed dynamically by sending it a message. In this case, the Mailbox Manager can be notified to order messages by increasing virtual dates; it will store messages in the actor mailbox following this instruction until a new message specifies it not to do so.

Keeping Track of the History

In the metalevel architecture, the Execution Manager is in charge of anything regarding the processing of messages. Thus, it may be notified to keep track of the actor's history, as shown in Figure 8.6, i.e., to maintain a queue of pairs <Behavior, Message>, as well as the flow of messages sent by these successive behaviors.

Launching the Rollback

This is the Execution Manager that is in charge of the coherence of the computation as well. Therefore, before processing a message, it will check the Local Virtual Time coherence. If it detects an incoherence, the Execution Manager decides to launch the rollback.

8.7.3. Summary of the Third Step

The third step introduces reflection in the actor universe. It shows how rollback, as any specific computation requirement, can be notified in a reflexive architecture at the metalevel without any permanent change of the interpreter. Time-warp mechanisms can be implemented independently of any simulation. In a reflective architecture, the implementation of time warp and rollback is based on reflection and on the same idea as reversible interpreters defined by Lieberman [19].

8.8.   AGENTS, FROM SELF-CONTAINMENT TO ECOLOGIES

A new form of computation is emerging. Propelled by advances in software design and increasing connectivity, distributed computational systems are acquiring characteristics reminiscent of social and biological organizations. These open systems, self-regulating entities which in their overall behavior are quite different from conventional computers, engage in the asynchronous computation of very complex tasks, while their agents spawn processes in other machines whose total specification is unknown to them. These agents also make local decisions based both on imperfect knowledge about the system and on information which at times is inconsistent and delayed. They thus become a community of concurrent processes which, in their interactions, strategies, and compeition for resources, behave like whole ecologies [13].

The fourth step needs an introduction to agents as a step ahead in actor programming. Using the metaphor introduced by Huberman, an agent is a community of concurrent processes behaving like a whole ecology in its interactions, strategies, and competition for resources with its neighbors. Agents can make local decisions based on imperfect knowledge about the whole system or on inconsistent and delayed information.

Agents are used to define a framework for *ecosimulation*: "*the simulation of the behavior of an ecosystem, based on object-oriented concurrent programming.*" Ecosimulation relies on the concept of ecosystem: "*a system involving the interactions between a community and its nonliving environment.*" To be aware of its ecosystem, an agent is provided with a reflective dimension from which it can reason about the ecosystem where it belongs, in order to *adapt* according to evolving circumstances, i.e., eventually change it or change itself.

These new concepts are applied to an example already used in the first step: the example of the beehive revisited. In an agent context, bees become aware of their surroundings, i.e., the environment described as an ecosystem. The beehive simulation keeps individual modeling and interactions between an individual and an ecosystem at a rather simple level. This application of the agent simulation framework to an ecological system of the real world demonstrates how concurrent computer systems get cues from the simulation of ecosystems, and achieves the validation of both sides of the ecological metaphor.

8.8.1. The Ecological Metaphor

The ecological metaphor is used to explain ecological system behavior in terms of concurrent computation: What computer system concepts would help improve the simulation of real ecosystems, and therefore deepen their understanding? How can these concepts be integrated in order to achieve this goal? The results of some experiments well suited for *ecosimulation* (simulation of the behavior of an ecosystem) should help find answers to some of these questions.

Traditional AI travels back and forth from human to computer behavior, making an intensive use of the "computational metaphor" based on the analogy between brain and computer [4]. From cognitive to computer science, cognition theory supplies models for intelligent computer applications; from computer to cognitive science, the so-called "computational metaphor" takes the sequential computer for the model of cognitive processes. These exist similar family connections between ecological and *concurrent* computer systems so that each of those fields helps to provide deeper knowledge about the other. Several examples show that shift, from psychological insights up to either sociological or ecological ones:

- Hewitt searches for hints through social or business organizations instead of taking cues from individuals. He uses these analogies to build up open information system semantics for concurrent and distributed systems [13].

- Minsky's *Society of Mind* proposes the reverse analogy, and traces a path from computer systems to a model of intelligence. He introduces the concept of agent, and describes intelligent behavior as the result of interactions among many "computational" agents described in terms of a society [22].

Traveling both directions calls for expressive tools integrated into a general framework:

- to explore the first direction, via modeling and implementing realistic and truthful concurrent simulations of ecosystems, i.e., of systems involving the interactions between a community and its nonliving environment;

- to implement open concurrent applications inspired by theories in ecology.

The framework proposed further on in this section expresses both ecological and computational research models within the same formalism. The obvious advantage is to make one side directly inherit from discoveries in the other without much effort. The main purpose of its design is the study of *adaption* within both ecological and concurrent systems: adapation appears as a major dimension of ecosystems, as well as a crucial property for Open Information Systems (OIS) interacting with a fluid reality.

8.8.2. Open Information Systems

Hewitt's work on OIS is inspired by knowledge of societies and organizations [11]. OISs deal with large quantities of diverse information and exploit massive concurrency. OISs are characterized by: 1) concurrency, 2) asynchronicity, 3) decentralized control, 4) inconsistent information, 5) arm's-length relationships, and 6) continuous operation.

> The components of an open system are at arm's-length relationships: The internal operation, organization, and state of one computational agent may be unknown and unavailable to another agent for reasons of privacy or outage of communications. Information should be passed by explicit communication between agents to conserve energy and maintain security [13].

The openness of OISs forces their design to take into account their own evolution since they are confronted with unpredictable events coming from the environment into which they are open. An OIS must adapt in order to overcome the narrowness and the rigidity of most traditional systems. When faced with unexpected situations, only an adaptive system has a chance to evolve on its own instead of breaking down. In addition, a system able to adapt does not need the intervention of designers or users to tackle such events. Aside from smoothing the interactions, adaptation may also ease the integration and the cooperation of several heterogeneous systems, and thus facilitate the construction of complex systems.

8.8.3. Actors as Parts of OIS

Most of Hewitt's work belongs to the actor paradigm, formally defined in Agha's actor model of concurrent computation, presented in the first step. At this point, one aspect appears important: the model exploits concurrent processes without making any assumptions on their location over a network of processors; message passing is asynchronous, and the arrival order of messages is nondeterministic. Knowledge in OIS is essentially local; the notion of global state is nonsense. Agha's actor model provides an efficient framework for partitioning complex systems into independent concurrent entities, and in this sense, it stands as a good basis for the representation of OIS and ecosystems. However, actors provide only the lowest layer needed to model ecosystems because they do not take into account the link between an actor and its environment.

8.8.4. Agents, from Self-Containment to Ecologies

From actor to agent, the road is direct: an agent is an organization of actors embedded in an ecosystem. Under the Distributed Artificial Intelligence (DAI) paradigm [6], the concept finds its roots in a social conception as well as in a biological one:

- From a social point of view, an agent knows about local goals to satisfy, and deals with its environment and other agents to reach these goals. The global solution of a problem emerges from the interactions between these entities.

- From a biological point of view, the intelligence of a system emerges as a side effect of the interactions between local entities, generally lacking intelligence.

Nevertheless, actors and agents capture only part of the essence of the real world: the real world is dynamic, and its entities evolve with time. Then, the ecosystem as a whole has to be modeled, and individuals must be able to modify themselves and evolve. ALife provides a model of the environment, while reflection provides actors and agents with self-manipulation and self-adaptation capabilities.

8.8.5. To Set Up the Landscape: ALife Patches

As Bateson [2] mentions, it is not possible to understand the evolution and the behavior of a living being without linking it to the evolution and the behavior of other living beings in its environment. The evolution of the horse is closely related to that of the herbs on which it feeds. In the same spirit, *situated activity* supposes that one is always in relation with its environment in which one adopts a local perspective. In this context, the environment is a set of external surroundings in which a plant or animal lives, which tends to influence its development and behavior. This concept is central in ALife, even if usually defined in a simplistic way as simple sets of *patches* [5], [23].

ALife is a blend of biology, ethology, and computer science. Unlike biology and ethology, ALife gathers explanations about animal behavior and evolution from the creation and observation of artificial robotics animals. ALife departs from traditional AI or cognitive science since it does not try to model the functionality of a single, centralized, highly complex system, such as the human brain, but rather chooses to model simpler entities whose conjunction will result in self-organization as an emergent effect. An example of self-organization is provided by bees collecting pollen, ants building their nests or looking for food, birds moving together in a flock, or larvae of coleopteran aggregating in clusters. Another example of ALife, helping to understand adaptive systems and evolution by natural selection, is provided by a simplistic simulation of the antibodies and antigens from the human immune system [23].

8.8.6. Toward Adaptive Behavior: Reflection

Let us recall that intelligence is often defined as the ability to adapt to situations or, also, as the capacity to choose a suitable behavior, according to the circumstances. Bateson defines adaptation as a *"feature of an organism whereby it seemingly fits better into its environment and way of life. The process of achieving that fit."* Reflection is a mechanism that allows one to easily implement adaptive behaviors [10].

Let us recall that, to be reflective, the base system (denotation) requires at least a representation of itself (metasystem) fit for manipulation and modification. Any modification of the metasystem must have an immediate impact on the behavior of the base system itself, and conversely, any modification of the base system is reflected on its description at the metalevel; this link embodies the causal connection between a system and its metasystem. Therefore, reflection appears as a key to adaptation since an entity can modify its behavior through modifications brought to its metasystem.

8.8.7. Toward Ecosimulation

Work on OIS, DAI, and ALife is concerned with the behavior of groups of entities, whether they be actors, objects, or robots working together.

OIS, DAI, ALife, and reflective architecture supply all the tools and insights necessary to model ecosystems, i.e., to realize ecosimulation models:

- From OIS, ecosimulation borrows the actor paradigm which integrates the notions of objects and concurrency.

- From DAI, ecosimulation borrows agents that consider actors as members of an ecosystem.

- From ALife, ecosimulation borrows patches that represent a reification of the environment.

- A reflective architecture provides mechanisms that enable the implementation of adaptation in order to cope with the dynamic nature of the real world.

8.9.   THE FOURTH STEP: A GENERAL FRAMEWORK FOR ECOSIMULATION

Ecosimulation emerges as a new trend of research whose purpose is to model individuals or living organisms in relation to the environment in which they live in order to study the rules regulating their behavior. Even more generally, ecosimulation is concerned with all kinds of phenomena, either quantitative or qualitative, related to life [29]. It can be, for instance, a test bench for the exploration of the rules and behavior of an oceanic ecosystem [21].

Ecosimulation takes into account conditions ruling the real world: things usually evolve concurrently, objects do not stand on their own, etc. With these conditions as a first hypothesis, this section shows how current research in computer science can help bring out a model for realistic and truthful ecosimulations. Each of the research fields sketched in the latter section, DAI, OIS, and ALife, has a specific target contributing to the development of ecosimulation:

- DIA is about problem solving

- OIS is about robustness and the adaptability of concurrent computer systems

- ALife is about the creation and the observation of artificial animals.

Nevertheless, they all aim at providing a framework for thinking about *how systems behave*:

- How does the complex behavior of an ant colony emerge from the simple actions of individual ants without any central control?

- How does the finality of a distributed operating system emerge from the cooperation of many dedicated agents?

Ideas like *feedback* and *emergence*, stemming from cybernetics and all kinds of systemic approaches, apply to physical systems, natural or artificial, as well as social ones.

In order to build realistic ecosimulation, one needs to give an account of the following considerations:

- the real world is composed of objects

- the real world is an open system: real systems are connected to the external world and communicate with it

- the real world is concurrent

- an entity belongs to an environment and evolves in it

- an entity needs to adapt to changing situations.

This framework integrates the concepts of actors, agents, environment, and reflection into a single perspective. Its implementation is realized in the Reactalk programming environment [8], [10].

Many viewpoints on ecosystems are valuable, depending on one's goals, but all of them use *a reification of their structures*. The overall structure of the world is described as a set of interacting recursive microecosystems embedded into higher level ones.

8.9.1. Model of an Individual

The ecosimulation architecture maintains the relation link between an agent and the ecosystem where it belongs. Reflective levels are perceived as ecosystems of agents, linked by three kinds of reflective links. Each one expresses a given perspective on the actor:

The reflective link. An actor is described in a causally connected way as an individual by a personal and private meta-actor, ecosystem of agents evolving along the time: agents can join, disappear, be replaced, and the same applies to relations. Since its meta-actor reifies its behavior, the actor can access its own behavior through the reflective link. The reflective link can be used as well conversely: a modification of the structure of the metalevel ecosystem changes on the fly the behavior of the actor. The reflective link models the *somatic behavior* of an actor. Modifications of a meta-actor affect only one actor at the base level.

The generic link. Since the structure of an actor is reified through the generic structure to which it refers (prototype, generator, or class), modifications of the generic structure change the behavior of bunches of actors. The generic link models the genetic phylum of the actor.

The systemic link. A macroscopic view of an actor would show it as an agent belonging to an ecosystem. A reflective link allows it to access the reification of the ecosystem in which it evolves (its environment) and gives it a handle on this ecosystem.

8.9.2. Model of an Ecosystem

An ecosystem maintains a description of its inhabiting agents and of the rules governing their interactions. An ecosystem is formalized by a directed labeled graph $<A, R>$ evolving dynamically by the addition/deletion of vertices and edges. The set of vertices A contains agents. The set of directed labeled edges R defines relations among agents in the context of the ecosystem: a communication path between two agents is a triple $<S, D, P>$

> where S is the source agent
> D is the destination agent
> the label P is the agent managing the communication.

A relation $<a1, a2, a3>$ means that agent $a1$ can communicate with agent $a2$ through the communication protocol defined by agent $a3$. A directed graph naturally expresses such a distinction: agent $a1$ may be able to send messages to agent $a2$, while the converse is not true. The role of $a3$ is crucial because the exchange of information is subject to many constraints: $a3$, the communication agent, is responsible for making them explicit. It is often possible to transmit sequences of symbols with a perfect syntactic precision, but these symbols would have no meaning unless the transmitter and the receiver have agreed on their meaning. Any information sharing presupposes a semantic convention. The role of communication agents is to reify (make explicit) the semantic convention of the agents.

8.9.3. The Beehive Revisited

A Closer Look at the Actor Beehive Simulation

This beehive simulation presented in the first step (see Section 8.2.4) focuses mainly on two aspects of the beehive: the search for food and feeding of the queen. This simulation had three main purposes:

- to study the expressiveness of the actor paradigm

- to explore delegation and inheritance, two paradigms of knowledge sharing
- to show the plasticity of the model, for instance, to study the modification of the knowledge of a bunch of bees on the fly.

This simulation has shown that, extended to discrete-event simulation, the actor paradigm greatly improves the isomorphism between the conceptual model and the code itself, making design, maintenance, and debugging much easier. It also showed that a differential approach like delegation is easier for interactive simulation than the usual one, based on the abstract concept of class, and finally, that delegation is more efficient when the behavior of some model components is subject to dynamic changes.

A Portable Model

How could this model, originally run in Plasma, a pure actor-based language lacking classes, be transposed in Smalltalk-80, a class-based language? The solution is obvious in a reflective ecosimulation architecture: reflection releases an actor from its inheritance hierarchy in such a way that delegation becomes available through metalevel modification of the actor's computation model [9].

How about the Hive?

The actor solution presented in the first part of the chapter presents some flaws related to the expressiveness and the adequate representation of the simulation world to the real world. Those flaws find their roots mainly in the absence of agent hood:

> The arrival order of bees in the queen's feeding file is encoded within the behavior of single bees, when it is clear that it should be expressed at the beehive level, i.e., at the metalevel. As a matter of fact, nature would dictate to express behavior related to the creation of bees at a global beehive level, while a single bee's behavior should be encoded at a local level, the bee level. Similarly, the simulated time should also be expressed and handled at the metalevel.

The ecosimulation architecture offers a solution where, at first, *the beehive is reified*. This gives an opportunity to express important simulation concerns at the beehive level, such as statistical laws, simulated time, etc., that affect the whole ecosystem behavior.

The reflective link of any agents to the ecosystem gives bees access to such information when needed. Then, it is easier to collect statistical data on topics such as the effect of an overflow of population on the whole beehive. It is also easier to express global constraints, e.g., limitations of resources such as: "no more than 60,000 bees can live within the beehive at the same time. . . ."

While the actor paradigm eases the modeling of individuals, the beehive simulation in a reflective agent architecture demonstrates that it supports ecosystem modeling and individual agent hood in such a way that knowledge is always expressed at the correct level, either global or local.

8.9.4. From Ecosimulation to Concurrent Computation

The actor and the ecosimulation architecture better satisfy *the correspondence principle* embedded in Winograd's *physical system hypothesis*. Knowledge arises from the manipulation of symbolic representations referring to objects and properties of the real world. On the other hand, underlying an ecosimulation architecture, a metaphor links ecosystems and concurrent computer systems. It is expected that insights from the simulation of ecosystems would serve for the design and implementation of concurrent computer systems, and that both—ecosimulation and concurrent systems—could be expressed with an ecosimulation architecture as a unifying framework. Until this point, we have sketched how this architecture supports rather realistic simulations based on concrete ecosystems such as a beehive. In this simulation, ecosystems are modeled as distributed computational systems, taking advantage of one direction of the metaphor.

8.9.5. Limitations

An example of ecosimulation has been realized under *ParcPlace Systems' Objectworks®Smalltalk-80*™ whose *release 4* graphic facilities sped up the implementation of the overall architecture [9]. The programming toolkit appeared rather adequate for a prototype environment. However, the introduction of concurrency in the ST-80 raised many problems, mainly because of the ST-80's lack of fairness in process scheduling. The integration of the ST-80 Model-View-Controller (MVC) paradigm into a concurrent universe was not straightforward.

For simulations involving many actors, concurrent executions were often difficult to follow, understand, and debug: a snapshot of the system at run time appears as a large amount of unstable information. This information involves different levels (often very low) of the system, and quickly modifies as the system runs. More tools would have been needed to collect it and condense it in order to have a concise account of these modifications at our disposal. Ecosystem programming seems interesting, but an emerging global behavior is hard to predict. This programming style is more intuitive than systematic. Further experiments are necessary for a methodology to emerge.

8.9.6. Summary of the Fourth Step

The fourth step explores the infancy of an "ecological metaphor." It links distributed computer systems and ecological systems in the same way as the computational metaphor links cognitive sciences and artificial intelligence. The ecosimulation architecture proposes a framework for the exploration of both sides of the "ecological metaphor link" (simulation of ecosystems/design of concurrent systems).

The ecosimulation architecture borrows from different research fields:

- to OIS, actors (*objects + concurrency*)
- to DAI, agents (*actors in an ecosystem*)
- to ALife, environment (*the world around the agents*)
- to reflection (*introspection and self-modification*).

It describes the world as a set of recursive (i.e., embedded in higher level ones) microecosystems interacting with one another. It proposes a model of ecosystems as concurrent computational systems where each kind of knowledge (local/global) can be specified at the proper level. It supports simulations of natural ecosystems like beehives or anthills, as well as more abstract ones [10].

8.10. CONCLUSION

This chapter studies the application of concurrent object-oriented techniques and reflection to discrete-event or behavioral simulation problems. In a constructivist style, it goes from simple actors up to whole ecologies of reflective agents. Different aspects of object-oriented concurrent programming—knowledge representation, concurrency, reflection, ecologies of reflective agents—are presented as a succession of conceptual steps, problem-driven rather than technology-driven.

Each step is introduced as an improvement to the solution of a given problem. Throughout the chapter, a beehive model example illustrates the different steps, from standard actor programming to ecosystem programming. The progression strives to follow the evolution of concurrent object-oriented programming techniques, and to show how simulation can take advantage of their application.

The first step details two basic knowledge representation mechanisms—inheritance and delegation—used by both object and actor systems for sharing knowledge and behavior, and points out their impact on discrete-event simulation programs. Then, it introduces specific extensions of the actor message-passing paradigm: time-referenced and conditional messages. Two examples, a beehive and a steam machine, illustrate their application to simulation problems.

The second and third steps introduce concurrency issues to improve the efficiency of the whole framework. A classical time-warp system and a rollback mechanism based on the history of the actor are implemented in a message-driven system. Reflection provides the tools to dynamically restore the state of an actor. In this paradigm, reflection is a solution to rollback implementation, providing an actor with a data version of its registers through which the effect of a given message can be cancelled by an antimessage.

The last parts of the chapter introduce agents to improve the beehive example by making bees aware of their surrounding environment. Using the ecosystem metaphor introduced by Huberman, it shows that agents can make local decisions based on imperfect knowledge about the whole system or on inconsistent and delayed information. Agents appear as a community of concurrent processes which, in their interactions, strategies, and competition for resources, behave like whole ecologies. The reflective scope is enlarged: an actor could only use it to change its own state; an agent can change not only its own state, but the state of some other agents of its surroundings. Some research work, currently under development, tries to introduce *emotions* as a metaphor for control structure and as a regulating mechanism for interruptions in an agent world.

Object-oriented concurrent programming and reflection provide a flexible toolkit for different kinds of discrete-event or behavioral simulation problems. In the state of the art, flexibility is often at the price of much of the support usually found in larger industrial systems. From another point of view, pure actor systems belong to the domain of advanced research, and usually provide a poor programming environment. In some cases such as Actalk, this weakness has been overcome since the ST-80 strong programming environment remains available in Actalk. However, Actalk is more of a system for testing actor architecture than a robust actor system able to face industrial applications. The actor theory is new; most of the research in the area of parallel language has been practical, but with limited formal basis. When it is formal and theoretical, it is too often at the expense of realism. In spite of this, large-scale simulation systems such as air traffic control have been developed on top of an actor substrate supporting agent programming, and the examples presented here show that actors, reflection, and agents provide a promising background for qualitative simulation.

References

[1] G. Agha, *Actors: A Model of Concurrent Computation in Distributed Systems*. Cambridge, MA: M.I.T. Press, 1986.

[2] G. Bateson, *Mind and Nature: A Necessary Unity*. Toronto: Bantam Books, 1979.

[3] J. P. Briot, "From objects to actors: Study of a limited symbiosis in Smalltalk-80," LITP 88-58 RXF, Université Paris VI, 1988.

[4] A. diSessa, "On *learnable* representations of knowledge: A meaning for the computational metaphor," AIM 441 (Logo Memo 47), A.I. Laboratory, M.I.T., Sept. 1977.

[5] A. Drogoul and J. Ferber, "A behavioural simulation model for the study of emergent social structures," in *Proc. European Conf. Artificial Life, Toward a Practice of Autonomous Syst. (ECAL'91)*, M.I.T. Press/Bradford Books, 1991.

[6] L. Gasser et al., "Representing and using organisational knowledge in DAI systems," in *Distributed Artificial Intelligence*, Vol. 2, L. Gasser and M. N. Huhns, Eds. San Mateo, CA: Morgan Kaufmann, 1989.

[7] S. Giroux and A. Senteni, "Reactalk, A reflective version of Actalk," in *OOPSLA'91 2nd Workshop on Reflection and Metalevel Architecture in Objected-Oriented Programming*, Phoenix, AZ, 1991; to be published as a Xerox Tech. Rep.

[8] S. Giroux and A. Senteni, "Taylorising the behaviour of an actor: An organizational approach of computational reflection," in *East EurOOpe'91 Proc.*, SIGS Publications, 1991.

[9] S. Giroux, "Agents et systèmes, une nécessaire unité," Ph.D. thesis, Département d'Informatique et de Recherche Opérationnelle, Université de Montréal, 1993.

[10] S. Giroux and A. Senteni, "A distributed artificial intelligence approach to behavioural simulation," in *Proc. SCS European Simulation Multiconf.*, 1991, pp. 89–94.

[11] C. Hewitt, "Open information systems semantics for distributed artificial intelligence," *Artificial Intell.*, vol. 47, no. 1–3, pp. 79–106, 1991.

[12] C. Hewitt, "Viewing control structures as patterns of passing messages," *Artificial Intell.*, vol. 8, pp. 323–364, 1977.

[13] B. A. Huberman, Ed., *The Ecology of Computation*. Amsterdam: North-Holland, 1988, 342 pp.

[14] S. Jagannathan, "A reflective model of inheritance," in *Proc. European Conf. Object-Oriented Programming, ECOOP'92*, 1992.

[15] D. Jefferson, "Virtual time," *ACM Trans. Programming Languages and Syst.*, vol. 7, pp. 404–425, 1985.

[16] W. Kreutzer, *System Simulation: Programming Styles and Languages* (Series in Computer Science). Reading, MA: Addison-Wesley, 1986.

[17] G. Lapalme and P. Sallé, "Plasma II: An actor approach to concurrent programming," in *Proc. ACM Sigplan Workshop Object-Based Concurrent Programming*, vol. 24, no. 4, 1989, pp. 81–83.

[18] G. Lapalme and A. Senteni, "Une application de la méthodologie acteur à la définition d'une interface conviviale," Tech. Rep. Departement d'Informatique et de Recherche Opérationnelle, Université de Montréal, 1987.

[19] H. Liebermann, "Reversible object-oriented interpreters," in *Proc. ECOOP*, Paris, France, June 1987, pp. 13–21.

[20] P. Maes, "Concepts and experiments in computational reflection," in *Proc. OOPSLA'87*, Orlando, FL; Special Issue of *SIGPLAN Notices*, vol. 22, no. 12, pp. 147–155, 1987.

[21] T. Maruichi, T. Uchiki, and M. Tokoro, "Behavioural simulation based on knowledge objects," in *Proc. European Conf. Object-Oriented Programming, ECOOP'87*, 1987, pp. 257–266.

[22] M. Minsky, *The Society of Mind*. New York: Simon and Schuster, 1985, 339 pp.

[23] M. Resnick, "Children, computers, and artifical life," in *Proc. Annu. Conf. Comput. Education Group of Queensland*, Australia, June 1990.

[24] P. Sallé, "Langages d'acteurs et langages objets: le langage Plasma," in *Proc. Interkibernetik'87*, Tarragona, Spain, 1987.

[25] A. Senteni, P. Sallé, and G. Lapalme, "Simulation with actors using time-referenced message-passing," in *Proc. SCS European Simulation Multiconf.*, 1989, pp. 109–114.

[26] B. C. Smith, "Reflection and semantics in Lisp," in *Proc. 1984 ACM Principles of Programming Languages Conf.*, 1984, pp. 23–35.

[27] T. Tanaka, "Actor reflection without meta-objects," TRL Res. Rep. RT-0047, IBM Res., Tokyo Res. Lab., Aug. 1, 1990.

[28] J. Vaucher, "A wait until algorithm for general purpose simulation languages," in *Proc. SCS Winter Simulation Conf.*, 1973, pp. 77–83.

[29] T. Winograd and F. Flores, *Understanding Computers and Cognition: A New Foundation for Design*. Reading, MA: Addison-Wesley, 1987.

[30] A. Yonezawa and M. Tokoro, Eds., *Object-Oriented Concurrent Programming*. Cambridge, MA: M.I.T. Press, 1987, 282 pp.

Key Words

About the Editors

George W. Zobrist received the B.S. degree in Electrical Engineering from the University of Missouri, Columbia, Missouri, in 1958; the M.S. degree in Electrical Engineering from the University of Wichita, Kansas, in 1961; and the Ph.D. degree in Electrical Engineering from the University of Missouri, Columbia, Missouri, in 1965.

He has been employed by USNOTS, China Lake, California (1958–59); by the Boeing Company, Wichita, Kansas (1959–60); by the University of Missouri, Columbia, Missouri, as an Associate Professor in Electrical Engineering from 1961–69, by the University of South Florida, Tampa, Florida, as a Professor in Electrical Engineering (1969–76). He spent the year of 1970–71 as Chairman and Professor of Electrical Engineering, University of Miami, Florida, and the year of 1972–73, on leave of absence, at the University of Edinburgh, Scotland, as a Research Professor. He was Chairman and Professor of Electrical Engineering at the University of Toldeo, Ohio, from 1976 to 1979 and Director of Computer Science and Engineering for SSOE, Inc., Toledo, Ohio, from 1979 to 1982. Since 1982 he has been a Professor of Computer Science at the University of Missouri—Rolla and Chairman of the Computer Science Department since 1994.

He has been employed as a consultant in the areas of network performance evaluation, computer-aided analysis, design and simulation by Wilcox Electric, Kansas City, Missouri; Bendix Corporation, Kansas City, Missouri; ICC, Miami, Florida; Defense Communications Agency, Washington, DC; Naval Research Labs, Washington, DC; NASA, Kennedy Space Center, Florida; Prestolite, Toledo, Ohio; Avionics Lab, WPAFB,

Ohio; ESMC, PAFB, Florida; IBM, Lexington, Kentucky; and various insurance firms, electrical contractors, and attorneys.

He has organized and/or participated in numerous continuing engineering education seminars. Topics have included filter design, computer-aided design, applied communications systems engineering, Fortran programming, simulation using SIMSCRIPT and GPSS, electrical calculations based on National Electric Code and Review of National Electrical Code, and software engineering. He has also presented seminars on microprocessor architecture, computer-aided design, and software engineering in Brazil, South Africa, and Yugoslavia.

His current research interests include: simulation, computer-aided analysis and design, software engineering and metrics, and local area network performance evaluation. He is presently editor of *IEEE Potentials Magazine, VLSI Design, and International Journal in Computer Simulation.*

Dr. Zobrist is a member of Eta Kappa Nu, Tau Beta Pi, Phi Eta Sigma, Pi Mu Epsilon, Sigma Xi, Upsilon Pi Epsilon, IEEE (Senior Member), and SCS (Member), and is listed in *American Men of Science* and *Who's Who in America.*

James V. Leonard received his Bachelor of Electrical Engineering degree from the University of Akron in 1961; he received an MSEE (Power) from Washington University of St. Louis in 1966; and he received an MSEE (Digital) from the University of Missouri—Rolla in 1976 and a Professional Development degree from the University of Missouri—Rolla in 1984. He is currently employed in industry as a Senior Principle Engineer and is a consultant in St. Louis, Missouri. He has been in industry for 35 years and is currently responsible for the aircraft integration of a US Navy missile into both US and foreign aircraft. He received the 1984 IEEE Centennial Medal, the 1986 USAB Achievement Award, the 1991 Region 5 Outstanding Member Award, and the 1991 US Navy Reliability, Maintainability, and Quality Assurance Award (Salty Dog). He has 24 published papers, a two-volume reference series on "Progress in Simulation" (Ablex Publishing), has produced the IEEE video "Your Future After Graduation" for Region 5, and is a registered professional engineer in Ohio and Missouri.

IEEE ACTIVITIES
  (S'60-M'62-SM'81)
  OFFICES: Board of Directors, 1992–93; Region 5 Director 1992–93
  COMMITTEES/BOARDS: Vice-Chairman USAB, 1993–94: USAB

OPCOM, 1992–94; USAB Member-at-Large, 1994–95; Pensions Committee, 1991–95 (Chairman, 1995); USAB Student Professional Awareness Committee Chairman, 1989–90; Membership Development Committee, 1993–95; RAB Section/Chapter Support Committee, 1992–93; IEEE Executive Quality Committee, 1992–93; USAB Opinion Survey Committee, 1993–94; RAB Awards and Recognition Committee, 1992–93; USAB National Government Activities Committee, 1992; Member/Customer Service Advisory Ad Hoc Bod Committee, 1994–95; Chairman, USAB Government Procurement and Regulations Committee, 1986–88

REGION: Director Region 5, 1992–93; Region 5 Bylaws and N&A Committee, 1994–95; PACE Chairman, 1988; East Area Chairman, 1985–87

SECTION: St. Louis Section Chairman, 1980–81; Section PACE Chairman, 1988–93; Section Membership Development Chairman, 1994–95; Section Student Activities Chairman, 1981–85

SOCIETIES: Organized the St. Louis Chapter of AESS in 1994; Interim Chairman, 1995

CONFERENCES: Co-Founder of the St. Louis Section "Missouri Conference" and designated a Fellow of MOCON in 1995

REPRESENTATIVE: United States Department of Defense Microcircuit Obsolescence Committee, 1988–90

Lightning Source UK Ltd.
Milton Keynes UK
UKOW030202120313

207468UK00001B/57/P